The
Complete
Book of
Firearms

S. MASINI   G. ROTASSO

The Complete Book of Firearms

PORTLAND HOUSE
NEW YORK

The publisher would like to thank the following museums for their invaluable assistance: the Museo Nazionale di Castel Sant'Angelo (Rome), the Museo Nazionale di Capodimonte (Naples), the Museo Storico della Fanteria (Rome), the Museo d'Artiglieria (Turin).

Thanks are also extended to the following for the kind loan of material: Astra-Unceta y CIA; Carl Walther GmbH; Colt Collection of Firearms; Edibase-Enrico Bartocci Editore; Editoriale Olimpia; Empresa Nacional Santa Barbara de Industrias Militares S.A.; FN-Fabrique Nationale Herstal; Heckler & Koch Gmbh; Jane's Publishing Company Ltd.; J.P. Sauer & Sohn GmbH; Matra Manurhin Defense; Oesterreichische Nationalbibliothek; Prima Armi; Pietro Beretta; R.L. Wilson; Royal Ordnance; SIG Swiss Industrial Company; Springfield Armory Inc.; Steyr; Sturm, Ruger & Company Inc.; Webley and Scott Ltd.

Originated by ERVIN s.r.l., Rome
under the supervision of ADRIANO ZANNINO
editorial assistant: SERENELLA GENOESE ZERBI

Photography by Ruggero Bacciali
Line drawings: Valeria Matricardi
Pencil drawings: Cecilia Giovannini

Translated by Valerie Palmer

© 1987 Arnoldo Mondadori Editore S.p.A., Milan
© 1988 Arnoldo Mondadori Editore S.p.A., Milan, for the English translation

This 1988 edition published by
Portland House, a division of
dilithium Press, Inc., distributed by
Crown Publishers, Inc., 225 Park Avenue South,
New York, New York 10003.

Library of Congress Cataloging-in-Publication Data

Complete book of firearms,

    Reprint. Originally published:
Mondadori. c1988.
    1. Firearms—History.
TS533.066 1988   683.4   88-9823
ISBN 0-517-66947-1

h g f e d c b a

Printed in Italy by Arnoldo Mondadori Editore, Verona

CONTENTS

9 HANDLING FIRE

12 Matchlock weapons
17 The Battle of Pavia
18 The wheel-lock system
34 Innovation and progress
38 The flintlock mechanism
41 Armament and reform in the Sweden of King Gustavus Adolphus
51 The eighteenth century
59 French Army Uniforms
60 Weapons, Wars and the Industrial Revolution
66 Pistol-duelling in the first half of the nineteenth century
70 In the New World
79 Modern Weapons
80 The eventful history of the cartridge
84 Famous pistols
86 Weapons of the Second World War
91 Hunting weapons
92 Target weapons
93 Bibliographical Notes

95 ARMS FROM THE MID EIGHTEENTH CENTURY TO THE PRESENT DAY: historical and technical survey

97 FROM MATCHLOCK TO FLINTLOCK

98 Mechanisms
103 Terminology

125 FROM PERCUSSION TO BREECH-LOADING

126 Mechanisms
129 Terminology

173 REPEATING AND AUTOMATIC WEAPONS

174 Mechanisms
236 Weapons of the street and tavern

239 CONTEMPORARY WEAPONS

244 Automatic and semi-automatic rifles
254 Sub-machine guns
259 Pistols
275 Glossary
279 Index by country
281 General index
285 Bibliography

INTRODUCTION

A history of weapons covering the development of personal firearms from their origins to the present day, and mainly intended for readers investigating this complex area of man's technological achievement for the first time, is something which has not been available in many countries in the past. Although the period involved is a relatively short one – from the fifteenth to the twentieth century – the scientific, social and economic transformations which it has witnessed have radically altered man's environment and human relations in general. In this context of massive change, weapons and their use in war and civilian life have played, and continue to play, an essential part.

In order to provide a useful reference source for those carrying out research in this field who may lack a detailed knowledge of the subject, the publishers approached two experts: the first is an authority on the history of military institutions who has made a detailed study of the intricate relationships between society, economic factors and the armed forces; the second is an expert on the history of weaponry who has also handled most of the weapons described in this book.

The authors began with a major photographic campaign in three large national collections of old weapons: the National Artillery Museum in Turin, the National Museum at Castel Sant'Angelo in Rome, and the Infantry Museum, also in Rome. In addition to the results of this research, illustrations have been provided from private archives, specialized publications and art collections.

While the illustrations were being assembled, one of the authors set to work on the historical text while the other prepared the caption material. The cross-referencing of data and information involved in this exercise benefited both sides, and the result is a thorough guide that will be appreciated even by readers who have never picked up a weapon in their lives. It is at the same time of enormous interest and value to those already familiar with the subject but who, up to now, have not had access to detailed descriptions of weapons which have at best been the subject of occasional specialist attention.

So here in one book readers will find material for which they would otherwise have had to read several volumes: the text summarizes the history of individual firearms from their origins to the end of the nineteenth century; it presents a series of historical and technical profiles from the mid eighteenth century to the present day, including several more or less undisplayed types alongside the more familiar models; illustrations show how the principal types of mechanism in the history of individual firearms worked, together with a survey of the different types of cartridge in use from the mid seventeenth to the end of the nineteenth century; a bibliography provides a ready reference for those wishing to pursue their research further; and, finally, a glossary guides readers through the different technical terms.

It goes without saying that a book which has such broad textual and pictorial terms of reference as these cannot include detailed information on all weapons produced in the space of more than six hundred years. For that, one would need to refer to publications which concentrate on one or at most two centuries. The authors have therefore aimed to produce a book covering a number of areas of interest which, in the past, have all too often been relegated to the footnotes of historical enquiry.

The authors would like to express their gratitude and appreciation to the directors and staff of the museums in which the weapons shown in the photographs are housed. They also extend thanks to Alfredo Bartocci, Cesare Calamandrei, Romano Onorati, Angelo Parodi, Rossana Picciati, Luciano Salvatici and Sergio Zannol for their kind assistance and invaluable advice. Finally, they dedicate this book to their wives, who have helped and supported them throughout the entire project.

One of the first representations of a firearm, from the illuminated manuscript *De Nobilitatibus, Sapientiis et Prudentiis Regum*, by Walter de Milemete, in the library of Christ Church, Oxford. This British manuscript, dated 1326–7, shows a mortar shaped like a large pot, supported by a trestled mount. The artilleryman, who is protected by a coat of mail, has just lit the gunpowder by holding a fuse on a pole close to the touch-hole. A more refined version of this device was subsequently developed and known as a linstock. The projectile fired from the weapon is clearly not a ball but a metal bolt.

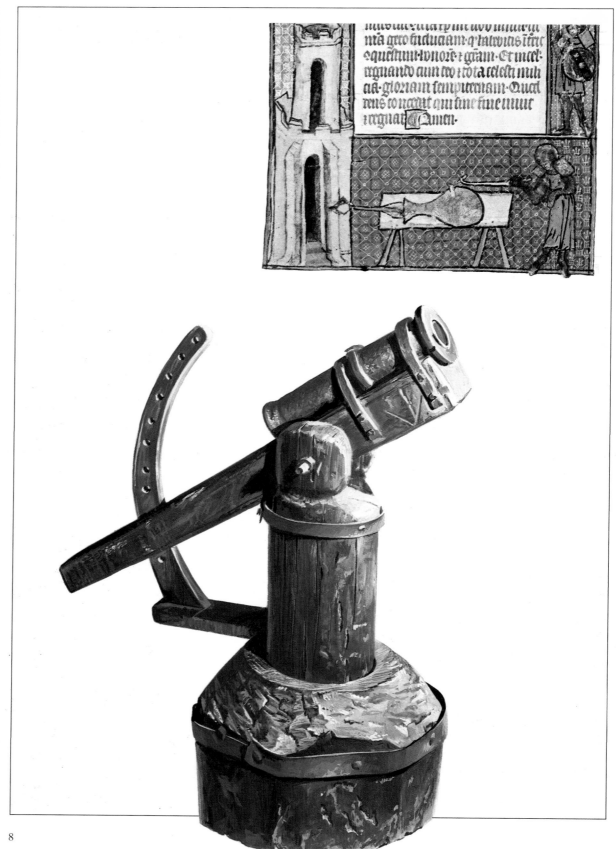

Cannon from the late fourteenth or early fifteenth century, belonging to the Bernisches Historisches Museum, Berne. The support has been reconstructed from a drawing dated 1390–1400. Note the simple device for altering the angle of elevation of the piece, which can be pointed in any direction.

HANDLING FIRE

Those precursors of modern chemistry, the alchemists, knew how to mix the elements together and studied their properties. They used fire to separate minerals from slag; they boiled and distilled organic matter, and melted metals in their crucibles. Those who had taken up alchemy because they wanted to make their fortunes searched for the Philosopher's Stone or, intent on quicker results, for a method of obtaining gold from base metals. Many others, however, were genuine scientists who, with the makeshift means at their disposal and often at risk of being taken for sorcerers or servants of the Evil One, attempted to discover the basic laws by which nature was governed. Of these alchemists, the Franciscan Roger Bacon, Marcus Graecus and Albertus Magnus (who was even proclaimed a saint) have been credited if not with the invention of gunpowder, then at least with having known about it. This was in the second half of the thirteenth century – at a time of cultural diffusion, when it was possible for a limited number of scholars (mostly churchmen) to communicate the results of their researches to each other through writing. They used symbols and allusions, anagrams and conundrums when the secret being divulged was a particularly sensitive one which they did not want to fall into the wrong hands. This, some people say, is why Roger Bacon used an anagram to conceal the formula for gunpowder.[1] Nevertheless, in a treatise he wrote sometime between 1266 and 1268, he describes as a "child's toy" the mixing together of saltpeter, sulfur and charcoal in a small receptacle for making rudimentary firecrackers. When these devices are set alight, he wrote, they can make "such a noise that it seriously distresses the ears of men ... and the terrible flash is also very alarming ... if an instrument of large size were used, no one could stand the terror of the noise and the flash. If the instrument were made of solid material, the violence of the explosion would be much greater."[2]

Little did he know how prophetic those words would turn out to be. And are we to believe that there really was another monk, known as Black Berthold (Berthold Schwarz was indeed his name) who, either in his native town of Freiburg or somewhere else in Germany, discovered the explosive properties of Bacon's compound by grinding these ingredients together in a mortar with a pestle and causing a reaction which sent the pestle hurtling into the air like a projectile? We do know for certain that in many parts of Europe at the beginning of the fourteenth century they used iron pots with perforated bases, into the

One of the many popular illustrations of the legend of Berthold Schwarz, the monk who "invented" gunpowder. The unwary inventor is being guided in his research by the Devil.

bottom of which the mixture we now call gunpowder was packed. These crude devices could fire iron bolts and stone or metal balls – it only needed a firebrand or red-hot poker to come into contact with the black powder inside the pot and the charge would go off in a totally unpredictable direction and over a limited range. Nonetheless, the psychological effect was still remarkable, and the projectile, if it hit its target, was certainly capable of killing a man or knocking down a door.

This was the birth of the cannon. From the start, cannons were obviously not something which just anyone could manufacture or own. Metallurgy was sufficiently well developed for these guns to be made in the forge, and it was soon realized that spherical projectiles were more effective than bolts; but the production costs were so high that only the great feudal lords, cities, and, above all, princes and kings could afford to manufacture and maintain large stocks of artillery. It also needed an expert to undertake the highly dangerous task of mixing the three components together; these substances were in fact kept in separate barrels until shortly before they were to be used. Often the manufacturer of the cannon was also a master gunner and provided an on-the-spot service of concocting the gunpowder and priming and aiming the weapon to be fired. In those days, of course, the basic laws of ballistics were virtually unknown: everyone aimed with the naked eye, using what each of them imagined to be the right method. In the early days, the cannon was used above all in sieges: its deployment in battle was initially very limited and had little effect. Such an artillery piece was moved about with great difficulty and was mainly employed to knock down walls and destroy towers. For these

ends it proved an excellent weapon and brought about radical modifications in the design and construction of castles and fortifications.

The power of this new weapon, however, was such that even those with more limited resources tried to make use of it – for instance the owners of the castles of Tannenberg in Hesse,[3] or Mörkö in Sweden,[4] or Vedelspang in Lower Silesia.[5] Weapons have been found in these castles which were the forerunners of what later came to be known as the arquebus. This word almost certainly comes from the German *hackenbüchse*, made up of *hacken* (a hook) and *büchse* (a generic word for firearm). When in use, these mini-cannons were rested against a wall and held steady by a strong hook, which was in a single piece with the gun barrel and so could absorb most of the recoil.

We are talking here of the period between the end of the fourteenth century and the beginning of the fifteenth, when small "hand gonnes" were first used by infantrymen and horsemen – horsemen, that is, as opposed to knights on horseback. Even during the era which had already witnessed the horrors of the Hundred Years War, a noble knight in armour would not have dreamt of using a weapon which fired from a distance. Mercenaries armed with bows and crossbows, on the other hand, were frequently deployed as light cavalry in support of the real knights on horseback who wore heavy armour and carried a lance and a sword. These common soldiers could also be entrusted with new instruments of death, although they were hardly much use, considering the difficulty of operating even a small gun without spilling the gunpowder while holding a lighted fuse in one hand and reining in a horse, terrified by the noise and flash from the firearm,

Chambered petrary *c.*1460–70, in the Bernisches Historisches Museum, Berne. It is a small-scale piece with a limited range, but for its time it could be fired quickly, thanks to the loading system used. It fired stone balls or charges of smaller stones. Depending on the size and characteristics of the weapon, the projectile could be loaded from the muzzle or the breech, or put straight into the chamber.

with the other. At best, it would have been possible to fire one shot only. It could hardly have been any easier for the foot-soldier to use one of these either, since he did not even have a horse on which to escape to a safe distance; and if he wanted to fire more than one shot he would have

One of the earliest pictures of a matchlock mechanism on a hand-held gun, MS 3069, f. 38 v., Österreichische National-bibliothek, Vienna.

had to keep close to the powder keg in order to reload the weapon or have another gun ready loaded (which would obviously have been very risky). All this is quite apart from the fact that there were not many commanders who saw anything to be gained by strengthening the offensive capability of the infantry at a period in history still dominated by the prestige of the cavalry. There were, of course, crossbowmen and archers, but training them was a long and costly business. In any case the knights on horseback had steadily increased the weight and thickness of their armour in order to avoid any repetition of deplorable episodes like the battles of Crécy and Agincourt, where the English peasant archers had decimated the flower of the French nobility.

One interesting theory argues that the use of personal firearms *en masse* was tested for the first time during the Hussite Wars between 1420 and 1434. The Hussites were Bohemian heretics who supported the preacher Jan Huss and were motivated by an intense desire for political and religious freedom. They were led by Jan Zizka, a man expert in war who put together an army designed to employ defensive tactics when it first engaged with the enemy, using for cover a barricade of wagons in a manner closely resembling that adopted four hundred years later by the white settlers in the Wild West when attacked by Red Indians. The line-up along these wagon barricades included cannon, crossbows and also men armed with hand guns, which all poured concentrated fire on the enemy cavalry coming toward them. With the enemy thus thrown into disarray and suffering heavy losses, they could then unleash a second wave, this time of infantry armed with farm implements and tools trans-

11

formed into lethal weapons, together with small numbers of lightly armed men on horseback whose task it was to pursue the survivors.[6]

Whether it was something the Hussites had set in motion or the result of technical progress in general, the development of the earliest gadgetry geared to making the individual firearm a much more effective weapon came in the first half of the fifteenth century. A manuscript dating from 1411 and now kept in Vienna[7] illustrates the functioning of a matchlock mechanism, later called a "serpentine." This basically consisted of a lever pivoted to the side of the wooden stock of a weapon which, with a little imagination, could be described as an early arquebus. There is a striking resemblance between this lever and the ones with which contemporary crossbows were fitted. But in the case of the arquebus in this particular manuscript, the purpose of the S-shaped lever was to hold at one end a piece of burning cord primed with saltpeter – the fuse. By pulling the lever towards him, the arquebusier brought the fuse closer to the touch-hole – the small aperture which connected with the powder charge inside the barrel. In this way, it was possible to steady the weapon and at the same time take aim, or rather have at least some idea of the direction in which the shot was to be fired. In another and much later manuscript (1468),[8] a centaur is shown firing a more refined version of the weapon and, in particular, taking careful aim and adopting the proper attacking stance.

Matchlock weapons

From this point onwards, a series of technical innovations evolved, which were to turn the arquebus, and also the musket (a larger member of the same family), into manageable and functional weapons. The first improvement was the wooden structure which supported the barrel. From being just a length of wood in which the iron tube was more or less embedded, it developed into a proper butt which could be rested on the shoulder, with another part jutting out from it which wholly or partly supported the barrel. The barrel

Pages 12–15. Details from a set of tapestries designed by Bernaert van Orley and woven by the tapestry-maker J. Gheetels in Brussels c.1530, now in the Museo di Capodimonte, Naples. These magnificent tapestries illustrate the progress of the Battle of Pavia which was fought on 24 February 1525 between the forces of the French king, François I, and the army of the Holy Roman Empire led by Ferrante D'Avalos, Marquis of Pescara. The Spanish arquebusiers decided the outcome of the encounter, which proved fatal for the French troops. François I was taken prisoner by the imperial forces and the famous *gendarmerie* was largely destroyed. This detail shows a scene during the battle.

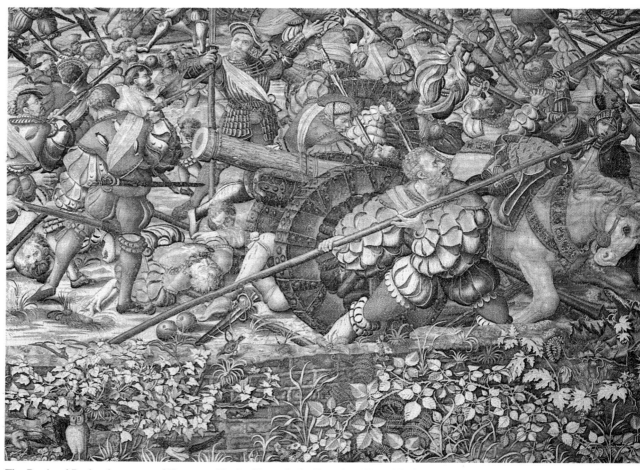

The Battle of Pavia: the troops of Emperor Charles V attack the French artillery. Having moved forward into Mirabello Park, where the French forces engaged in laying siege to Pavia were encamped, the imperial army initially found itself at a disadvantage as it came under fire from the formidable enemy artillery. François I, anxious to conclude the encounter in accordance with the traditions of chivalry, put himself at the head of the *gendarmerie* and the flower of the French nobility and charged against the enemy cavalry and infantry on the left flank of the imperial battle-lines. Under the sheer thrust of this charge, the battle's outcome seemed already decided, but the Marquis of Pescara sent in his arquebusiers, who wiped out the French cavalry, thus giving the imperial cavalry time to regroup and return to the offensive. In their turn, the landsknechte (foot-soldiers) and the Spanish overwhelmed the enemy infantry and swooped down on the artillery. The figure wearing the white sash behind the cannon in the picture is Georg von Frundsberg, leader of the imperial landsknechte.

itself was forged in the form of a tube open at both ends, one end of which was then closed by a large screw later known as the "breech-block." The touch-hole became a finer hole drilled into one side of the barrel, and next to it was a cavity, the priming pan, designed to hold a small amount of priming powder. From then on, the ignition process involved this small quantity of powder which was protected by a small lid, the pan cover, which was only removed at the point of firing. Lastly, the barrel changed from being held to the stock by metal bands fixed with nails, to being joined to it by a number of perforated lugs set into the wood; pegs were pushed through the stock and the lugs, thus making the whole structure stronger and firmer.

Apart from the mechanism, which was destined to change over the course of the centuries, most of the component parts of the long individual firearm were already in evidence towards the end of the fifteenth century and would remain the same until almost the end of the nineteenth. The shape of the weapons, however, underwent necessary modifications or was altered to satisfy the whims of the owners or manufacturers. But among the changes which were the result of genuine technical improvements, there were two types of snap-matchlock ignition which made it possible to hold the fuse well away from the touch-hole without having to pull the lever manually.[9] In both cases, a trigger was introduced, one in the form of a button and the other as a small lever which released the spring holding back the fuse arm. We are now looking at a mechanism of some sophistication. It needed a support-plate which was screwed into the stock of the arquebus,

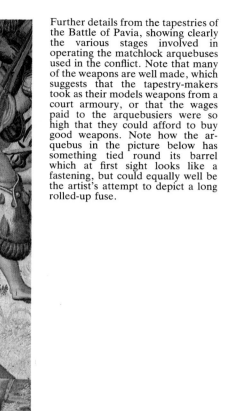

Further details from the tapestries of the Battle of Pavia, showing clearly the various stages involved in operating the matchlock arquebuses used in the conflict. Note that many of the weapons are well made, which suggests that the tapestry-makers took as their models weapons from a court armoury, or that the wages paid to the arquebusiers were so high that they could afford to buy good weapons. Note how the arquebus in the picture below has something tied round its barrel which at first sight looks like a fastening, but could equally well be the artist's attempt to depict a long rolled-up fuse.

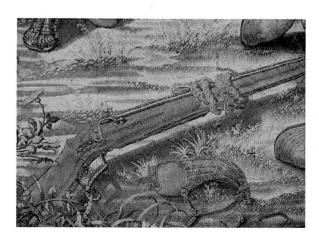

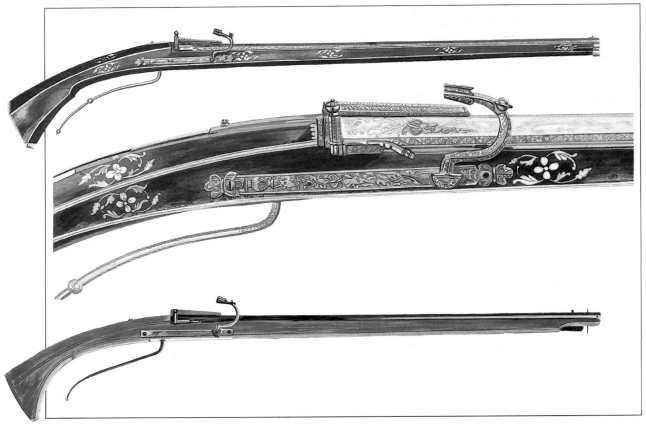

and for this to fit properly and house the springs and levers which made it work quite a deep hollow was made in the wood.

Technology had created a multi-purpose instrument within the reach of many people's pockets. On the one hand, those who hunted for a living or for pleasure had a new weapon for killing game, especially medium-sized game; on the other, the soldier of fortune, who cared little for the knightly code of conduct, could now equip himself with a weapon which put him on a par with the noble knight mounted on his horse and fully armed. There was no longer any need to obtain a heavy suit of armour in order to stay alive on the battlefield or to practice with the crossbow or bow for the rest of one's days. All that was needed were two strong arms and a modicum of skill to become a good arquebusier, and keep well away from the pikemen formed up in their squares. The Italian wars, fought from the end of the fifteenth and throughout most of the sixteenth century, showed for the first time just how effective, useful and mobile the individual firearm could be, especially when it was deployed *en masse* and at close range against an enemy which could not move about with ease. But although everything went smoothly when the target consisted of rank upon rank of Swiss mercenaries or landsknechts,

there were cries of outrage and recrimination when the victim of the common soldiers' lead shot was the flower of chivalry armour – clad and mounted on their chargers.

"Accursed and abominable machine/fashioned in the depths of Tartarus/by vile Beelzebub's own hands," thundered Orlando in Ariosto's epic poem of the same name[10] (although Ariosto actually lived at the court of Ferrara, a city well known for its cannon factories under the personal direction of the dukes of the house of Este). In his *Commentaries*, Blaise de Monluc,[11] a captain in the service of François I of France, later wrote: "Would it had pleased God that this accursed instrument had never been invented: I would not now bear the scars from which I suffer even to this day, and many bold men and true would not have died, often at the hands of the most cowardly and contemptible type of soldier, such as would not dare to look full in the face those whom they struck down from a distance with their accursed shot. But these are inventions of the Devil, to make us kill each other more efficiently."

There were other distinguished captains at the beginning of the sixteenth century who sent

Matchlock musket for firing from fixed positions. Octagonal barrel dating from the sixteenth century. Museo Nazionale di Castel Sant'Angelo, Rome.

Above, top: sixteenth-century matchlock arquebus (Italy, c.1570). The barrel is square all the way along and decorated with floral motifs, arms and grotesque masks. Judging by the coat of arms and inscriptions on the breech, the weapon must have belonged to Count Niccolò Gambara. Royal Armoury, Turin. Center: a detail of the mechanism of the same weapon. Note the tubular sight, which is engraved and gilded like the long, thin lock plate and sickle-shaped serpentine. Bottom: sixteenth-century matchlock arquebus (northern Italy, c.1570). From the information available, it appears that this weapon came from the Uboldo collection in Milan, which was dismantled by insurgents during the Five Days of Milan (the five-day revolt against the Austrians) in 1848. The barrel is square, with a tubular sight. National Artillery Museum, Turin.

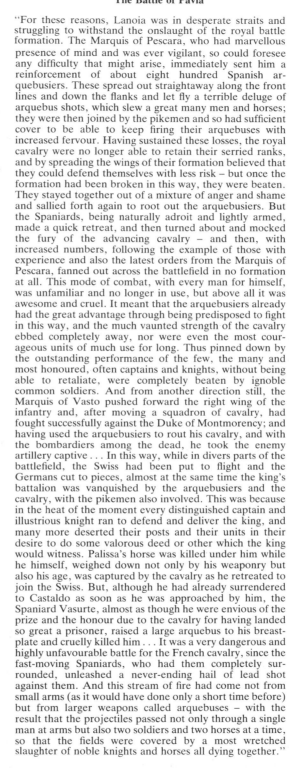

The Battle of Pavia

"For these reasons, Lanoia was in desperate straits and struggling to withstand the onslaught of the royal battle formation. The Marquis of Pescara, who had marvellous presence of mind and was ever vigilant, so could foresee any difficulty that might arise, immediately sent him a reinforcement of about eight hundred Spanish arquebusiers. These spread out straightaway along the front lines and down the flanks and let fly a terrible deluge of arquebus shots, which slew a great many men and horses; they were then joined by the pikemen and so had sufficient cover to be able to keep firing their arquebuses with increased fervour. Having sustained these losses, the royal cavalry were no longer able to retain their serried ranks, and by spreading the wings of their formation believed that they could defend themselves with less risk – but once the formation had been broken in this way, they were beaten. They stayed together out of a mixture of anger and shame and sallied forth again to root out the arquebusiers. But the Spaniards, being naturally adroit and lightly armed, made a quick retreat, and then turned about and mocked the fury of the advancing cavalry – and then, with increased numbers, following the example of those with experience and also the latest orders from the Marquis of Pescara, fanned out across the battlefield in no formation at all. This mode of combat, with every man for himself, was unfamiliar and no longer in use, but above all it was awesome and cruel. It meant that the arquebusiers already had the great advantage through being predisposed to fight in this way, and the much vaunted strength of the cavalry ebbed completely away, nor were even the most courageous units of much use for long. Thus pinned down by the outstanding performance of the few, the many and most honoured, often captains and knights, without being able to retaliate, were completely beaten by ignoble common soldiers. And from another direction still, the Marquis of Vasto pushed forward the right wing of the infantry and, after moving a squadron of cavalry, had fought successfully against the Duke of Montmorency; and having used the arquebusiers to rout his cavalry, and with the bombardiers among the dead, he took the enemy artillery captive . . . In this way, while in divers parts of the battlefield, the Swiss had been put to flight and the Germans cut to pieces, almost at the same time the king's battalion was vanquished by the arquebusiers and the cavalry, with the pikemen also involved. This was because in the heat of the moment every distinguished captain and illustrious knight ran to defend and deliver the king, and many more deserted their posts and their units in their desire to do some valorous deed or other which the king would witness. Palissa's horse was killed under him while he himself, weighed down not only by his weaponry but also his age, was captured by the cavalry as he retreated to join the Swiss. But, although he had already surrendered to Castaldo as soon as he was approached by him, the Spaniard Vasurte, almost as though he were envious of the prize and the honour due to the cavalry for having landed so great a prisoner, raised a large arquebus to his breast-plate and cruelly killed him . . . It was a very dangerous and highly unfavourable battle for the French cavalry, since the fast-moving Spaniards, who had them completely surrounded, unleashed a never-ending hail of lead shot against them. And this stream of fire had come not from small arms (as it would have done only a short time before) but from larger weapons called arquebuses – with the result that the projectiles passed not only through a single man at arms but also two soldiers and two horses at a time, so that the fields were covered by a most wretched slaughter of noble knights and horses all dying together."

(P. Giovio, *Le vite del Gran Capitano e del Marchese di Pescara*, edited by L. Domenichi, Bari, 1931.)

17

captured arquebusiers to the gallows or ordered their hands to be cut off. These extreme measures obviously did not prevent the deaths of several of the nobility from firearms – like Gaston de Foix who was shot at Ravenna in 1512, or the many knights who fell at Pavia in 1525 under fire from the Spanish arquebusiers, whose role in that battle between the armies of François I of France and the Emperor Charles V was decisive.

The use of individual firearms appears to have spread more rapidly through the lands of the Holy Roman Empire than in France. This may have been due to Charles V himself, who had made no secret of his preference for this new weapon for hunting and self-defense too. His sumptuous armoury, part of which he inherited from his father Maximilian,[12] contained some exquisitely crafted and richly decorated pieces.[13] Many incorporated highly progressive features developed by the brilliant German gunsmiths, whose skill, together with that of their Italian, Spanish and Flemish rivals, will be discussed later.

So the start of the period when the individual firearm found fame can be pinpointed to the early years of the sixteenth century.

Wheel-lock plate in the Portuguese style from a wheel-lock arquebus possibly made in Italy (*c.*1620) and now in a private collection.

Pistol with double wheel-lock. The stock is made entirely of metal, and the grip has a circular cross-section. Nuremberg, *c.*1560.

The wheel-lock system

I t was the invention of the wheel-lock system which increased the interest of the ruling classes in firearms. The slow-match system was cumbersome and dangerous. What the nobleman out hunting needed, as did the hired assassin and the rich man anxious to defend himself against sudden attack, was a weapon which was ready to fire right away, not one that required the firer to hold in his hand a lighted fuse – awkward, unsafe and visible at night – and then insert it in the serpentine at the last minute. Thus it was that, roughly at the same time, various inventors came to exploit the mineral iron pyrites, which produces sparks when rubbed against metal.

The invention of the wheel-lock is attributed by some to Leonardo da Vinci, who made a drawing of one in his *Codex Atlanticus*. Others believe that German craftsmen made the breakthrough.[14] It was in fact in Germany that the main centers for producing these devices grew up, and the mechanism found on a number of combined gun-and-crossbows in the Dieci Armoury in Venice was apparently German-made and dated from around 1505.[15] These weapons were loaded by putting the gunpowder and projectile down the mouth of the barrel; then the cock was put in the safe position. The cock – on the Italian and French weapons at least – was a movable arm screwed next to the small wheel with two jaws at the end which gripped the piece of iron pyrites[16] producing the sparks: "putting the catch on" involved lifting it away from the pan and then keeping it there by means of a spring. The next stage was to put the cock fully on by means of a small toothed wheel on one side of the "tiller" which was connected to a large spring. When the spring was tightened, it caused the small wheel to turn, by means of a key, and then locked it by a toothed wheel which engaged with a notch at the edge of the wheel. At this point the priming powder was put into the pan.

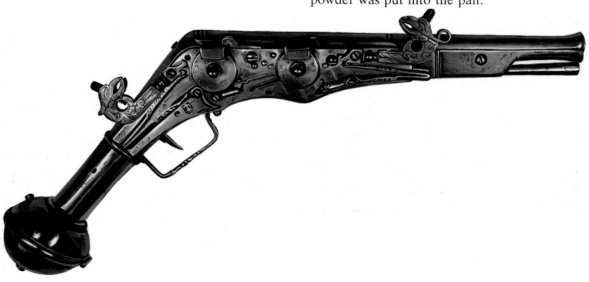

Wheel-lock arquebus with an octagonal barrel. Germany, first half of the seventeenth century. Museo Nazionale di Castel Sant'Angelo, Rome.

Unlike the priming pan on matchlock weapons, the pan on wheel-lock models had a slot at the bottom, through which the top of the small wheel – now locked – projected. This feature assisted in the ignition process. In fact, after the primer had been covered by the lid of the pan, the weapon was ready to fire. To cause ignition the pan cover was shifted and the cock lowered with the result that the iron pyrites held by its jaws brushed against the top of the toothed wheel projecting from the bottom of the pan, and the trigger was then pulled. The sear stud, which had locked the small wheel, withdrew from the hole, and the wheel itself, pulled by the relaxing spring, spun round. Whereupon the pyrites rubbed against the teeth of the wheel and produced a stream of sparks which ignited first the priming powder and then the main charge. The interval between the

production of the sparks and firing of the shot was minimal.

In the space of a few years, wheel-locks became widespread throughout Europe, despite the large number of decrees forbidding or limiting their use.[17] A number of improvements were made: the working parts were fitted inside the stock of the gun; strong grooves took the place of fragile teeth in the wheel; a way was found of opening the pan cover by pressing a button rather than moving it by hand; the lock spring was made stronger and more flexible by giving it two arms of equal or unequal length; and various safety measures were implemented to enable the weapon to be carried ready loaded without undue risk. Thanks to the wheel-lock mechanism, it was also possible to reduce the size of firearms, thus enabling the pistol to be developed. Although examples of

Above, from the top down: wheel-lock plate with key combined with powder measure; a snaphance lock; and a Roman-style lock.

Opposite, from the top down: a Portuguese- or Iberian-style lock (only a dozen or so of these mechanisms are known to be in existence); wheel-lock with two cocks; Portuguese-style lock. Museo Nazionale di Castel Sant'Angelo, Rome.

Right: wheel-lock pistol with etched decoration on the plate, Germany, first half of the seventeenth century. Museo Nazionale di Castel Sant'Angelo, Rome.

matchlock pistols do exist,[18] the wheel-lock system undoubtedly made it much easier to fire a weapon with just one hand. In fact, since the new weapons could be loaded in advance and then kept at the ready for an indefinite period, as long as certain precautions were taken, the practice developed of carrying two or more wheel-lock pistols in special pockets on a horse's saddle.

Pair of wheel-lock pistols. Augsburg, last quarter of the sixteenth century.

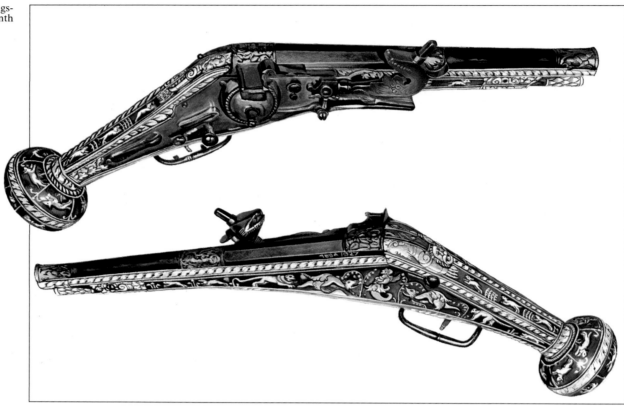

Wheel-lock plates were manufactured in various countries, above all Germany but also Italy, France and Spain. It is in fact possible to distinguish different types, which varied according to the time and place of production. The German lock plates originally had a cock spring which stretched round much of the wheel; then they had V-springs, with arms of equal length or with a shorter bottom arm. The cock originally had a very big arm, and then, from the second half of the sixteenth century onward, became almost flat, subsequently reverting to more upright, baroque forms; safety catches to immobilize the trigger and prevent the weapon from going off by mistake also became more common.[19]

In Italy the province of Brescia was the main center for the production of wheel-locks. In fact, during the period in which wheel-locks became more established, Brescia's main output was of gun barrels, in accordance with a kind of international division of labour which gave Germany a virtual monopoly of firing mechanisms. Those wheel-locks which were undoubtedly of Brescian make reveal many similarities to the German ones but lack some of the features of those on which they were probably modelled. They are, however, more pleasing to look at, often softened by the addition of a curl motif to the upper jaw of

the cock, while the lower jaw was mobile.[20]

As for the French wheel-locks, the main difference was that the axis of the wheel passed right through the stock of the weapon and ended on the opposite side in a kind of dummy lock plate called the "side plate." The big wheel spring was fitted inside the stock itself, separate from the plate. Lastly, French wheel-lock weapons had a noticeably bulging stock because of the wheel inside them.[21] The locks, manufactured in the city of Teschen on Bohemia's northern frontier (now divided into the Czech city Ceský Těšín and Polish Cieszyn), are worthy of special mention. It was from the name of that city that the weapons made there came to be called *Tschinke*. They

22

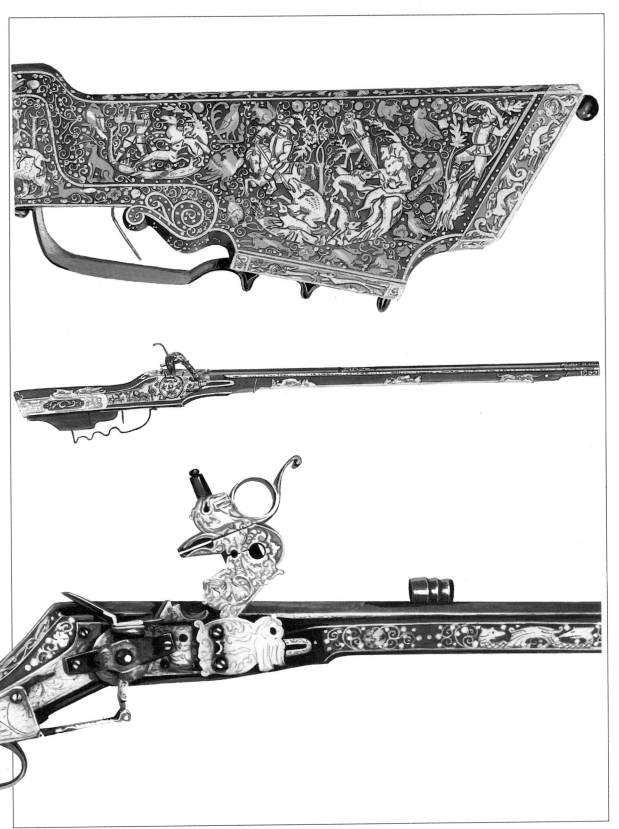

Detail of the butt of a wheel-lock arquebus made by Johannes Harttel, Teschen, 1666. Museo Poldi-Pezzoli, Milan.

Rifled wheel-lock arquebus, belonging to the Grand Duke of Tuscany, Ferdinand II, dated Munich 1628. Museo Nazionale del Bargello, Florence.

Detail of a *Tschinke* wheel-lock carbine, Silesia, c.1630. Squared barrel, tubular sight. The lock plate, the plate covering the main spring and the bridle of the lock spring are decorated with engraved floral motifs, while the stock is inlaid with bone and mother-of-pearl. The barrel has a rifled bore, with eight clockwise grooves. Royal Armoury, Turin.

23

Short-barrelled pistol (or puffer), first half of the seventeenth century, Saxony. Double-barrelled; stock and handle in walnut inlaid with bone, and with a graffito of vine-shoots and animal figures. Museo Nazionale di Castel Sant'Angelo, Rome.

were very lightweight arquebuses for hunting, with rifled barrels and wheel springs fitted outside the stock to reduce the weight of the weapons and make them easier to maintain – the disadvantage of this being that the weapon was more delicate as a result. Despite their antiquated appearance, these weapons were accurate and remarkably easy to handle, and well suited to hunting wildfowl and small game. The tail of the external spring was covered by a broad plate to protect the handler's fingers.[22]

Strange as it may seem, the wheel-lock system did not arouse the same feelings of contempt and fear as the matchlock had done. This difference in attitude may have been due to the fact that the wheel-lock weapon was always an expensive item, although the preference shown by a number of princes for this kind of technological "toy" may well have had some influence as well. One should also remember that the wheel-lock weapon was not widely used by the military to begin with, because of the difficulty of repairing one that was damaged anywhere near the battlefield. On the other hand, the popularity of these weapons for hunting and self-defense led to an exceptional development in specialist craftsmanship which brought prosperity to several parts of Europe. It should be made clear at this point that the early firearms were not made by just one craftsman or factory[23]: the more complex and ornate a weapon was, the more people would have been involved in producing it. In order to make a barrel, for example, the first person needed was a "master welder," who would take the red-hot sheets of steel from the furnace and forge them into tubes. This was the most important and the most difficult operation: if a badly welded barrel were to burst open, it could well cost him his life. The master welder or master gun-barrel maker would then hand the tube over to the borers, who in turn delivered it to the "levellers" responsible for finishing off the inside of the barrel. By now the product was a proper gun barrel and was passed next to the screwmakers who fitted the big screwed plug at the breech. Only then was it handed to the polishers and "furnishers," as an early seventeenth-century work described them. It was they who most often added their signatures to the gun barrels. As for the lock plates, they too could be the work of several craftsmen: the various marks stamped on the plates could have been put there either by the owner of the workshop or by the vendor of the finished weapon. Those craftsmen who had the best chance of leaving a personal mark on the product were perhaps the inlayers and decorators of the stocks, although some of them, like the so-called *Meister der Tierkopfranken* (Master of Vine Shoots in the Form of Animal Heads),[24] have remained anonymous and have been given, as in this case, descriptive titles by scholars to identify them. Needless to say, the owner of the weapon, especially if he came from a noble family, was another who did not miss an opportunity of engraving his initials or coat of arms wherever possible – which does not always make it easy to date a weapon. Various studies have been published on the identification of punch marks on lock plates and barrels, the most important being the monumental work by Johan F. Støckel: *Haandskydevaabens Bedømmelse.*

The spread of wheel-lock hunting weapons prompted gunsmiths to develop different types of stock for arquebuses. Stocks with a short butt which was rested against the cheek and not on the shoulder were widely used. Strange as it may seem, this method was not painful for the user, because in this type of weapon the recoil was felt mainly in the firearm itself and in the hands holding it. Another kind of weapon with an unusual butt by modern standards was the "petronel" (from the French *poitrine*, chest), so called because the butt was shaped to be rested against the chest, which took the force of the recoil. Weapons were also made specially for left-handers, which created considerable problems with the shape of the butt, resulting in some curious designs. As for pistols, people were very much taken by the idea of a pistol butt ending with a large pommel in the shape of a sphere or an onion.[25] This end-part of the weapon was not

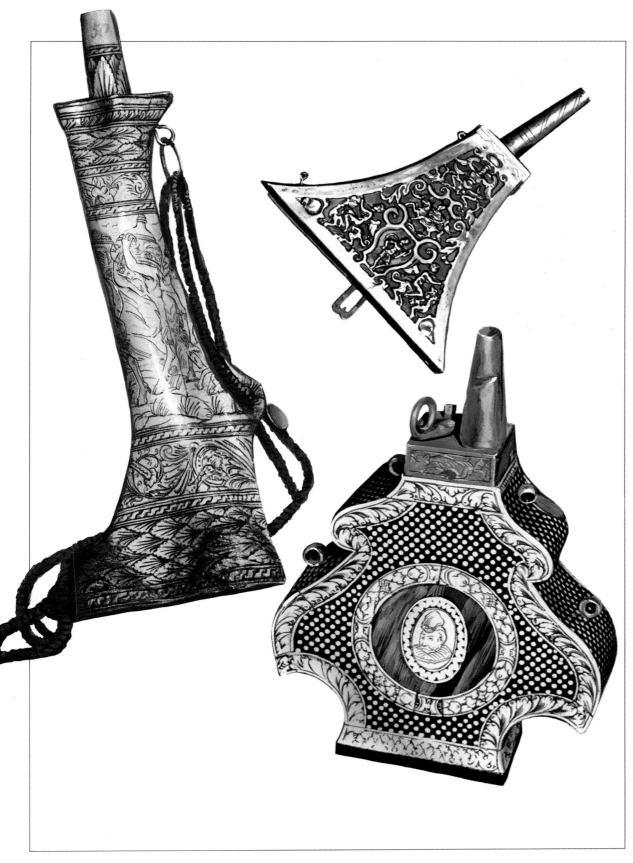

A horn and two flasks for gunpowder, richly decorated. The horn is made of bone and engraved with a scene from mythology (satyrs carrying wine and fruit) and floral motifs. Northern Italy, second half of the sixteenth century. The flask at the top of the picture is covered in hide and pierced metal, with characters in Roman armour and winged figures riding gryphons. Northern Italy, c.1600. The flask at the bottom is decorated with dotted inlays in bone and plaquettes with floral motifs, with the figure of a man at the center; it matches a wheel-lock and a matchlock arquebus made in southern Germany around 1570. All three items are from the armoury of Konopiste Castle in Czechoslovakia. Most of the weapons there belonged to the dukes of the house of Este and were inherited by Archduke Franz Ferdinand of Hapsburg in 1875.

meant as a club in hand-to-hand fighting, but rather to provide a firmer and more even grip – an essential feature, especially for those firing from horseback.

Which brings us back to the question of how individual firearms were used in battle. Soldiers on horseback had no way of defending themselves against infantrymen who were armed first with arquebuses and then with the heavier muskets, both fitted with the unsophisticated but reliable matchlock mechanism. Increasing the weight and thickness of a horseman's armour was not the answer: there came a point where his horse would have been slowed to a walk and the rider would have been incapable of handling his weapons properly. Taking their cue from illustrious characters like Emperor Charles V, who was not averse to using a pistol in the heat of battle, noblemen on horseback began arming themselves with wheel-lock pistols, and their example was soon followed by their retainers, who in the past had followed behind them on lesser breeds of horse and sometimes armed with bow or crossbow. These mounted soldiers, who were capable of being more mobile in battle than foot-soldiers, were especially common in Germany. About halfway through the sixteenth century, they began organizing themselves into compact units which used the combined fire-power of the three or four wheel-lock pistols which each man had at his disposal to take on and get the better of cavalry armed with lances and infantry hampered by their own solid battle formations. This new type of soldier soon came to be known by the German name *Reiter* (rider). Reiters employed a highly individual tactic known as the "caracole:" drawn up in formations twenty to thirty horsemen wide and fifteen to thirty deep, they would move forward at a trot or even at a walking pace until the enemy were within range of their pistols. The front row would fire and then withdraw to bring up the rear, the next row then being free to fire, while their comrades reloaded their weapons or prepared another pistol. For a long time, this tactic was successful – until it was realized that the reiters were very vulnerable in close combat. These over-specialized troops were thus replaced by mounted soldiers who could also use swords. In the process, however, these mounted marauders had dealt the *coup de grâce* to the great chivalric traditions, as may be gathered from this account written by Captain François de La Noue between 1580 and 1585:

"Those who are men-at-arms by profession state that there is no doubt that a unit armed with lances must get the better of a unit carrying pistols; and it would appear that, if anyone dared disbelieve them, he would be considered a most

Drawings from an instruction manual for members of the cavalry by J. J. Wallhausen, commander at Danzig (Frankfurt, 1616). It gives instructions to the arquebusier on how to load and handle his weapon on horseback.

Wheel-lock arquebus of the Farnese family with two cocks. The barrel has a smooth bore; the lock plate and breech have chiselled ornamentation depicting mythological and hunting scenes; the stock is walnut, and ornamented with steel plaquettes, mounted on *à jour*, showing rural scenes, jousts, geometrical designs and plant volutes. Northern Italy, 1590–1620. Museo Nazionale di Castel Sant'Angelo, Rome.

Details of the Farnese arquebus. Left, a close-up of the wheel-lock with the two cocks. The wheel cover has been worked *à jour*, and is held in place by two screws; the reserve cock is the one on the left, behind the wheel. Below right, detail of the butt, the shape of which is typical of that used by late sixteenth-century Italian gunsmiths. Weapons similar to this one, housed in the Armoury in Windsor Castle and in the Musée de l'Armée in Paris, definitely belonged to the Farnese family, and, in several places, bear the lily of the coat of arms of this powerful family. The mythological figure in the center of the butt is Apollo.

Far left: a view from below of the trigger guard and firing mechanism. The trigger guard is pierced with a design of two Farnese lilies. This arquebus is thought to be one of a number made for the Farnese family between 1595 and 1605.

ill-informed soldier . . . Nonetheless, one must recognize the fact that reiters were the first to introduce the use of pistols, which I regard as extremely dangerous if one knows how to handle them properly. This is a breed generated by the arquebus, and, if the truth be told, all these instruments are diabolical, dreamed up in some malevolent workshop for the purpose of decimating kingdoms and republics and filling the cemeteries with dead. However, human wickedness has made these weapons so necessary that one cannot do without them. Now to benefit from them much care must be devoted to the subject, and no nation has more (pistols, I mean) than the Germans, whom I would regard as in the vanguard in this field, and those who have most distinguished themselves in this sort of cavalry which carries such arms. I will not embark here on a detailed description of all the arms at the reiters' disposal because they are all too well known. Suffice it to say that the effectiveness of their defensive weapons is on a par with that of the lancers, while their offensive weapons are stronger, because a gendarme can only use his lance for one hit, whereas a reiter carries two pistols from which he can get six or seven shots, capable of causing serious damage if he takes good aim. Each of them also carries a sword, the effects of which can be similar. Seeing that the pistol can fend off defensive weapons and the lance cannot, one must conclude that the reiter has the upper hand in attack and is equal in defense.

It may also be said in the lancer's favour that he is better mounted and has a more stable balance, besides which the sight of a lance being brandished from afar with its pennant streaming can strike terror in the hearts of men. My response to this would be that the massive formation of serried ranks adopted by the reiters makes up for the weakness of their horses and equipment. As for being afraid of a lance, that is as nothing when compared with the alarm caused by the sound of a pistol exploding at close quarters."[26]

De La Noue was well aware of the power of firearms: a blast from an arquebus caused him to lose his left arm, after which he had himself fitted with a mechanical device which earned him the nickname *bras de fer* (iron arm).

Wheel-lock arquebus with two cocks and a small wheel-lock arquebus. Hunting weapons, typical of the Brescian style of arms manufacture in the first half of the seventeenth century. The semi-circular notch, which can be seen near the front end of the plate, below the cock spring, was probably put there originally to make it easier to dismantle the plate, but this notch subsequently became a hallmark of arms made in the province of Brescia. Museo Nazionale di Castel Sant'Angelo, Rome.

What the infantry were able to come up with in response to this new fighting technique was mainly force of numbers and better organization. During the Thirty Years War, however, between 1618 and 1648, new types of combatant made their appearance who were able to use the arquebus and musket on foot, and sword and pistols on horseback. These crack troops, who were known as Dragoons in many armies and were sometimes concentrated in special corps like the famous Musketeers of the King of France, could take on any kind of adversary with strength and cunning, as demonstrated by the hero of Grimmelshausen's *Der Abenteuerliche Simplicissimus*, who was forced to fight a duel against a cuirassier on horseback, armed with pistols:

". . . I had already given some thought to the way in which I should go into combat with a well-armed cuirassier if one were ever to attack me in the open and I were on foot and armed only with a musket. When we reached the place where our Beggars' Dance was supposed to begin, I had already loaded my musket with two balls, put a new fuse ready and greased the pan cover with tallow, as vigilant musketeers are wont to do on rainy days to prevent the touch-hole and the powder in the pan from getting wet. Before the fighting started, our respective aides established between them that we should do battle in the open and that, to this end, we would enter – one from the west and the other from the east – a walled field, and then that each of us would behave to the other as a soldier who has an enemy in front of him . . . When I entered the field from the side which had been allotted to me, I had a double fuse lit. The moment I saw my adversary in front of me, I made as if to throw away the old fuse as I was walking along, but in fact shook priming powder only on to the lid of the pan, then blew, and put two fingers on the pan in the customary way. Then, before I was close enough to see the whites of the eyes of my opponent, who was watching me closely, I took aim at him and let my decoy fuse burn away on the lid of the pan. My foolish adversary took this to mean that the musket had failed to go off and that the touch-hole was blocked, so he charged straight at me full of zeal with a pistol in his hand under the impression that he could make me lose my nerve and do me to death. But, before he knew what was happening, I had opened the pan and taken fresh aim; and the welcome I gave him was such such that the shot rang out, and he fell, at one and the same moment."[27]

From left to right: wheel-lock pistol from Germany, first half of the seventeenth century, with walnut stock inlaid with bone motifs featuring animals, plant volutes and flowers, and ending in a pommel with six inlaid concave sides; arquebus with an internal wheel, Germany (Suhl), first half of the eighteenth century; small wheel-lock arquebus, Germany, first half of the seventeenth century, with walnut stock inlaid with ivory, mother-of-pearl and horn; short-barrelled wheel-lock pistol (or puffer). Museo Nazionale di Castel Sant'Angelo, Rome.

Right: a double-firing wheel-lock arquebus, Brescia, early seventeenth century. Double-barrelled; the stock is of walnut and decorated by barrel bands with pierced iron rosettes. The wheel is modestly decorated. The inside of the plate bears the mark "A.M." Also shown are a "left-handed" duelling dagger and a powder flask covered in metal applied *à jour*. Museo Nazionale di Castel Sant'Angelo, Rome.

From wheel-lock to flintlock. Two wheel-lock arquebuses from the end of the seventeenth century, manufactured in northern Italy or Austria, alongside a flintlock weapon with a Roman-style lock probably made in Brescia at about the same period. Note that the lock plate of this last weapon appears to have been used originally on a wheel-lock gun, which would indicate that the weapon was converted when the new ignition system was introduced.

Behind the weapons is a powder flask dating from the same period. Museo Nazionale di Castel Sant'-Angelo, Rome.

Innovation and progress

The episode described above would have occurred in about 1635, but around the same date considerable progress had been made in the science of arms, if only in the development of prototypes. The most important single innovation was the technique of rifling. Tradition has it that this was the work of Gaspard Kollner, a Viennese gunsmith, or August Kotter of Nuremberg, who are thought to have introduced it some time between the end of the fifteenth century and the beginning of the sixteenth. The first conclusive evidence of this method of working the inside of a weapon can be seen in an arquebus dated 1542 in the Tøjhusmuseet in Copenhagen. The punch mark on the lock plate could be that of Wolf Danner, a famous armourer from Nuremberg.[28] In any case, rifled weapons, which were mainly used for hunting, began to be more common in the second half of the sixteenth century. They still had no military role, because of the difficulties in loading them. Some maintain that in the early days the rifling grooves were designed to collect gunpowder residue and only later was it discovered that weapons with this type of furrowing were more accurate than those with a smooth interior to the barrel. This is an interesting theory, but without much foundation. It is much more likely that the idea came from the practice of making bolts (known as "quarrels") for crossbows in such a way that they would spin in flight. This could be done by modifying the tip of the bolt or by fixing oblique feathers to the shaft. It was observed that bolts prepared in this way hit the target more easily, and someone must have thought that a similar system could be used to solve the problem of the inaccuracy of firearm projectiles.[29] A spherical ball, slightly smaller in diameter than the smooth gun barrel into which it had been inserted, would strike the walls of the barrel from the moment it was fired until it emerged. As a result its trajectory became unpredictable and was largely determined by the last ricochet it had made before leaving the barrel. In a rifled barrel the same projectile, which had first been firmly pushed down with a ramrod and sometimes a hammer as well until it was right at the breech (the rear end of the barrel connected to the touchhole), would spiral along the rifling grooves once it had been fired and assume a straight trajectory in accordance with laws of ballistics which were not drawn up until many years after the introduction of rifling. It was vitally important that the projectile, if it was to keep strictly to the grooves all the way, be thrust down hard inside the barrel: this led to problems, such as deformation of the ball, risk of the ramrod breaking, and slowness of

Detail from a painting by Velasquez, *Philip IV hunting*, Prado, Madrid. Painted around 1635, this portrait shows the King of Spain armed with a rifle which has a Catalan-style or "miquelet" lock.

Hunting rifle with Florentine-style lock, an example of eighteenth-century Italian craftsmanship from Tuscany or Emilia. The butt is richly decorated in low-relief silver. An iron escutcheon is fitted to the knuckle, and a figure is engraved on the breech. The aiming system consists of a backsight notch mounted on an engraved and perforated silver plate; the gun is double-barrelled.

Detail of the Florentine-style lock with a "swan's neck" cock and a steel, the arm of which consists of a small female figure. Museo Nazionale di Castel Sant'Angelo, Rome.

loading. One widely used expedient consisted of wrapping the shot in hide or cloth smeared in grease to make insertion of the projectile less violent, since it was the surface of the wrapping material and not that of the bullet which kept to the grooves inside the barrel in this case. The little compartments found in the stocks of some old rifles were in fact put there to house a number of these pieces ready for use.

Rifled weapons were obviously more expensive than those which had a smooth bore (interior to the barrel). As the ballistic principles which made projectiles fired from rifled barrels more steady in flight had still not yet been discovered, some craftsmen increased the number of rifling grooves to give their customers the impression that the weapon was highly accurate. The system could

not have caught on everywhere, above all for technical reasons: to be really effective, the grooves would have had to be very wide and deep and spaced out exactly round the circumference of the barrel. Such precision was well beyond the capabilities of a craftsman of the sixteenth or seventeenth century, however skillful.[30]

At that time, all those who could afford to would purchase arms of this sort. While peasants continued to go hunting with matchlock guns, noblemen, armed with wheel-lock arquebuses, often with rifled barrels, went in for some real massacres of game. The Elector of Saxony, Johann Georg I (1585–1656), killed 116,906 animals in his lifetime, according to contemporary records, which was about 5,000 more than his son Johann Georg II (1613–1680) managed.[31] But we must realize that the spread of hunting, although not responsible for these excesses, did lead to a fundamental change in the art of hunting by switching the emphasis from physical strength to skill as the first requirement in a hunter. It was no longer necessary to be stronger than the prey, to have the strength to draw a bow or hurl a javelin: instead, what mattered was the ability to aim accurately and keep a steady nerve. The rest was done by the arquebus and its projectile.

It was, however, desirable to have a weapon which would not misfire, always a possibility with a sophisticated wheel-lock mechanism. This is why in top quality arquebuses it is not uncommon to find two cocks with a single wheel,[32] or to discover opposite the cock holding the pyrites a cruder but ever reliable slow-match serpentine.

Not even this could satisfy the needs of the gun-handler who, when out hunting and especially in battle, wanted the use of a second shot without having to take two weapons with him. Thus it was from the mid sixteenth century onwards that, obviously, among the well-to-do or those with the necessary sleight of hand (weapons could always be stolen), the "diapason" pistol made its appearance, with two barrels and two locks one above the other; as did pistols and arquebuses with two barrels side by side, and more than two; and weapons with superimposed charges, or the facility for inserting several balls into one barrel, each with its own dose of gunpowder, and with several ignition devices to fire them.

In the second half of the sixteenth century two further inventions appeared: the revolver and the breech-loader. In fact, light cannons with rotating barrels and breech-loading systems had already been seen during the fifteenth century, in the first phase of artillery history.

The breech-loading system in particular had been used on small and medium-sized guns and sometimes on very large pieces too. It was especially useful when one did not need either a long range or great power, but speed of firing was of the essence. It basically involved putting the gunpowder charge and projectile into a kind of

How to load and fire a musket. From a series of etchings by Jacob de Gheyn, published at The Hague in 1608:
1 After firing, the musketeer grasps the musket rest and the loose end of the slow-burning fuse with his left hand.
2 He removes the fuse from the serpentine.
3 Holding the fuse at a distance, he refills the pan with priming powder and then closes it again.
4 He takes one of the wooden containers hanging from his bandolier and pours gunpowder from it into the barrel.
5 The musketeer takes a ball from the pouch beneath his arm and inserts it into the barrel. He then removes the ramrod from its housing under the barrel and pushes the projectile to the far end of the barrel.
6 He blows on the fuse to make it burn again.
7 He places the fuse in the serpentine and reopens the priming pan.
8 With his index finger on the trigger, the musketeer is ready to fire his weapon.

2   3   4

6   7   8

pot with a handle, which was placed between the breech, the opening of which was at the back of the actual gun, and a wood or metal support which was in a single piece with the load-bearing structure of the weapon. Once this "chamber" had been inserted, it was pushed closer to the gun by driving a wooden wedge between its base and the fixed structure of the weapon. Then the fuse was put to the touch-hole drilled in the chamber, and the weapon was fired. An artilleryman who had several of these chambers prepared could, in this way, fire almost repeatedly, obviously for as long as the weapon could stand it. The system was abandoned because, as already mentioned, the weapon was only accurate over short distances, given that the breech did not close hermetically and this let some of the gases from the explosion escape. This was a less serious problem in the case of a wheel-lock pistol or arquebus, in which the chamber could be replaced by a small metal tube inserted into a compartment in the breech by an ingenious slot-in system rather like a forerunner of the modern cartridge.

Obviously the cost of a weapon of this kind was prohibitive, as was that of the first guns with revolving barrels, where, instead of the interchangeable metal tubes for use with a single barrel, there were several barrels which had to be rotated by hand, or rudimentary "cylinders" or groups of cylindrical chambers which were also turned by hand so that each one was lined up exactly with the barrel and touch-hole. These were basically experimental models which were not widely adopted, with the possible exception of the breech-loading wheel-lock pistol, of which a number of examples have survived.

All this technological fervour may well have contributed to the development of the mechanism which was to replace both the matchlock and wheel-lock in the course of the seventeenth century: i.e., the "flintlock," which was to dominate the hunting scene, street-life and battlefield until the first half of the nineteenth century.

The flintlock mechanism

Flint is a type of chalcedony, the colour of which varies from yellowish or grayish to reddish brown; it occurs in the form of pebbles in various localities from the north coast of France to Belgium, Britain and Texas. Its properties, like those of pyrites, have been known since ancient times, as can be seen from the following quotation from Cicero: *lapidum ictu ignem elicere* (to produce fire by striking stones together). An exhaustive description of the properties of *lapis focaria* is also to be found in a text from the Middle Ages, when Isidoro of Seville, at the beginning of the seventh century, wrote: "There is another type of common pyrites called living stone, which when struck by iron or stone emits sparks which are collected with sulfur or certain fungi or leaves, and by this means fire is kindled more rapidly. The people call it flint." The substance used to "collect" the fire was known as tinder; tinderboxes, which exploited the characteristics of flintstone, were certainly made at the time of Dante, who wrote in the *Inferno*: (canto XIV, v. 38–39) "... whereby, like tinder under flint, the sands were kindled ..." and in 1347, in a commentary on this passage, Boccaccio explained the practice of striking flintstones together to

Pistol with Catalan-style or miquelet lock. Barrel is worked in high relief. M. N. Loys, Spain, first half of the seventeenth century. Right: detail of the mechanism with the cock in the post-firing position.

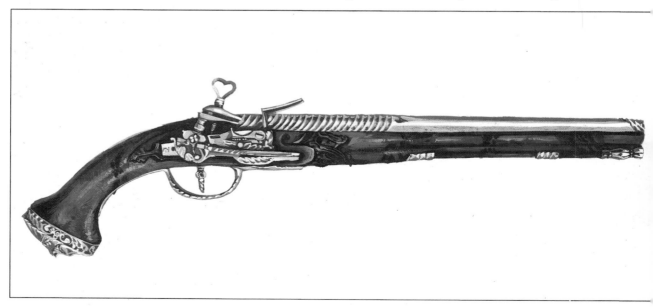

produce sparks for fire-lighting. In spite of all this, there is no firm documentary evidence of the existence of flintstone ignition systems until a Swedish inventory of 1547, which refers to *snapplås*, or the Swedish name for the flintlock mechanism.[33] To begin with, therefore, it consisted of a cock with a piece of flint between its jaws fitted opposite a steel plate supported by a turning arm. Even in the first types of flintlock the cock is placed on the left of the mechanism. When the weapon has been loaded, the cock is turned back towards the handler until a stud engages to block the device. The priming powder is then tipped in and the small steel plate (the steel) is positioned above the priming pan so that the flat part is opposite the cock. When the trigger is pulled, it frees the powerful spring of the cock, which snaps forward. The flint strikes the top of the steel and, as it pushes it back, slides down it with a rasping movement, producing numerous sparks which ignite the priming powder, thus firing the shot. This type of lock is known as the Scandinavian type and is found on the oldest model of flintlock weapon: an arquebus, its barrel marked Nuremberg, which was probably one of thirty-five arquebuses mentioned in an inventory of the Swedish Royal Army of 1556.[34]

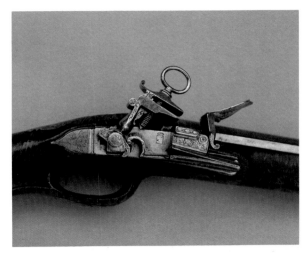

Right: hunting rifle with Roman-style lock, Rome, eighteenth century. Walnut stock, engraved silver furniture. Double barrel. Lock with gold touch-hole; escutcheon on knuckle; trigger guard fashioned out of the wood of the stock. Above, right: detail of the Roman-style lock. The breech and lock plate are stamped with the mark of Sirani & Corset, armourers to the papal court in the eighteenth century. Museo Nazionale di Castel Sant'Angelo, Rome.

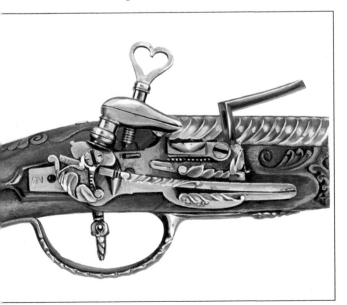

The death of Gustavus Adolphus of Sweden (1594–1632) at the Battle of Lützen. Painting by De Jonge.

Flintlock arquebus; Nuremberg/ Sweden, c.1556. Livrustkammaren, Stockholm.

Armament and Reform in the Sweden of King Gustavus Adolphus

R ich in ferrous metals and so situated that she commanded the shipping routes of northern Europe, Sweden was soon the crossroads for an important traffic in firearms for military use. In 1556, King Gustavus Adolphus of the Vasa dynasty issued an order for the fitting at the royal arsenal of Arboga of thirty-five flintlocks to the same number of barrels which had been produced at Nuremberg. One of these guns, pictured above, is considered the oldest flintlock weapon in existence. With a few modifications, which are the subject of some controversy among scholars, the type of lock fitted to this arquebus came to be used throughout Scandinavia and the Baltic, as shown by the other arquebus, dating from about 1650. This too was probably for military use and featured a safety device in the form of a screw which enabled the steel to be turned 180° horizontally. While local craftsmen made guns for rural use, the first Swedish arms industries devoted themselves to the production of military weapons, in line with a martial tradition of which King Gustavus Adolphus

was the greatest exponent. This sovereign initiated various military reforms which turned the Swedish militia into the first wholly national army, with men enlisted for military service and stationed in regimental districts corresponding to the old rural provinces. He also introduced some important improvements to his soldiers' armament. The weight of the musket was reduced so that it no longer needed a rest; the percentage of musketeers to pikemen was raised, and the rate of fire was also considerably increased. Gustavus Adolphus was responsible for the first, true field artillery, and also the famous experimental, ultra-lightweight "leather guns" which were in fact never used on a large scale.

After a series of local wars for control of the Baltic and the North Sea, the Swedish king became involved in the Thirty Years War, landing at Peenemunde on 6 July 1630. After two years of victories against the imperial army, he was killed at the Battle of Lützen (16 November 1632). In this brief period he had nonetheless managed to save German Protestantism and turn Sweden into a great power.

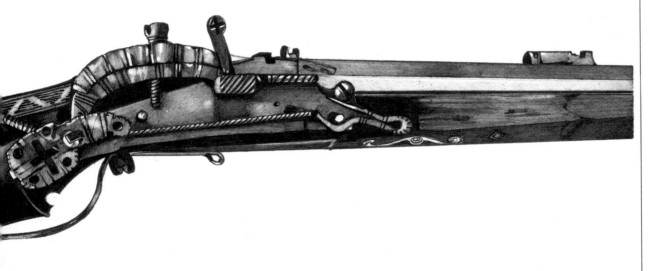

Arquebus with Baltic lock; Sweden, c.1650. Livrustkammaren, Stockholm.

The type of lock now known as *snaphance, snaphaunce* or *chenapan* was probably derived from the Scandinavian models. As Blackmore explains,[35] this term was originally used to describe all flintlock mechanisms. At the beginning of the nineteenth century, however, it was used to describe just those mechanisms which resembled the Scandinavian lock. Be that as it may, the snaphance type was a great improvement on its predecessor. New features included the fact that the instrument which blocked the cock, the technical term for which was the tumbler, now also caused the priming pan cover to open automatically; furthermore, a projection on the lock plate prevented the cock from falling down into the priming pan, which would have soon worn out the flint. Another characteristic of many snaphances was a big "button" covering the pan, whose function was largely decorative. This was around 1570–5 and we know that in 1575 the arquebusiers of the Guard of Duke Emanuele Filiberto of Savoy were armed with flintlock arquebuses. A manuscript by Giovanni Antonio Cornaro in the Biblioteca Ambrosiano, Milan, dated 1594, also mentions the same flintlock arquebuses and compares different types in a dialogue between two imaginary people: Tirone, who praises the wheel-lock "especially those in the Flemish style, which are exceeding fine and cost twenty-five scudi apiece" and the Veteran, who replies: "they are as easily broken as they are hard for the poor soldier to come by. Such arquebuses are only used by great men. One can accomplish the same end, by placing above the arquebuses a sort of flintlock of little cost, made just of a few metal parts, but which are sure not to break or spoil and so easy of operation that even in the hands of the clumsiest fellow, he will immediately learn how to use them and do so safely, the fire which they produce falling in the midst of the powder, certain not to fail and with any least stone they can be fixed above ordinary arquebuses without altering or spoiling the stock."[36]

The practicality of the flintlock mechanism was demonstrated by the various types which spread across Europe: snaphances were produced in the Low Countries, in France, Scotland and Russia; in Italy, Florentine or Bolognese locks were produced for a long time – another elegant and sophisticated form of snaphance, in which the arm of the cock was shaped like a swan's neck. Another big improvement was a type of flintlock mechanism developed between the end of the sixteenth and first half of the seventeenth centuries: the Catalan-style or miquelet or Biscay type. This had a "frizzen," or a steel and pan cover forged in one piece, at an angle of approximately 90° one from the other. Furthermore, the spring of the cock was fitted externally and exerted pressure on the rear, bottom part of the cock known as the heel. Opposite the heel was a type of foot called the toe, which fitted between the lock plate and spring of the cock, just resting against the edge of the lock plate. Two sear lever studs blocked the toe in two distinct positions when the cock was turned backwards. The first was the safety (half cock) position, which prevented any risk of accidentally firing the weapon; the second position was reached by turning the cock back further (full cock) to prepare it for firing. The toe rested on the sear stud, consisting of a small rectangular plate. When the trigger was pulled, the stud was retracted and the powerful spring pushed the cock against the frizzen, which was knocked upwards to expose the priming pan.

Officially, the Catalan type of lock originated in Spain at the end of the sixteenth century, but some authors believe it was invented in Italy,[37] while others prefer to call it the Mediterranean lock,[38] of which there were two distinct versions: Spanish and Italian. The one described by Hayward as the Italian version, commonly known as the Roman lock, is, however, documented later than the miquelet and differs from it in some respects. It has a similar frizzen, but the action of the external spring is different, as this pushes downwards on the toe of the cock. Two sear studs operate inside the lock, the first on the toe of the cock, in the half-cock or safety position, and the second on the heel, in the full-cock or ready-for-firing position. The second stud is withdrawn when the trigger is pulled and releases the spring on the toe of the cock, instead of the heel as in the Catalan lock. Furthermore, the steel normally slopes forwards in the Roman-style frizzen.

These two types of flintlock remained in use until the beginning of the nineteenth century, the

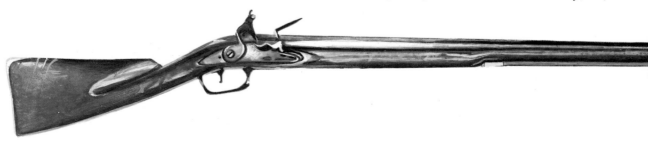

Detail of the lock plate of a flintlock pistol, Paris, c.1680. Museo del Palazzo di Venezia (National Odescalchi Collection), Rome.

design proving so sturdy and reliable that craftsmen continued to fashion them in the same way.

But the mechanism which was to prove the most successful and widely used was invented in France between 1600 and 1610, or at least that is the date attributed to a superb gun preserved at the Heritage Museum at Leningrad,[39] signed "M. Le Bourgeoys à Lisieul," which must refer to the craftsman Marin Le Bourgeois, who was born in Lisieux and died in 1634 and was active at the French court as a painter, sculptor and maker of musical instruments and firearms.[40] The gun in Leningrad carries the number 152 of the inventory of the *Cabinet d'Armes* of Louis XIII, but according to some documents in the archives could have been made for Henri IV, in which case the date would have been prior to 1610, making Marin Le Bourgeois the first historically authenticated inventor in the history of firearms.

A characteristic of the French-style mechanism, also known as the modern-style lock, is a sear fitted internally which acts on a tumbler connected to the cock. The tumbler has two notches: the first one for the half-cock and the second for the full-cock position. The sear, connected to the trigger, works vertically instead of horizontally, pivoting on the notches when the cock turns. On the outside is a single spring, which assists movement of the frizzen. Other types of lock with mixed characteristics were in use at almost the same period: the "Baltic" lock for example, in which the risk of accidentally firing the gun during loading was precluded by a frizzen in which the steel was joined to the pan cover, but so designed that it was shifted to one side when the gun was carried loaded;[41] and the "English" lock, with a horizontally-acting internal spring as in the snaphance, an L-shaped frizzen as on the French lock and a safety catch called a dog, which was released by hand, to hold the cock in the half-cock position.

All in all, flintlock weapons were much more economical than the wheel-lock type. They were also quicker and easier to load. Although wheel-locks continued to be produced, flintlock guns very much took over, both for civil and military use. As for English locks, these are undoubtedly what Antonio Petrini is referring to in his *Arte*

Fowling piece, 7 ft (2.13 m) long, from the Hudson Valley (late seventeenth century). H. I. Peterson Collection.

43

Fabrile (The Art of the Blacksmith) of 1642, where he says "they are made in great number, as also in England, being grossly and ill fashioned, and yet they are excellent for making fire."[42]

"Excellent for making fire" not only in war, but also in peace, it should be noted. In the first half of the seventeenth century the English sporting gun, the fowler or fowling piece, was invented, measuring from 5 to 6 ft (1.5–1.8 m), in the belief (disproved only a long time later) that a long barrel, with a powerful explosive charge, could give a longer range and straighter trajectory.[43] What counted was the fact that in the relatively free political and social climate of England, this weapon was affordable by practically everyone, and this led to a great increase in game shooting, above all among the middle classes, who until then had spurned the dangerous matchlock arquebuses and had been unable to afford the costly and delicate wheel-lock types.

Fowlers remained in use for a long time, and were taken by the colonists to North America. For during this same period, many were seeking their fortune or room for their political and religious beliefs in the New World, where they were confronted by a wilder natural environment and hostile inhabitants. The fowlers proved far superior to matchlock and wheel-lock guns for hunting and defending the settlements. The first half of the seventeenth century saw the development of whole schools of gunsmiths. In France,

Henri IV was responsible for the construction of the Great Gallery of the Louvre, where artists and craftsmen worked for the Court, and they always included a gunsmith. The first was Marin Le Bourgeois, already mentioned, and even outside Paris renowned and capable craftsmen were at work like Pierre Bergier in Grenoble, or J. C. Tournier de Massevaux in Alsace, or Le Bourgeois himself, who had a workshop at Lisieux in Normandy with his brother Jean.[44]

The French gunsmiths of the mid seventeenth century and the catalogs which illustrated their art were responsible for the diffusion throughout Europe of lock plates with rounded surfaces. Of the pattern books of chiselled ornamentation intended for gunsmiths and the collectors of the time, a volume produced by C. Jaquinet in 1660 can be considered one of the first forms of printed publicity by a craft workshop in this area.[45] The book in fact specifies that all the designs are taken from the works of Thuraine and Le Hollandois, "*Arquebusiers Ordinaires*" to His Majesty the King of France. As for Germany, we have already mentioned a few names in connection with wheel-lock guns, but they are worth reiterating, given the great number of weapons of German origin preserved in museums throughout the world. Unlike France and England, Germany was not a unified state in the seventeenth century, but a mosaic of principalities, duchies and palatinates whose courts were, in many cases, so prosperous

A lock-maker (left) and a stocker (right), from sixteenth-century engravings of gunsmiths' workshops.

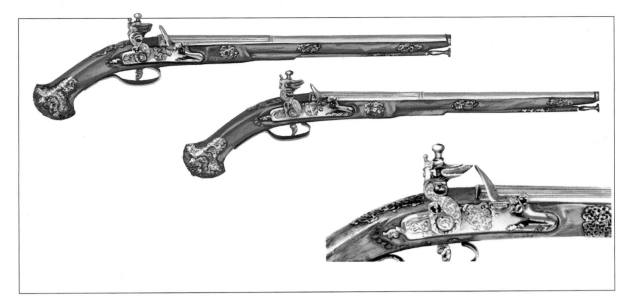

Pair of flintlock pistols with "modern-style" lock. The barrels are double, polygonal towards the breech and octagonal with ribbing and with a ring around the muzzle for ornamentation and reinforcement. They are signed "Lazarino Cominazzo," who was a famous master polisher and finisher. The weapons have pierced and engraved steel mounts. They are fine examples of the work of some famous master craftsmen from the province of Brescia and date from about 1660. Tower of London Armouries, London.

that they could afford to support the work of whole schools of gunsmiths. Two main styles developed: that of the west and northwest, with its main center in the Rhineland; and that of the south and east, with centers at Augsburg, Nuremberg, Munich and Dresden. The weapons produced in this second group included the *Tschinke* wheel-lock carbine (at this period, the term "carbine" referred to any type of long, rifled weapon smaller and lighter than a rifle). The city of Teschen, not far from Dresden, was "visited" by troops from various countries during the Thirty Years War, and the elders of the city offered the officers of the different armies models of their weapon for hunting birds. Bavaria, and particularly the ducal court of Munich, had great numbers of gunsmiths, prominent among whom were the brothers Sadeler and Caspar Spät, gun-

Seventeenth-century engravings showing the production of barrels and gunpowder.

stock decorators Adam Vischer, Hieronymus Borstorfer, David Altenstetter, Elias Becker and the anonymous, but very famous, *Meister der Tierkopfranken*. The Thirty Years War also caused the craftsmen who produced these weapons to move around. Thus after their city was burned in 1634, the members of the Klett family, originally from Suhl in Thuringia, moved to Salzburg-Ebenau in Austria, where they devoted themselves to the invention of repeaters and breech-loaders.

In Italy, the town of Gardone Val Trompia in the province of Brescia, well known for its gunsmiths since at least the beginning of the sixteenth century,[46] was the most important center for the production of firearms at that period. The Brescian arms were renowned for their elegant shape, fine chiselled ornamentation and perfect barrels. The most important manufacturer in the seventeenth century was the company run by the Cominazzi family. A very large number of weapons have barrels marked with the punch of Lazzarino Cominazzo or one of his relatives or descendants. However, many of them are forgeries, as the products of this "firm" were known to be of such high quality that gunsmiths from other localities tried to pass their weapons off as products of the dynasty from Lake Garda. Another famous family was that of the Francini, notable among whom was Giovanni Battista Francino, active between 1630 and 1660. The Cominazzi, the Francini and other influential families around Lake Garda were always at loggerheads; contemporary records speak of frequent gun battles and Lazzarino Cominazzo himself was in fact killed by a shot from an arquebus on the evening of 21 August 1641.[47] However, these continuous feuds did not harm the fortunes of the Brescian arms. When a master gunsmith was exiled for homicide beyond the boundaries of the Most Serene Republic of Venice, to which the territory of Brescia belonged, he could always find some prince who was willing to receive him and provide him with workshops and materials. As for the South of Italy, a great deal of research remains to be done on the gunsmiths active in Naples: they were undoubtedly influenced by Spanish culture, but according to Hayward were particularly skillful at chiselled ornamentation of guns.

Ever since the time of Henry VIII, England had provided a rich market for gunsmiths from all

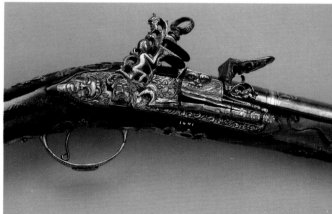

Above right: flintlock gun with Roman-style lock, from the end of the seventeenth century. A sophisticated product from the Mediterranean area (probably central Italy). Walnut root stock, engraved, pierced and embossed silver furniture, with traces of gilding; gold damascening on the barrel. Right: detail of lock, with the arm of the cock consisting of a Cupid surrounded by plant volutes. Museo Nazionale di Castel Sant'Angelo, Rome.

Eighteenth-century Italian hunting weapons. Several important families were noted for the production of very high quality hand-crafted firearms for hunting and self-defense. They included the Beretta, Cominazzi, Toschi and Zanotti families, who had been renowned for their work since the previous century. Museo Nazionale di Castel Sant'Angelo, Rome.

over Europe on the look-out for illustrious clients. Many curious weapons, which were undoubtedly avant-garde at the time (the first half of the sixteenth century), are housed in the Tower of London Armouries. The English monarchs managed to attract a growing number of gunsmiths to the country who had been forced to emigrate for religious reasons or had come in search of higher earnings, and these foreigners were later integrated into the workshops run by English gunsmiths. We have already followed the fortunes of the English lock. Towards the middle of the seventeenth century, the production of carbines and pistols with turn-off barrels developed in England (although the principle was already known in Germany, Holland and France). This method deserves some attention, because it was basically a type of breech-loading system. The barrel of the weapon was unscrewed at a point directly in front of the breech, where there was a chamber into which a ball was inserted of slightly larger diameter than that of the barrel. The projectile offered greater resistance to the initial force of the charge, but, once this resistance had been overcome, its velocity was greater than that of a ball loaded through the muzzle. Furthermore, with this system it was possible to use rifled

Hunting weapon with Florentine lock, made in Tuscany or Emilia in the eighteenth century. Double barrel, carved butt; figures applied to lock plate. Museo Nazionale di Castel Sant'Angelo, Rome.

barrels without having to force the projectile down them, therefore making the trajectory more precise. Lastly, it was possible to measure the gunpowder charge more accurately, which also gave more regular results.

Prince Rupert, commander of the cavalry of King Charles I during the Civil War, performed a number of heroic feats with weapons of this type. His trusted armourer Harman Barne had serious problems during the government of Oliver Cromwell, but this record of political persecution won him the position of royal armourer during the reign of Charles II, who restored the monarchy to England.[48]

Another very famous armourer who was active in England in the second half of the seventeenth century was Caspar Kalthoff, a member of a family of gunsmiths from Solingen who, together with his parents working in Copenhagen, was responsible for developing a repeater which may be regarded as the first of its kind.[49] In the Kalthoff gun, the bullets are housed in a cylindrical container inside the stock, below the barrel; the gunpowder is kept in another container in the butt. The trigger guard pivots, and moving it backwards or forwards causes the breech of the gun to turn in such a way that a bullet falls into it; at the same time, a measure of powder drops down from the rear container in the butt; the breech is then closed and the priming powder dropped into the pan. Finally, the wheel-spring is loaded or (in the case of flintlock weapons) the cock is raised ready for firing. The Kalthoff family and its imitators produced various versions of this weapon, some of which had as many as thirty charges: a formidable instrument in the hands of private individuals or highly trained marksmen like those of the Royal Danish Foot Guards, who made good use of them during the wars fought by their country in the second half of the seventeenth century. However, it was a little ahead of its time and the intricacy of its mechanisms made it very delicate and difficult to repair in the event of breakdown or blockage by gunpowder residue. A variant of the Kalthoff system made until the beginning of the nineteenth century, mainly by English gunsmiths but also by Americans, was the so-called Lorenzoni system, later modified by the Englishman Cookson, in which loading was controlled by an external lever instead of the trigger guard. The process was slower than in the Kalthoff system, but needed fewer mechanical parts and was therefore more economical. On the other hand it was less safe and many weapons of this type have come down to us with the butt shattered, a sure sign of an explosion, which was probably fatal for the unfortunate users.

Other countries produced some outstanding weapons at this period. Some of them were veritable works of art, like certain Scottish products which are much sought after by collectors, or the work of Dutch craftsmen such as Jan Knoop and Swiss, such as Felix Wender and the Meunier family in Geneva; not to mention Peter Kalthoff, brother of Caspar, who is regarded by many as the inventor of the gun which bears his surname. In Russia too, partly thanks to Swedish influence, firearms were doing quite well at this period, even if they were somewhat behind western models. Our survey would not be complete without mentioning the products of the Far East and, in particular, India and Japan. In these areas, matchlock weapons predominated, largely imported by the Portuguese and then produced locally. In Japan in particular, following the progressive isolation of the country by the Tokugawa dynasty of Shoguns, the matchlock system was perfected and weapons were pro-

A pair of Scottish flintlock pistols, of the eighteenth-century type (second half). All-metal stock, with "ram's horn" grip and trigger in the shape of a flattened acorn.

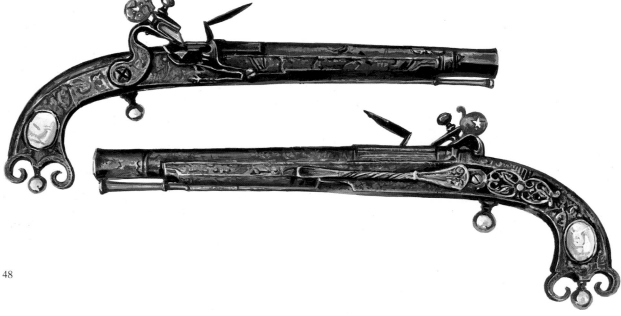

duced with finely decorated stocks and barrels, with the family emblems (*Mon*) clearly in evidence.[50] However, before the Tokugawas took over completely, matchlock weapons had already played a decisive role in the battles of Japanese history. The most dramatic example was the battle of Nagashima, between the Takeda clan and Oda Nobunaga and his ally, Tokugawa Ieyasu. The Takedas launched their *samurai* warriors, mounted and armed with long lances, in a charge over the rough ground dividing them from the enemy. Anticipating this move, Oda Nobunaga had positioned 3,000 crack arquebusiers in three lines behind a palisade. When the horsemen were within range, the arquebusiers opened fire and, according to many accounts of the battle, even did so in sequence, giving the line which had just fired time to retire behind the other two and reload.[51] The consequences for the attackers were appalling. The *Ashigaru*, who were relatively indifferent to the ideals of the *Samurai*, completely destroyed their opponents. It is doubtful whether Nobunaga accomplished the maneuver of firing in three lines, characteristic of a number of European armies of the eighteenth century. However, as early as 1522 at the Battle of the Bicocca, Prospero Colonna had ordered fire by 4,000 Spanish arquebusiers in four lines who, by firing in sequence, had mowed down the square formations of their Swiss adversaries.[52] The Japanese war lords may originally have heard of such tactics from their European arms suppliers.

Let us now return to the battlefields of Europe,

which we left at the beginning of the seventeenth century. From halfway through the previous century, the not very powerful matchlock arquebus had been replaced by the cumbersome musket, which weighed up to 20 lb (9 kg) and needed a forked rest (sometimes useful as a final means of defense). Throughout the first half of the seventeenth century, the musket was the principal firearm used by the infantry, who also included a fair number of pikemen, although increasingly fewer than the gun users.

An important innovation was the use of granular gunpowder, which was obtained by soaking the mixture of sulfur, charcoal and saltpeter and then passing this compound through a sieve.[53]

Guns for hunting and self-defense, from the eighteenth and nineteenth centuries. Museo Nazionale di Castel Sant'Angelo, Rome.

Another novelty was the introduction of pre-packed charges in wooden containers. These packs were suspended from a special bandolier, which also held the flask with the priming powder, and were known as the "twelve apostles," as this was the number soldiers chose to take with them to the battlefield, partly for reasons of practicality and partly out of superstition.

A few accounts of battles from the first half of the seventeenth century speak of very sparing use of muskets. At the battle of Kuisyingen in 1636, the slowest soldiers only managed to fire seven rounds in eight hours; in 1638, at Wittenmergen, the musketeers of the Duke of Weimar fired just seven times in a battle that lasted from midday to eight o'clock at night.[54] These may be extreme examples, or perhaps just bad use of the potential

of firearms, but when one considers that the flintlock mechanism was being developed at this time, one cannot help being amazed at first by the conservatism shown by the commanders of the Senate of the Most Serene Republic of Venice who in 1657 dismissed wheel-lock arquebuses as "ineffective in combat and unbefitting the soldier" and advised the captains of the city to revert to matchlock muskets, which had recently been made lighter and easier to handle.[55] The fact is that the arsenals were already full of matchlock weapons, and even flintlocks were considered too costly and delicate for the ordinary foot-soldier.

The eighteenth century

The slow but steady spread of the French lock led, however, to the adoption of flintlock guns by all European armies within the first few years of the eighteenth century. The pikemen were very much superseded at this time, thanks to the adoption of the bayonet, a type of long knife which was fixed to the firearm to transform it into a short pike in case of need. The first bayonets were of a "plug" type, that is, they had a handle which fitted into the muzzle of the gun.[56] But by

On the left, a blunderbuss with folding bayonet; England, early nineteenth century. Walnut stock, brass triple barrel. English dog lock with safety catch behind cock. The breech is signed "Twigg," and marked "London," with two London proof marks. To the right, a folding arquebus of the "scavezzo" type made in Brescia at the end of the seventeenth century. It was a long weapon with a hinged butt to enable it to be concealed beneath clothing. The gun is marked "FB" and signed "Domenico Bonomino." Museo Nazionale di Castel Sant'Angelo, Rome.

On the left, a double-barrelled gun using the Wender turn-over system; France, mid seventeenth century. This system consists of two barrels rotating around a central axis. Pressing the sprung trigger guard frees the friction discs, allowing the large caliber (21 mm at the muzzle) barrels to be moved. On the right is a hunting weapon which works on compressed air using a similar mechanism to the Girardoni system; Cortina d'Ampezzo(?), late eighteenth century. Bartolomeo Girardoni, invented a pneumatic repeating rifle which was adopted by the Austrian Army and called the *Repetierwindbüchse*. The reservoir is a truncated-conical metal container which acts as a butt. On the right of the barrel is a cylindrical container for spherical projectiles. A transverse slide in the breech feeds the round into the barrel. Cocking the hammer compresses a device; when the trigger is pulled, this device knocks open the valve of the reservoir, letting out enough air to expel the ball. The gun here is a civilian version, with rococo-style engraving; rifled barrel, with double notch and sight.

Above: mechanism of *Wender*-system gun, signed "Claude Roux à Lion" on the elaborately engraved lock plate.

Below: mechanism of Girardoni-system gun, with hammer cocked. Museo Nazionale di Castel Sant'Angelo, Rome.

Above: detail of "scavezzo"-type folding arquebus. The butt hinges open and is held back by a sear. Below: six-shot cylinder hunting rifle; France, nineteenth century. Butt made of walnut root, with a carving of a lion's head on the bottom part. Twisted, polygonal barrel engraved "RUBANS D'ACIER." A scroll with gold and silver damascening is inscribed "J. J. HERMAN BREVETE." Right: detail of the cylinder with the barrel turned up ready for loading from the front. Nipple-type ignition system. Museo Nazionale di Castel Sant'Angelo, Rome.

53

the beginning of the eighteenth century, "socket" type bayonets were already in use, or ones with an external bush which fitted around the muzzle. In this way, the gun could be fired with the bayonet "fixed," ready for immediate use in case of emergency, when there was no time to reload the weapon or when the infantry were relying on the deterrent value of a bayonet attack.

The combined use of guns and bayonets radically altered fighting tactics. First of all, people tried to exploit the relative simplicity of the firearm to speed up and regularize the rate of fire of troops through the mechanical repetition of a certain number of movements. If the troops were well disciplined, an enormous volume of fire was available compared with a few decades previously. The infantry was generally arranged in three lines: the first kneeling, the second standing and the third reloading the weapons. Normally only the front row on foot would fire, but two lines of fire could be ordered, with the second row firing over the heads of their companions. This obviously gave a much more powerful burst of fire. As most of the guns were smooth-bore without sights, the infantry formations behaved like ships firing a broadside. The essential thing was to break the solidity of the enemy formation and then disperse it by advancing with bayonets drawn. A famous incident in history was the "exchange of courtesies" between Lord Charles Hay, commanding the British First Foot Guards, and the Comte d'Auteroches, grenadier-lieutenant in the French Guard. At the Battle of Fontenoy in 1745, the Englishman apparently said to the Frenchman: "Gentlemen of the French Guard, fire first!" To which the Frenchman apparently replied: "No, Sir, the French Guards never fire first; please to fire yourselves."[57] This invitation was, however, dictated not so much by courtesy as by the strict regulations which forbade the French toops to fire the first shot against approaching enemy infantry, the reason being to avoid return fire or, worse still, a bayonet attack while the men were engaged in the twenty-four movements considered necessary at the time to reload their weapons. Observance of the rules in that corner of the field of Fontenoy proved disastrous for the French, but in most cases it was essential to maintain the cohesion of the troops. Now that the initial reluctance to use firearms had been well and truly overcome and the false security of armour abandoned for ever, the minor nobility, forced to obey the national monarchies, had agreed to form the backbone of

Powder flask made of boiled leather and a leather bandolier with bullet pouches. The flask has a metal top with a spring-operated spout for dispensing the gunpowder charge. Italy, seventeenth century. Museo Nazionale di Castel Sant'Angelo, Rome.

the new armies, in which soldiers of fortune, runaway peasants and unemployed townspeople no longer had an opportunity, as had happened in the Thirty Years War, of enriching themselves and improving their social status. Encouraged to sign up on false promises, press-ganged or enlisted, the poorest section of the population, the so-called "dregs" of the society of the Enlightenment, became automata in the hands of their commanders. An exception to this were the elite troops: the various guard regiments, the grenadiers, dragoons, and most of the cavalry. Not that the discipline was less hard, but they did at least receive higher pay and were armed with better weapons. In this situation, which remained more or less unchanged up to the Napoleonic Wars, the first big national weapons factories appeared. In France, in particular, the factory at Charleville produced the first regulation model gun for the infantry in 1717. In Britain various private individuals under license from the Board of Ordnance, whose headquarters were in the Tower of London, supplied from 1725 onwards the first documented examples of the famous Brown Bess – the "long musket" used by the British army.[58] As for Prussia, a standard infantry rifle was produced from the beginning of the eighteenth century – a sturdy, functional weapon which among other things had a steel ramrod, which was heavier but certainly less liable to break than the wooden ramrods of the French and English guns. With the aid of the steel ramrod, the Prussian fusiliers could easily fire at least three rounds a minute. Their tactical abilities were such that they could persuade even attentive observers such as Voltaire to exaggerate them. In a letter of 8 January 1758 from Lausanne, the great philosopher wrote to Monsieur d'Argent:

"I agree with your dim view of the King of Prussia, but he possesses the foremost of talents in the game he is playing – speed. The nucleus of his army has been trained for forty years. Just think how regular, vigorous, hardened machines must fight, who every day see their leader acknowledge them with a raise of the hat and exhort them to do their duty. Remember . . . how they turn the cartridges, how they fire from six to seven shots a minute."

Voltaire may well not have understood weapons as he did philosophy, literature and history, but these remarks of his do at least provide a record of another important innovation, the cartridge. Before its adoption by soldiers and civilians, the firer had to carry a flask of gunpowder around with him, plus a smaller flask of finer, priming powder. The only improvement, as we have seen, had been the "twelve apostles" suspended from a bandolier. Cartridges made it possible to fire many more rounds in relative safety. The cartridge in its original form consisted of three parts: the spherical projectile, the gunpowder and the strong paper wrapping. By means of the small flash produced by the casting process which always projected from the lead bullet, the ball could be attached to the paper wrapping containing the powder. The other end of the paper was then tied with fine thread and the cartridge was complete.[59] To use it, the soldier had to tear open the opposite end from the one containing the bullet with his teeth and pour a

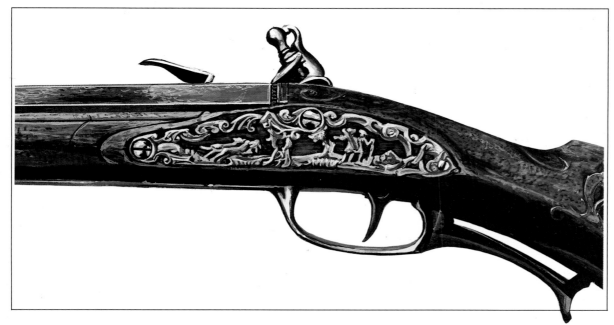

Detail of the side-plate of the lock of an early eighteenth-century Jäger rifle. It is engraved and embossed with a hunting scene and is the work of Paul Poser from Bohemia.

little of the powder into the priming pan. Having shut the lid on this, he would put the rest of the charge in through the muzzle of the gun, followed by the projectile with the paper still attached to it. After the whole lot had been pushed home with the ramrod, he then raised the gun to the firing position and was finally ready to fire it.

Certainly with this system, because the charge varied each time, firing could not be accurate (but for the infantry formations in use at the time, this was not a problem). Another serious drawback common on the battlefields of the eighteenth century and the early part of the nineteenth century was the raging thirst that soldiers experienced because their mouths were continually coming into contact with gunpowder. In spite of the regulations, soldiers tried every means imaginable to increase the rate of fire at the worst moments of the battle: with the ramrod, they would push the entire cartridge, once the bottom of it had been opened, into the gun with such force that a bit of the powder would find its way into the closed priming pan through the vent; or they would try to achieve the same result by hitting the butt of the gun on the ground; they would fire "with a rolling ball," or send the projectile down without the paper wrapping, thus eliminating any possibility of the bullet sticking to the walls of the barrel. Obviously, the results of firing with a rolling ball were even more erratic. Finally, the ramrod could be pushed into the ground, avoiding having to replace it in its housing each time – a dangerous expedient if the unit to which the fusilier belonged received the order to change position rapidly.

For most of the eighteenth century, there were no major innovations in the field of individual weapons. The cavalrymen were equipped with pistols and short carbines and a few units which specialized in preliminary skirmishes or marksmanship were given *Jäger* rifles (from the German word for hunter). A similar mechanism was already in use with wheel-lock arquebuses, but with the introduction of flintlocks it became more popular. It basically consisted of a double trigger. The first performed all the operations of cocking the gun and the second, which was fitted in front of the first, consisted of a thin lever which released the cock prepared by the main trigger on a slight pressure from the finger, thereby disturbing the aim of the shot as little as possible.

Both Jäger and ordinary rifles took much longer to load than smooth-bore guns. In some cases, the projectile had to be forced along the rifling grooves by hitting the end of the ramrod with a mallet.

Double-barrelled percussion-lock hunting weapon. Italy, mid nineteenth century. Museo Nazionale di Castel Sant'Angelo, Rome.

If the *Jägerstutzen* (Jäger rifle) was the most important contribution of civilians' use of guns to the armament of soldiers, the simplicity of the flintlock mechanism encouraged many craftsmen to experiment with technical solutions which had already been tried with matchlock and wheel-lock weapons. Unlike what had happened in the past, however, gunsmiths were now working for a much larger market, both because weapons had become more economical to use and because the rise of the middle classes in many European countries greatly increased the demand for arms which were easy to use, did not require a long period of training and were capable if not of killing one's adversary, at least of frightening him. A significant weapon from this point of view was the blunderbuss. This distinctive short gun, with its barrel which was flared outwards at the front, encouraged the belief in those ignorant of ballistics that the bigger the exit hole, the broader the "pattern" or spread of the projectiles on their way towards the target. According to this line of reasoning, a blunderbuss loaded with shot or metal fragments should have a better chance of hitting the target at close range than a weapon with a cylindrical muzzle and a single projectile in the barrel. In point of fact, even a pattern of pellets follows a more or less straight trajectory, apart from the inevitable ricochets against the walls of the barrel. The real advantage of the blunderbuss and pistols with similar characteristics was the fact that it was easier to load in the dark or on a moving vehicle. A coachman or guard on a shaking coach, obliged to defend himself against the highwaymen who infested the roads, or conversely, an outlaw lying in wait in the dark, used the flared shape of the barrel as a funnel to avoid spilling the gunpowder and help push the ramrod home. This real advantage of wide-mouthed guns is confirmed by the existence of flared "muzzles" which were made of brass and sold separately for fitting over the front end of normal firearms. The need to fire several shots with a single weapon, covering a wider area, was better satisfied by instruments like the "duck's foot" pistol, with four barrels in a fan shape connected to a single lock, or big guns like the one with seven barrels made for the Royal Navy by Henry Nock between 1780 and 1790.

Apart from weapons for hunting and self-defense, the production of duelling pistols provided a rich market for gunsmiths, especially in the second half of the eighteenth century. Although the sword continued to be favoured as an instrument for resolving questions of honour, pistols began to be preferred in some countries. This was particularly true in England, perhaps because a duel with a pistol did not require much expenditure of energy, ungainly movement or

French Army Uniforms

The development of national armies, culminating in the long period of wars between the end of the eighteenth and beginning of the nineteenth centuries, gave large sections of the European populations a taste for fine uniforms, which fostered a sense of national identity and patriotism. In the middle of the last century, a new "science" was born, devoted to the study of all aspects of militaria and the regulations controlling the clothing and equipment of soldiers of all periods. The exchange of information between militaria experts and arms historians has often proved invaluable in furthering our knowledge of military institutions. (Illustrations of uniforms taken from the treatise *Les uniformes de l'Armée française depuis 1690 jusqu'à nos jours* by Lienhart and Humbert, Leipzig, 1900).

shouting, which was more in tune with the temperament of the English gentleman. Furthermore, skill in handling a pistol could be acquired by careful practice, without the need for special equipment and exhausting training in swordsmanship by a fencing master. Thus pistol duelling was also suited to those with no military background.

Sure of their rich clientele, the English gunsmiths continued to perfect their weapons. Towards the end of the eighteenth century, round barrels, which were generally truncated-conical in shape and heavier at the breech, were replaced by octagonal ones, which were better balanced, and could therefore counteract the tendency of novices to fire upwards. At the beginning of the nineteenth century, further improvements were introduced, such as a new type of trigger guard with a spur for the middle finger, and a "saw handle" in which the hand was almost enveloped by the grip. With a handle of this type, providing purchase for the middle finger and a sensitive trigger to be pulled by the index finger, the pistol became a real extension of the arm, a lethal weapon, even in the hands of the inexpert, justifying the various precautions recommended to pistol duellers, such as positioning oneself in profile and drawing one's stomach in.[60]

The relative courtesy with which the opposing sides treated each other in the "Lace Wars," as the wars of the eighteenth century were called, began to diminish with the threat of revolution.

The Master General of Ordnance in the United Kingdom certainly had no qualms about producing, from 1776 onwards, the guns created by the Scottish Captain Ferguson by perfecting a system invented at the beginning of the century by Isaac de la Chaumette, a Huguenot exile in England.

Weapons, Wars and the Industrial Revolution

Ferguson's system consisted of a large, perpendicular screw passing through the breech of the gun and connected to the trigger guard at the base. Turning the trigger guard lowered the screw just enough for it to act as a trapdoor through which the bullet and gunpowder charge were introduced. The trigger guard was then turned back, closing the breech again.

Ferguson refined la Chaumette's original model by adding vertical grooves to the screw. He also modified the pitch in such a way that a single movement was enough to open the trapdoor of the breech. These improvements minimized the risk of blockage by gunpowder residue and the rate and precision of fire could be greatly increased – up to seven rounds a minute.

Ferguson led a special unit of troops armed with his guns against the colonists in North America. The Battle of Brandywine Creek (21 September 1777) was a triumph for the Ferguson

rifle, but its inventor was gravely wounded. He returned to fight again six months later and was killed by a shot from a Kentucky rifle on 7 October 1780 on King's Mountain in North Carolina.

The real protagonist of the American War of Independence was the Kentucky, or rather the Pennsylvania rifle, because this was the region where such guns were produced to begin with. This long rifle was certainly not suitable for firing volleys in close ranks, but it was particularly good for breaking up the rigid formations of the British Infantry in wooded country, as Colonel Daniel Morgan's sharpshooters succeeded in doing during the first and second battles of Saratoga between September and October 1777 when, stationed in trees or behind bushes, they sowed panic among the redcoats and, in the course of the second battle, killed Brigadier General Simon Fraser.[61]

The only worthy adversary of the Pennsylvania rifle would have been the Jäger, used by the marksmen of the minor German principalities, whom the British enrolled as mercenaries. But these men arrived on the scene too late, and a fair number of them crossed over to the side of the colonists, guns included.

In Europe meanwhile, the most intense and dramatic series of conflicts in military history prior to the two World Wars was about to begin. Commonly known as the "Napoleonic period," it also included the wars fought by the armies born of the French Revolution.

The French, who were, needless to say, the protagonists, had recently adopted their Model 1777 musket. In 1800 to 1801, a similar model was issued, the Anno IX model[62] (corresponding to the period from September 1800 to September 1801, according to the revolutionary calendar). Apart from a few external differences, the 1777 and Anno IX models had the same strengths and weaknesses and, in particular, a tendency to fouling by gunpowder residue.

As for the British, who were to be the strongest opponents first of the Revolution and then of Napoleon, their original Brown Bess or Long Land Service muskets were few in number. Most of the guns were the less expensive India Pattern variant originally made for the troops of the East India Company and produced in Britain itself from 1797. However, the British weapons had one advantage over the French. Thanks to their slightly smaller caliber, they could use enemy ammunition, whereas the French type could not. The cartridges had been perfected, the charge and shot being wrapped in waxed or oiled paper. However, the professionalism of the troops had diminished, as had their ability. According to an estimate by B. P. Hughes, a battalion of 500 men, in two lines, with the soldiers 22 in (56 cm) apart, over a front of 150 yds (135 m), could fire from 1,000 to 1,500 rounds a minute, or from 6 to 10

Pennsylvania or Kentucky rifle, 1815–20, inlaid with brass and silver.

East India Company musket.

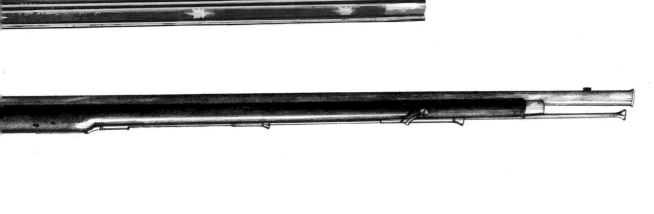

Model 1777 musket, restyled Model Anno IX (1800–1801), that is, modified and adopted in the ninth year of the French Revolution.

rounds a minute per yard, that is, on a front of less than one meter.[63] But as to the accuracy of fire, that was a very different matter. Colonel George Hanger, a veteran of the American War of Independence, wrote in his book *To All Sportsmen*, published in 1814:

"A soldier's musket, if not exceedingly ill-calibrated (and many of them are), will strike the human figure at 80 yards, but a soldier has to be most unfortunate to be wounded by a common musket at 150 yards, assuming his antagonist had aimed at him; and as for firing at a man from 200 yards, the odds against hitting the target are about as high as if you were to fire at the Moon."[64]

A few conservatives even suggested bringing back the bow and arrow and W. W. Greener in his book *The Gun and Its Development* mentions a contest which took place at Pacton Green in Cumberland in August 1792. Over a distance of a hundred yards, the bow put sixteen arrows out of twenty into the target, compared with twelve balls from an ordinary musket.

Be that as it may, there were no archers to be seen on the Napoleonic battlefields, but at best, crack shots with rifled guns like the British Baker, a few Prussian models and the Austrian 1807 model Jäger. The French used few rifled weapons. Their superiority lay in the courage and dash of the troops and the mastery with which they were led. When these qualities failed, numerical superiority and better training prevailed, as in Spain, at Leipzig and at Waterloo.

While Europe was caught up in the turmoil of war, the Presbyterian minister of the peaceful Scottish village of Belhelvie, Alexander John Forsyth, a keen gameshooter, was convinced that the birds managed to escape from him because they could see the flash of the priming powder of his gun before the main charge went off. Improbable as it may seem, it was enough to persuade him to turn to chemistry, which had been progressing by leaps and bounds since the end of the eighteenth century (one only need think of Lavoisier, Volta, Avogadro and Gay-Lussac). The characteristics of fulminates, salts obtained by treating metals with fulminic acid, had been known for some time: if subjected to high pressure, they exploded. Forsyth thought of using the explosion of fulminate of mercury to ignite the

Two luxury percussion-lock hunting carbines, converted from what were originally flintlock weapons. Jäger-type weapons, with two triggers. Würzburg, c.1740 (excluding the conversion to percussion lock). They were brought to Italy in 1814 by the Grand Duke of Tuscany, Ferdinand III of Hapsburg-Lorraine, as part of his personal armoury (see historical section on the Principality of Würzburg). Museo Nazionale di Castel Sant'-Angelo, Rome.

Dreyse Model 1862 infantry rifle with "needle-type" breech-block.

gunpowder charge. He therefore produced a small, flask-like object, dubbed the "scent bottle" on account of its shape, which was fitted to the external mechanism of the new gun in place of the pan and steel. In Forsyth's weapons the cock was replaced by a hammer – i.e., it no longer held a flint, but was fashioned in such a way that it struck a percussion pin fitted to the top of the bottle. Inside this, was a dose of fulminate, which exploded, igniting the main charge through the touch-hole, and thus firing the gun. The firer of the gun then turned the flask and a fresh dose fell into the little chamber, preparing the weapon for the next round.

Forsyth's system was cumbersome and even dangerous, but now the principle had been discovered. It was 1807 and the clergyman's invention was not an immediate success with the army. However, British gunsmiths like Joseph Manton, Joseph Egg and James Purdey understood its potential and set to work perfecting it. The number of civilian customers had grown and flintlock guns must have seemed too crude and complicated for the new users. Partially replacing the use of gunpowder by a modern chemical compound was bound to be a commercial success.

In the space of a few years, a number of improvements were made to the percussion system. A big step forward was the introduction of the percussion cap, attributed by most to Joshua Shaw, an Englishman who was active in the United States when news of the invention was published in 1814.

In the subsequent system, which used a nipple instead of a "scent bottle," a light metal cap containing the explosive compound at the back was placed over a hollow plug, which communicated with the breech of the weapon where the gunpowder was situated. When the hammer struck the cap, it compressed the fulminate of mercury inside it, and the flash from the explosion passed through the channel in the nipple and ignited the gunpowder, thus firing the shot.

At least, that was what was meant to happen. But, as anyone who has used a toy gun will know, the cap does not always work. And one can well imagine how inconvenient it was to position it properly each time.[65] Nonetheless, it was another step forward, very much in line with the times.

Industrialization was completely changing the

face of Europe and even the east coast of the United States. Everywhere, small shops where goods were both made and sold were being replaced by large workshops and factories; and for the first time, gunsmiths did not need the favour of monarchs or governments to enrich themselves and promote their products. Behind every arms industry was the initiative of a brilliant inventor, a skilled craftsman or at the very least, a tough businessman; but there were also whole teams of researchers and technicians, who were free to work for whoever would pay them best. In Europe, a typical example was Nikolaus von Dreyse. This skillful inventor, who was to figure prominently in the history of firearms, first worked in Paris for Johannes Samuel Pauly from 1809 to 1814. Pauly himself had had a number of brilliant ideas, but was less successful at putting them into practice than his pupil. In September 1812, for example, he was granted a ten-year patent for the first breech-loading guns in the world with ready-primed cartridges. Pauly's cartridge, composed of a tin base and a paper tube containing the gunpowder and projectile, was fitted at the back of the barrel, after a piston – the first "breech-block" – containing a needle, had been drawn back by means of an external lever. When the trigger was pulled, a spring thrust forward the needle, which struck the center of the tin base, detonating the compound with which the inside was coated, and thus igniting the main charge. A crack shot could fire several rounds a minute with a double-barrelled Pauly gun. However, Pauly was way ahead of his time and his weapons were mainly put to civilian use; improvements were researched and applied by Clément Pottet, who in 1829 patented an all-metal cartridge, and Casimir Lefaucheux, who replaced the needle by one which was an integral part of the cartridge. In Lefaucheux's cartridge, the hammer struck the top of this small needle which projected from one side of the base of the cartridge; the tip of the needle was driven against a compound of fulminate at the base of the cartridge, thereby causing the explosion.

To return to von Dreyse, at the same time as the French gunsmiths were carrying out their research, this German genius had managed, after numerous attempts, to produce a cartridge in which the cap of fulminate was positioned behind

French breech-loading revolver using center-fire cartridges; 10 mm caliber; six-shot cylinder. The barrel is inscribed "Lepage Moutier à Paris"; second half of the nineteenth century. Museo Nazionale di Castel Sant'Angelo, Rome.

Pistol-duelling in the first half of the nineteenth century

The use of the duel as a means of resolving private disputes originated from the "trial by ordeal" of the Germanic peoples. One must distinguish duels for personal reasons from the true chivalrous duel, which tended to settle any possible private grievances in the spectacle of a martial game. When the era of the great tournaments ended, the duel as a final means of defending one's honour was, paradoxically, forbidden by law, although in fact encouraged by custom, to the extent of being considered almost a symbol of social promotion. For a nobleman, the duel was one of the prerogatives of his class. For a man from the bourgeoisie, fighting a duel could win him a new dignity and recognition. Perhaps that is why duelling persisted for so long, despite numerous political, economic and social changes and increasingly heavy penalties. In a pistol duel, the injured party normally fired the first shot, at a distance agreed between the "seconds" of the two opponents. The second dueller would then answer the fire if he was still in a position to do so. The duel was ended if one of the two parties chose to give in or if witnesses and doctors considered that one of the duellers was unfit to continue. Agreement could also be reached on the number of shots allowed. Duelling to the death was considered dishonourable, but that of course did not prevent numerous gentlemen from meeting an untimely end over the centuries.

A pair of breech-loading target and duelling pistols in a "French-style" case (the items slot into compartments which exactly fit their shape), with accessories for loading and maintenance. Top to bottom: ramrod with charge extractor and screw tip for removing any bullets that got stuck in the barrel; bullet mould and crucible for casting bullets; screwdriver and tools for packing gunpowder into cartridges; percussion cap container; the two compartments in the corners hold bullets.

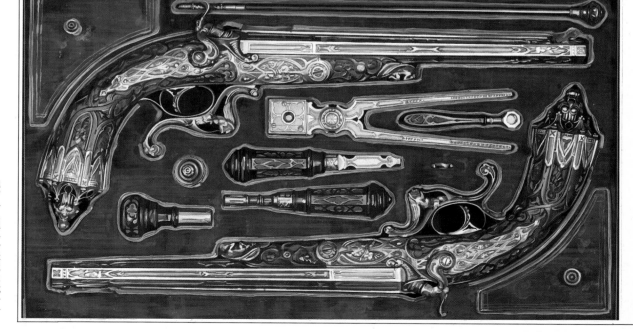

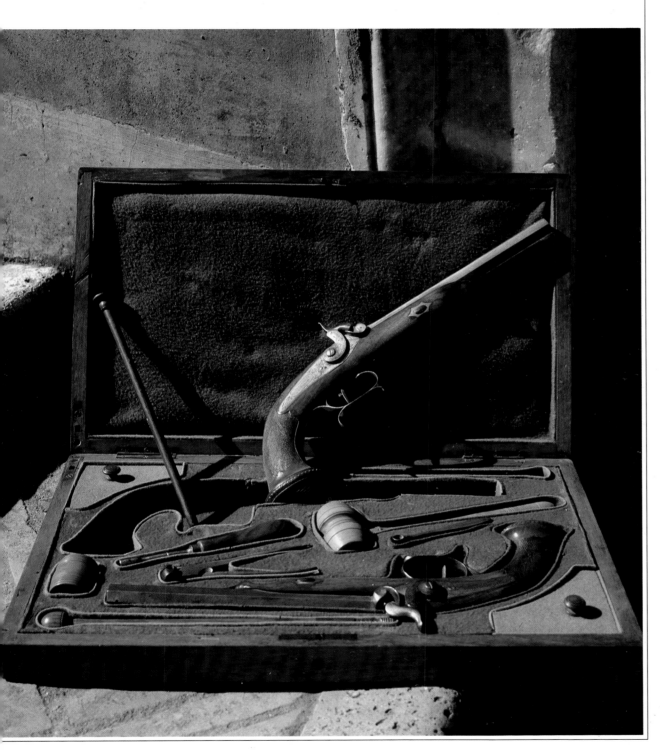

Pair of percussion-lock duelling pistols from the beginning of the nineteenth century. The case and accessories are similar to those shown opposite, but include a mallet for striking the end of the ramrod, to push home the bullets. Museo Nazionale di Castel Sant'Angelo, Rome.

the lead bullet and in front of the gunpowder charge. In the gun which his brother Rudolf tested before the Prussian authorities in Berlin in 1836, the paper cartridge was fitted in the breech and the breech-block consisted of a cylinder, with a handle to help pull it back at the moment of loading. Once the cartridge had been loaded, the breech-block was closed and the base of the handle, turned to one side, slotted into a recess at the side of the breech. Inside the breech-block, the usual needle was freed by operating the trigger and passed through the cartridge until it struck the cap at the base of the projectile.

Von Dreyse's gun had all the basic features of the single-shot breech-loaders which were later to dominate the battlefields. The King of Prussia himself understood the importance of the invention when he authorized mass production of the guns in 1841 and in 1848, described the invention as "a special decree by Providence to strengthen our national resources" and expressed the wish that the system might "remain secret until such

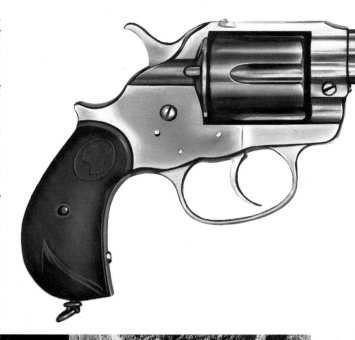

Three pepperbox pistols. Left, 11 mm caliber five-barrelled pistol; breech-loaded with pin-fire cartridges by means of a removable barrel block; the hammer, operated by the ring-shaped trigger, was fitted underneath and worked upwards. The case normally containing the weapon is marked "Caron, Arquebusier du Roi à Paris"; first half of the nineteenth century. Center, 8.5 mm caliber six-barrelled revolving pistol; nipple-type ignition with the hammer acting on the top barrel; probably made by Rigby in Dublin between 1830 and 1840. Right, a Belgian 9.5 mm caliber five-barrelled revolving pistol made at Liège by Mariette; nipple-type ignition; ring-shaped trigger, with screw-off barrels and percussion on the bottom barrel. Unusual features of this weapon, large numbers of which were produced from 1837, including many imitations, are the fact that the barrels were screwed on to the revolving cylinder individually, to line up with the nipple screwed in from the other side. Double-action firing mechanism. Museo Nazionale di Castel Sant'Angelo, Rome.

68

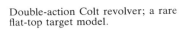
Double-action Colt revolver; a rare flat-top target model.

Pair of Colt revolvers with front-loading cylinders; "second model," ordered by a wealthy American businessman. Finely engraved, burnished weapons with ivory butts, kept in an elegant rosewood case, complete with accessories. The powder flask is solid silver.

69

time as the great role which it is destined to fulfill in history has associated it with the glory of Prussian arms and the expansion of the Empire."[66]

The Dreyse gun performed admirably when used to quell a revolutionary uprising in 1848–9 and, above all, against Denmark in 1864 and Austria in 1866 in what was known as the "Seven Weeks' War." It had a few serious defects: the bolt-handled breech-block was not fully airtight and the needle inside it corroded easily and had to be replaced from time to time. In Europe, however, at least until 1866, no other military gun could match it for practicality and rate of fire.

In the New World

Things were very different in America, where there were practically no restrictions on the use of individual firearms and gunsmiths were free to experiment. The one limitation was the patent system – a very important innovation designed to prevent the fruit of years of research and investment being compromised by some unscrupulous imitator. Paradoxically, however, in some instances patents actually hindered the progress of science and technology, particularly in the case of firearms. Patent offices could not keep pace with the countless innovations introduced virtually every day and this fact, plus a fair amount of political and financial pressure, blocked improvements to revolving arms for a long time, which were sold on a large scale by Samuel Colt and protected by clever patents.

With Samuel Colt, we are really entering the

firing pin had been popular since the end of the eighteenth century. Colt chose the opposite approach. The story goes that it was the mechanism for blocking a ship's wheel which gave him the idea for his revolving cylinder weapons, or guns with a number of chambers (five to begin with) in which the projectiles were placed, grouped together and fitted between the percussion system and the barrel.

These prototypes, made between 1836 and 1842, were "single-action": lifting the hammer by hand caused the cylinder to rotate, bringing a new chamber into line between the firing pin and the barrel. They were thus designed for those who needed repeated fire.

The most ardent – and influential – admirer of these powerful instruments of war was Captain Sam Walker, representing General Taylor for the purchase of arms for use in the war which broke out between the United States and Mexico in 1846. Thanks to the advice of Walker and the work of a few gunsmiths, Colt managed to produce – and sell – the Whitneyville-Walker 44 caliber, six-round, rifled model, capable of firing both spherical and ogival (cylindrical-conical) bullets, which were more accurate.

Up until 1857 Colt's patent blocked the market, but imitators were hard at work in both Europe and America. In fact, as early as 1851, Robert Adams was patenting a "double action" revolver in Britain, in which just pressing the trigger cocked the hammer, rotated the cylinder and caused the hammer to strike the new percussion cap. In 1856, it was the turn of Smith and Wesson world of modern inventors-cum-entrepreneurs in the field of firearms. "Pepperboxes" with three, four or five barrels which were lined up with the

Model 1860 Army single-action Colt revolver and English Dragoon Pistol 1851, single-action Colt revolver.

Two Colt sporting guns, with front-loading cylinders.

Various versions of the Colt "Single Action Army" revolver, with barrels of different lengths, and of the "Bisley" type.

Winchester Model 1866 repeating rifle.

to buy and perfect a patent for the use of metal cartridges in revolvers, and they managed to corner a section of the market with their models.[67] They were also responsible for the invention of rim-fire cartridges, in which the primer was distributed around the edge of the base.

The American Civil War was a perfect test bed for firearms. Few military arsenals were capable of producing their own weapons, whereas there were numerous voluntary military organizations wanting the latest and most efficient models, and the Unionist and Confederate governments were willing, with a little persuasion, to purchase large amounts of what was on offer from the manufacturers. Lastly, the sheer scale of the conflict and battlefields meant that the tremendous power of the new offensive weapons could be tested in a short space of time. Even a hybrid like the Springfield musket-rifle, various models of which were adopted by the Unionists, proved a lethal weapon. It was a percussion-lock, rifled muzzle-loader. It used the Delvigne type of bullet, renamed Minié even in the United States (popular name *Minnie ball*) after the French captain Claude-Etienne Minié who had helped perfect the system, which was then simplified by James Henry Burton, master gunsmith at the United States Harper's Ferry Armory.

In this rifle by the French captain Gustave Delvigne, in use from 1829, the breech where the gunpowder was placed formed the base of the barrel, but had a slightly smaller diameter than the latter, with the result that a thickness was created near the end of the barrel. The spherical bullet, which was slightly smaller than the internal diameter of the barrel, would run into this thickness when loaded through the muzzle of the gun. If the bullet was then tamped down with the steel ramrod, blocked by the breech, it would be

flattened against the walls of the barrel and stick to the rifling grooves, giving it – in theory at least – a more accurate trajectory. In order to prevent the blows from the ramrod deforming the gun, Colonel Thouvenin added a steel rod at the end of the breech, which acted like an anvil against which the base of the projectile was flattened by the ramrod. Thouvenin's bullet was also cylindrical-conical in shape, which increased its accuracy. This first type of rifle was used by the armies of various countries including France, Piedmont, Belgium and minor German states. Another big improvement was suggested by Delvigne himself, who observed that if the new, cylindrical-conical bullet were given a hollow base, it would dilate as a result of the action of the gases generated by explosion of the gunpowder.[68] Captain Minié, for his part, apparently took the Delvigne model and fitted a metal cup to the base, whose purpose was to receive the thrust of the gases and exert pressure on the inner walls of the projectile. At a later date, the American Burton removed this cup, fully realizing Delvigne's project, and the

Far right, Deane Adams five-shot continuous-action percussion revolver with a closed top to the frame. Britain, Model 1851.

Right, Kerr .44 caliber double-action percussion revolver. Britain, 1858–9; Royal Small Arms Factory, Enfield.

British, supervised by Burton himself, used American machinery to produce their 1853 model, later named the Enfield rifle, after its chief place of production.

At the time of the American Civil War, the Enfields and their American cousins the Springfields demonstrated a range of up to 875 yds (800 m) and a firing precision only found in sporting weapons. One must not forget that, at that period, all military guns were already provided with an accurate rear sight, which meant that after a short period of training even a recruit could hit the target a fair number of times. Bayonet charges of the Napoleonic type were doomed to failure, as happened at the battle of

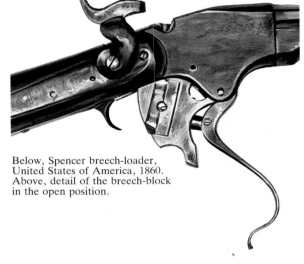

Below, Spencer breech-loader, United States of America, 1860. Above, detail of the breech-block in the open position.

Gettysburg (1–3 July 1863), but this lesson was learned by neither the Americans nor the European generals. People did realize, however, that the musket-rifle, with its old muzzle-loading system, was not entirely satisfactory either. Twelve thousand abandoned muskets were found on the Gettysburg battlefield, with two unfired charges inside them, and about 6,000 with more than three unexploded charges. One barrel contained no fewer than twenty-three unexploded charges, one on top of the other.[69]

With so many soldiers being called up from one day to the next, devoid of military instruction and destined to return to civilian life after a few years' service, new weapons were needed which reconciled the latest technology with limited human capacity. The increasingly high cost of wars also meant that they had to be concluded rapidly, using ever more efficient weapons. The conservatism of the army general staffs was swept away by political and industrial demand. Thus, while the Chassepot, the French answer to the Dreyse, was being perfected in France after the trials of the Austro-Prussian war, in the United States the Sharps breech-loader, the rugged Spencer seven-shot repeater and the Henry sixteen-shot repeater had already been tested on the battlefield. In ideal conditions the latter could fire 120 rounds in 5 minutes 40 seconds.[70] The Henry was an ancestor of the Winchester Model 1873, with a center-fire cartridge which was also used in Colt and Remington revolvers. Before this there had been the Model 1866 – an improved version of the Henry; and there were others too, notably the Model 1894. They all had lever-action loading

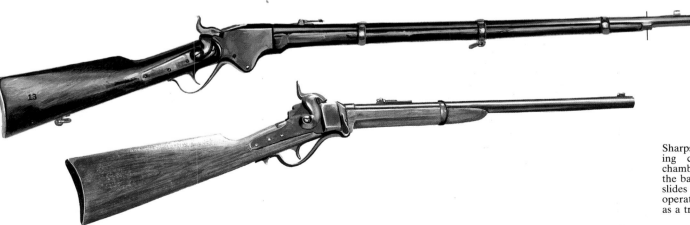

Sharps percussion-lock breech-loading carbine, Model 1863. The chamber in the breech is screwed to the barrel and a metal breech-block slides from top to bottom inside it, operated by a lever which also acts as a trigger guard.

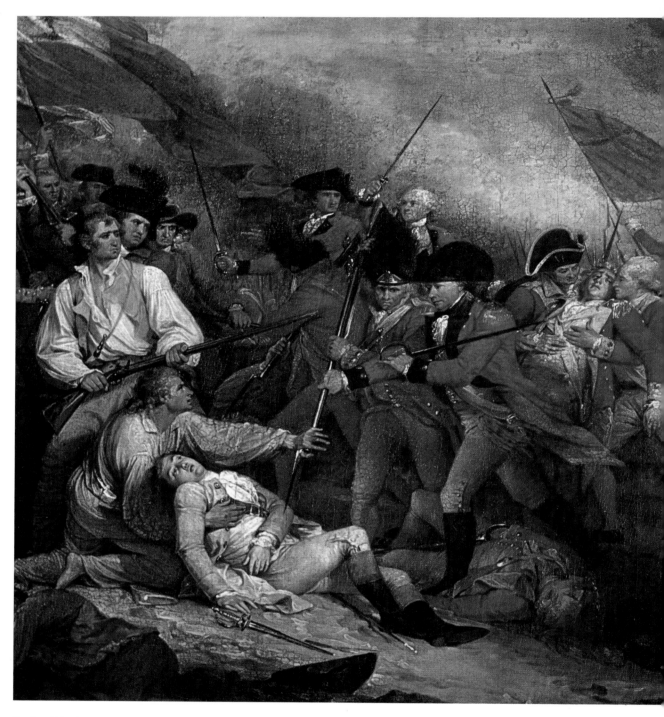

Battle of Bunker Hill by John Trumbull. On 17 June 1775, about 1,500 American volunteers resisted frontal attack by 2,500 regular British troops who were attempting to dislodge them from the heights of Bunker Hill and Breed's Hill, overlooking the city of Boston. The British, decimated by the accurate fire of the insurgents, only succeeded in forcing them into a retreat at the third attack. It was a victory achieved at the cost of 1,050 dead or wounded (forty percent of the British strength), compared with 445 casualties on the American side, and, as the latter were allowed to retreat undisturbed, the battle was seen as a victory for the cause of American independence. Much of this success was due to the long Pennsylvania rifles, later called Kentucky rifles, with which many of the freedom fighters were armed. Firing from fixed positions against an enemy advancing in close-order formation across open ground was the ideal way to use these weapons, which were not suitable for fighting in the open because of the time needed to reload them.

The Battle of Bull Run, at about 2 o'clock in the afternoon of 21 July 1861. On the orders of General McDowell, the Northerners prepare for a final assault on the Southerners' positions on Henry House Hill, but their artillery pieces are too close to the enemy, most of whom are armed with rifles. Stuart's cavalry charge against the "Zouaves" of the 11th New York, while the Federal cannon are at the mercy of the Confederate infantry. In the background, rather in anticipation of historical fact, the Federal infantry is seen retreating in disarray over the Stone Bridge. The disastrous Unionist retreat which put an end to the first battle of the American Civil War in fact took place from 4.40 pm onward following an attack on their right flank by the Southerners. The Battle of Bull Run cost the North about 1,500 dead and injured, and about 1,000 prisoners, apart from the loss of a great deal of equipment. The Southern forces lost a total of about 2,000 men, and at the end of the day the soldiers were too tired and disorganized to follow the enemy. For the first time, however, traditional military doctrine was rendered obsolete by the power and efficiency of rifled weapons.

The Battle of Gettysburg, at 3.30 pm on 3 July 1863. At the end of an extraordinary infantry charge of 15,000 Confederates on the orders of General Pickett, Brigadier General Armistead, at the head of 150 men from Virginia, managed to break through the Northerners' lines, only to meet his death a few yards further on. A few minutes later the Southern troops retired, leaving about 7,000 dead or wounded on the battlefield, who went to join the other 20,000 Southerners who were killed, wounded or captured in the three days of the battle (from 1 to 3 July 1863). The "Pickett charge," as it was immediately called, was the last attempt by General Lee to put the Northern forces to rout; but the advancing infantry was mown down first by the Northern artillery and then

by accurate fire from over 6,000 weapons. Apart from Springfields, some of the Northern soldiers were armed with Sharps single-shot breech-loading carbines and a few units even had Spencer seven-round repeating carbines, although it is doubtful whether the latter were issued to the troops used against Pickett's regiment. Be that as it may, the arms available to the infantry were more than enough to stop any other infantry, however valiant, attacking on completely open, sloping ground, although this lesson was not to be learned until the First World War.

From the work of the famous American artist George Catlin, dated 1830 and entitled *Chasing Back*. It shows a bison-hunter who was a poor shot. Luckily for him, he could count on the speed of his horse.

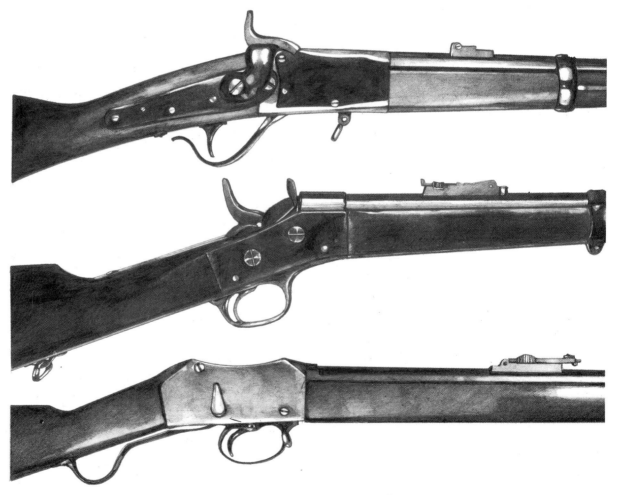

Peabody falling-block breech-loader.

Remington turning-block breech-loader.

Martini-Henry falling-block breech-loader.

system in which the projectiles were lifted towards the firing pin from a magazine below the barrel, the cartridge cases being expelled at the same time, that is, the part of the cartridge containing the detonator and gunpowder. An excellent gun which was too late to play a part in the Civil War was the single-shot rolling-block Remington breech-loader, subsequently used for hunting bison and big game.[71] In this gun, the hammer was cocked and a block in front of the breech was drawn back with the thumb, enabling the spent cartridge to be expelled. A new cartridge was inserted, and the breech-block was pushed forward with the finger and returned to its position without squashing the cartridge. At this point the trigger was pulled, freeing the spring of the hammer, which struck the firing pin inside the breech-block, detonating the explosive charge of the projectile.

Another interesting gun, if only for the part it played in the last colonial campaigns, was the Martini-Henry, adopted by the British Army in April 1871 after it had abandoned the previous Snider system. This weapon remained in service, despite mounting criticism, until 1891. It was one of the few breech-loading military weapons not to use a bolt-action breech-block, as tested on the Dreyse and Chassepot. The mechanism of the Martini-Henry was of the falling block type, with some improvements over the original model by Henry Peabody, patented in 1862.

The use of firearms in hunting big game has already been mentioned. British gunsmiths like Holland & Holland, Greener, Westley-Richards, Scott and the exclusive Purdey had been operating in this sector for some time. They, and many others, devoted themselves (and many still do) to the production of arms for use against medium and small game for a now huge world-wide clientele, both male and female. Incidentally, for the benefit of both women and a fair number of men who did not wish to advertise the fact that they were armed, the invention of the percussion lock and, in particular, the metal cartridge made it possible to buy small-scale weapons for self-defense, starting with the famous Derringer models, named after the first person to mass produce them.[72]

To return to sporting guns, the British and Americans were not the only ones in the market, particularly from the mid nineteenth century onwards. Spaniards, Belgians, Germans, French and Italians joined the fray, and many are still active – companies like Bernardelli, Famars, Francotte, Krag, Krieghoff, Merkel, Perazzi and Sauer, to name but a few.

While inventors and arsenals were developing new operating systems in the military field, nearly all the features required on guns available on the

"Hammerless" Italian double-barrelled hunting weapon, with internal hammers which are cocked automatically when the barrels are opened to insert the cartridges.

market today had been developed in the sporting sector before the end of the nineteenth century: choke bore tilting barrels, cardboard cartridges containing shot for small game and hammerless mechanisms. Above all, there was a strong preference for single-shot or double-barrelled weapons, both for greater power and precision and out of a sense of fair play and sportsmanship with regard to game shooting.

In the military sector, however, new technology was about to result in the development of firearms taking another big step forward.

Modern Weapons

Peter-Paul Mauser is rightly regarded as the father of the cylindrical breech-block system, although other capable engineers were studying the problem at the same time as he was. Mauser was lucky enough to encounter a government – that of the newly-formed German Empire – which after some initial hesitation gave free rein to his ideas.

In Mauser's system, when the breech-block is opened, a cam mechanism cocks a firing pin directly inside the bolt; the cartridge is inserted, the breech-block closed and the weapon is ready, with no risk of accidental firing. The first Mausers were produced in 1872, but back in 1867 production had begun of the Swiss Vetterli repeaters with a turn-bolt type of breech-block mechanism to replace the lever of the Henry-Winchester, of which the Swiss used the repeater system. The Italian Army was equipped with single-shot Vetterlis in 1871.

In the same year, Russia and Bulgaria adopted

The eventful history of the cartridge

1   2   3

The idea of predetermining the amount of gunpowder needed for each shot to speed up the loading process and make the weapon as accurate as possible soon occurred to users of firearms, whether for military or sporting purposes. The very etymology of the word cartridge shows that paper was chosen as the cheapest material for carrying a number of separate charges. Between the end of the sixteenth and the beginning of the seventeenth centuries, however, the most practical type of covering was found to be a wooden container, usually of boxwood. Between the end of the seventeenth and beginning of the eighteenth centuries, particularly for military weapons, the paper wrapping was used to hold the projectile as well, this being inserted into the barrel together with the empty wrapping as the final stage of the loading process.

The wars of the eighteenth century and Napoleonic period were fought using these types of cartridge. The idea of introducing the cartridge with the projectile directly into the loading system, to some extent anticipated by the first types of breech-loading individual weapons which used small metal "chambers," was certainly favoured by the adoption of the percussion lock. One of the most brilliant researchers in this field, the Swiss gunsmith Pauly, is regarded as the inventor of the modern cartridge. In 1812, he in fact patented a breech-loading system using a cartridge with a metal base, in the center of which the primer was placed. The system was subsequently perfected by Dreyse in his needle guns and throughout the nineteenth century efforts were made to perfect this new method of loading. It was immediately apparent that paper tended to leave so much residue behind that the weapon would block after a certain number of rounds. Accordingly, after experiments using papier mâché and cardboard, brass was chosen as the basic material for cartridges, cardboard only being used for hunting weapons. The primer was fitted in various different positions, until rim-fire and center-fire cartridges became established. The problems of connecting the various parts of the cartridge, choosing the shape of the projectile and, lastly, the type of propellant were also tackled. The invention of dynamite and its derivatives at the end of the nineteenth century enabled "smokeless pow-

ders" to be developed, and these are widely used in the manufacture of modern cartridges. Before this stage was reached, however, each loading system had its own type of cartridge, which obviously created problems over supply. The following pages give a necessarily limited idea of the great number of types in use up to the end of the nineteenth century.

THE FIRST CARTRIDGES

1 Wooden (normally boxwood) container for gunpowder charge which was attached to a bandolier and used in the late sixteenth and early seventeenth centuries.
2 Paper cartridge, used up to the mid eighteenth century.
3 Paper cartridge with three balls, eighteenth century.
4 Paper cartridge, used in western Germany and France, eighteenth century.
5 "French-style" paper cartridge, used in France and Prussia, eighteenth century.
6 Paper cartridge for sporting gun, 1846.
7 "Austrian-style" paper cartridge with tube of primer for percussion lock weapons, first half of nineteenth century.
8 "Dutch-style" cartridge, with cap for percussion weapon.
9 Papier mâché cartridge, with conical bullet, early nineteenth century.
10 Danish cartridge, 1849.
11 Danish cartridge, 1864.
12 Cartridge with conical bullet, used in Europe in the first half of the nineteenth century.
13 Cartridge with "Minié" bullet, Baden, mid nineteenth century.
14 Cartridge with "Minié" bullet.
15 Cartridge with conical bullet, Saxony, mid nineteenth century.

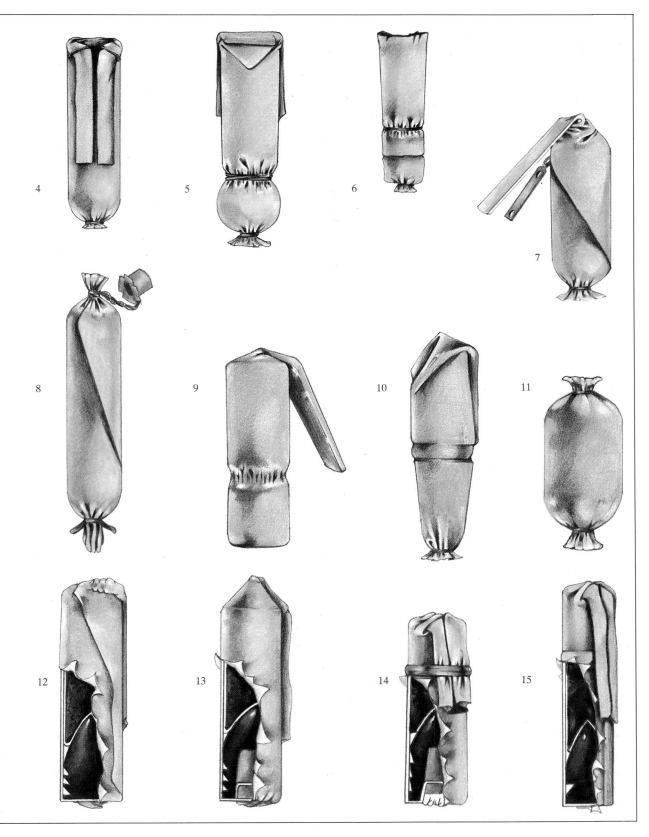

CARTRIDGES FOR BREECH-LOADING WEAPONS OF THE NINETEENTH CENTURY

1 Lefaucheux cartridge.
2 Cartridge for Roberts breech-loader (first type), 1831.
3 Cartridge for Montigny breech-loader, 1833.
4 Metal surround of cartridge used in Pauly breech-loader, 1812.
5 Cartridge used in Prussian Dreyse needle gun, 1847.
6 Cartridge with oval bullet for Dreyse needle gun, 1855.
7 Cartridge for final models of Dreyse needle gun.
8 Cartridge for French Chassepot needle gun, Model 66.
9 Cartridge for Einhorn needle gun, 1865.
10 Cartridge for Philipp needle gun, 1866.
11 Cartridge for French "Farington system" rifle, 1865.
12 Cartridge for hunting rifle, Baden, 1863.
13 Cartridge for infantry rifle from Saxony, 1865.
14 Cartridge for "Lindner system" rifle, Saxony, 1865.
15 Cartridge for "Lindner system" rifle, Austria, 1865.
16 Cartridge for "Lindner system" rifle, Bavaria, 1865.
17 Cartridge for "Marston system" rifle, 1860.
18 Cartridge for 'Westley-Richards system" rifle, 1862.
19 Cartridge for "Mont Storm system" rifle, 1860.
20 Cartridge for "Peabody system" rifle, with copper case, 1862.

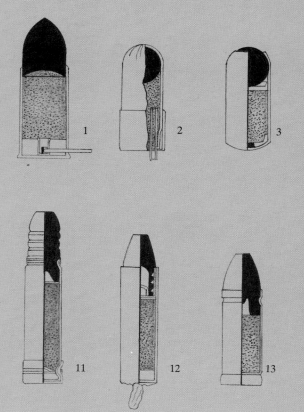

CARTRIDGES WITH METAL CASES

1 Cartridge for "Roberts system" rifle, 1867.
2 Cartridge for "Daw system," 1864; copper base, cardboard surround; Sylvester Krnka made a similar cartridge to this in 1855.
3 Cartridge designed by E. M. Boxer; paper-lined brass surround.
4 Cartridge for "Martini-Henry system" rifle, 1871.
5 Cartridge for "Berdan system" rifle, 1866.
6 Cartridge for "Werder system" rifle, Bavaria, 1868.
7 Cartridge for "Podewils system," Bavaria, 1871.
8 Cartridge for "Beaumont system," Holland, 1871.
9 Experimental cartridge for repeater weapons with tubular magazines.
10 Cartridge for Kropatschek-Chatellerault 74/82 repeater.
11 Cartridge for "Hebler system," 1887.
12 Cartridge for "Werndl system," 1867.
13 Model 77 cartridge for Mannlicher Model 82 repeater.
14 Mannlicher Model 1888 cartridge.

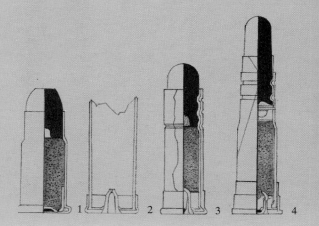

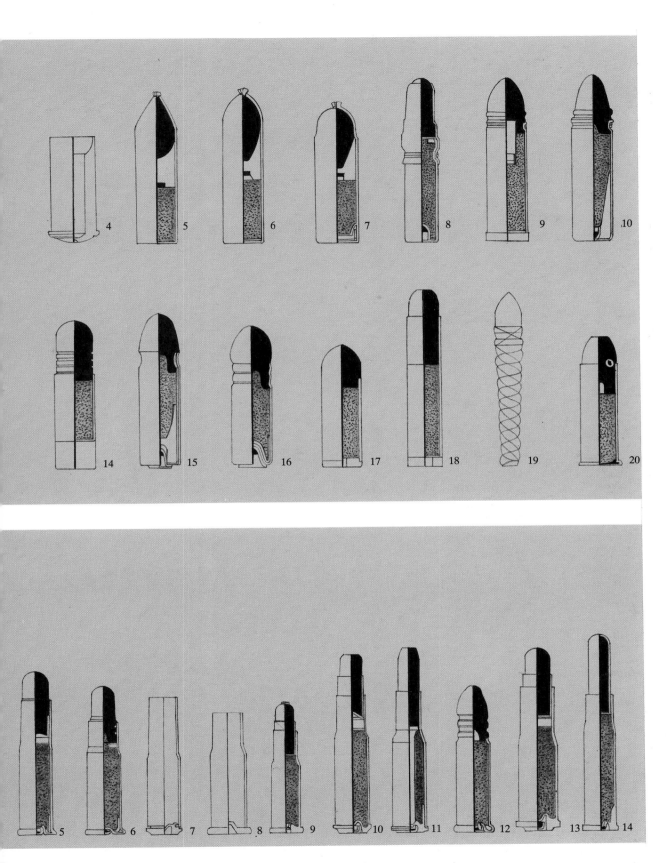

83

the Berdan breech-loading system; in 1874, the French converted the Chassepot to the Gras system in order to use a new metal cartridge. Technology was progressing in leaps and bounds. The massacre of Russians armed with Berdan and Krnka single-shot guns by the Turks, armed with Peabody-Martinis and Winchesters, at Plevna on 30 July and 1 September 1877 caused a sensation and in 1879 the American James Paris Lee patented a box-magazine for rounds which fitted into a special housing below the breech-block. Shortly afterwards, the magazine rifles of the Austrian von Mannlicher appeared. Here was another brilliant and prolific inventor who perfected a packet-loading system in 1885, according to which a group of cartridges joined together could be put into the magazine, thus simplifying loading.

Another improvement was the introduction of smokeless powders, which did away with the great clouds of smoke produced on battlefields by gunpowder once and for all and at the same time increased the power of the ammunition. The first powder of this type, made up of nitro-cellulose and picric acid, was produced in 1884 by the Frenchman Vieille after many years of experimentation to which chemists from all countries – including the inventor of dynamite Alfred Nobel – had contributed.

From this point onwards, only the illustrations and historical notes accompanying them can give an idea of the number of different models used by the armies of the leading nations of the world and produced by the many arms manufacturers.

The World Wars and numerous local conflicts which have caused so much bloodshed since the beginning of this century have aroused in many an understandable hatred of firearms, which are seen as the root of all evil – from imperialism to totalitarianism, and from organized crime to terrorism. In reality, what counts above all is the character of the person who is behind the weapon and intends to use it if need be to combat such criminal activity as illegal arms-trafficking for example, which constitutes a continuous and flagrant threat to world peace.

An important part of man's history can be traced through the use of firearms, which represent a very important chapter in the story of mankind. They marked the end of an era and, together with other fundamental scientific and technological discoveries, have carried us into this modern world.

Famous pistols

The first models of the semi-automatic pistol appeared at the end of the last century after many experiments, above all in Europe, by inventors and engineers like Borchardt, Schwarzlose, von Mannlicher and Bergmann. In 1896 the Mauser company patented its famous pistol. In 1900 DWM of Berlin began producing the "Luger" Parabellum M 1900, the first of a long series. Finally, in 1911, the United States Army adopted the Colt 1911, chosen from a number of competing designs and developed by a brilliant inventor, John Moses Browning, and the capable engineers of American industry.

In the Mauser system, the barrel and breech-block slide are connected by a vertically-moving block and recoil simultaneously at the moment of firing; after a few millimeters' travel, this block drops down, the barrel stops and the breech-block continues to recoil, expelling the spent cartridge case. In the Luger, the breech-block is articulated in three parts, and opens by a characteristic

(cont. p.86)

Luger Model 1917 with snail magazine.

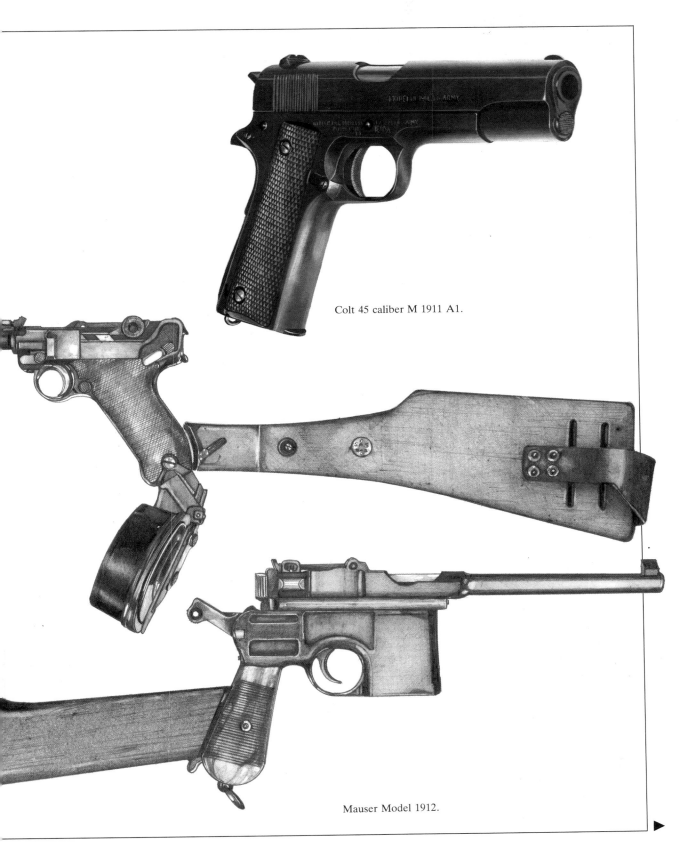

Colt 45 caliber M 1911 A1.

Mauser Model 1912.

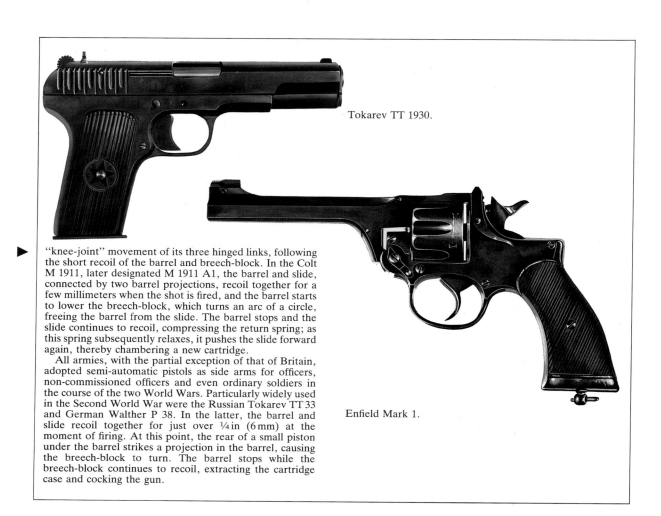

Tokarev TT 1930.

Enfield Mark 1.

"knee-joint" movement of its three hinged links, following the short recoil of the barrel and breech-block. In the Colt M 1911, later designated M 1911 A1, the barrel and slide, connected by two barrel projections, recoil together for a few millimeters when the shot is fired, and the barrel starts to lower the breech-block, which turns an arc of a circle, freeing the barrel from the slide. The barrel stops and the slide continues to recoil, compressing the return spring; as this spring subsequently relaxes, it pushes the slide forward again, thereby chambering a new cartridge.

All armies, with the partial exception of that of Britain, adopted semi-automatic pistols as side arms for officers, non-commissioned officers and even ordinary soldiers in the course of the two World Wars. Particularly widely used in the Second World War were the Russian Tokarev TT 33 and German Walther P 38. In the latter, the barrel and slide recoil together for just over ¼ in (6 mm) at the moment of firing. At this point, the rear of a small piston under the barrel strikes a projection in the barrel, causing the breech-block to turn. The barrel stops while the breech-block continues to recoil, extracting the cartridge case and cocking the gun.

Weapons of the Second World War

The experiences on the battlefields of the First World War and constant improvements to arms industries meant that most of the powers involved in the next World War were equipped with more up-to-date weapons, at least according to the standards of the war fought twenty years previously. However, the Second World War proved even more demanding than the First, both because of the size and variety of the battlefields, and the environmental and operational conditions with which the men and weapons had to cope. The various national industries were faced with the difficult task of adapting the quality and main characteristics of the guns and pistols with which their respective armies were equipped. They had to satisfy both tactical requirements, which favoured an increasing volume of fire per combatant, and demands of an economic nature, which had to take into account the difficulties over supply and over obtaining raw materials, as well as the need to produce an enormous number of weapons in a short space of time. In these circumstances, each country revealed the strengths and weaknesses of its own political and industrial system. Germany tested the ability of her engineers to the limit, both by constant research to improve the models already in production and by producing weapons which were completely new in design and operational capabilities, like the FG42 and StG, which were to serve as models for numerous imitations in the postwar period. Production was maintained at a high technical level even when the first defeats and

bombardments of the big industrial complexes began, an inevitable decline in quality coming only at the end of the war.

Italy entered the war with the '91 rifle, which was still a good gun, and some interesting and progressive weapons were put into production, such as the MAB; but growing disorganization and shortage of materials created serious problems of supply from the very first months of the war. Surplus stock and weapons stored in warehouses were used, after 1943, by the Germans, men of the RSI (Italian Social Republic) and the partisans.

Partly thanks to increasing support from the United States, Britain produced a great number of models, which were fairly similar to one another, and above all cheap weapons, like the famous Sten gun, which may not have been all that accurate and were certainly not good looking, but were perfectly functional in the hands of reasonably well-trained troops.

In the United States, after the initial difficulties of a strategic nature, a massive reorganization of industry took place, enabling military supplies of all kinds to be produced in

Opposite: weapons of the Axis. Mannlicher-Carcano Model '91 rifle and Mauser Model 1898 K (KAR 98K) carbine. Museo Storico della Fanteria, Rome.

Weapons of the British Empire. From left to right: Enfield no. 1 Mark III rifle (lacks the "magazine cut-off" device found on the original model); Enfield no. 4 Mark I rifle; Pattern 14 (P-14) rifle. Museo Storico della Fanteria, Rome.

a short space of time, which were enough to equip the armed forces of that country and the Allies. With regard to light arms in particular, the excellent Garand rifle was gradually distributed to all troops.

Finally, after the initial upheavals, the Soviet Union managed to equip increasing numbers of its troops with submachine guns which, when used in the massed attacks typical of the Eastern front, were rather like a more powerful descendant of the now useless bayonet.

At the end of the war, large amounts of military equipment fell into the hands of the victors and various items went to enrich military museums throughout the world, as well as numerous private collections: telling evidence of a tragic period in history, but one which produced a wealth of inventions. Most of these weapons were also reused to supply the armies of the countries which emerged from the break-up of the imperial colonies.

Italian weapons. From left to right: Mannlicher-Carcano Model 91/38 rifle, Mannlicher-Carcano Model 91/24 musket, Mannlicher-Carcano 91/38 cavalry musket. Museo Storico della Fanteria, Rome.

Model 1942 paratroop and light infantry rifle (Fallschirmjäger Gewehr 42). Museo Storico della Fanteria, Rome.

Automatic weapons. From left to right: Beretta Model 1938 A (MAB 38A) automatic musket; Thompson Model 1928 A1 submachine gun; Sten Mk II submachine gun. Museo Storico della Fanteria, Rome.

Hunting weapons

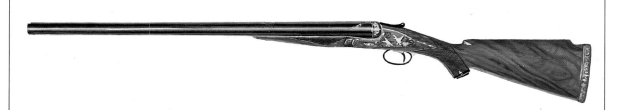

Purdey Luxury Model with over-and-under barrels (Britain)

If properly regulated, hunting does not deserve the strong criticism to which it is often subjected. Conserving the ecological balance is one of the top priorities of the sportsman, who does not want to risk running out of game. Modern sporting weapons are built to take account of the restrictions imposed by law, the type of game one intends to shoot and the lightness and ease of handling required by most users, the majority of whom are ordinary citizens who only go shooting at certain times of the year. Many people enjoy not just the competitive aspects of the sport; they also have a strong sense of aesthetics and prefer carefully finished, ornamented weapons, like the aristocratic owners of richly decorated arms of previous centuries. The end result, depending on the finances and tastes of the purchasers, is an enormous range of weapons which combine maximum functionality with sober elegance.

Manufrance Falcor Model with superimposed barrels (France)

Winchester automatic rifle (U.S.A.)

Marlin Model 336C repeating carbine (U.S.A.)

Target weapons

Taifun Model free carbine (U.S.S.R.)

Hammerli Model 150 pistol (Switzerland)

At all periods in history, man has vaunted his skill in handling arms, particular attention being devoted to target shooting. Firearms have been no exception, the archery contests with bow or crossbow of the Middle Ages being readily replaced by those using precision firearms. Particularly popular in central Europe, these competitions soon spread throughout Europe and before long to the New World as well. The newspapers and first popular magazines in the United States even invented the character of the crack shot who made a good living out of his skill with celebrated travelling shows like the famous *Wild West Show* of Buffalo Bill (William Frederick Cody). Characters who, in their time, were real "stars," like Doc Carver and Adam Bogardus, were the protagonists of countless challenges and demonstrations. At the same time, in both the United States and Europe, weapons manufacturers encouraged those who wished to emulate the great marksmen or use a shooting match to bolster their nationalistic pride, as happened in 1876 at the great meeting at Creedmor, in which Americans, Irish, Scottish, Canadians and Australians participated. This tournament, which was won by the American team, was followed almost blow by blow over the telegraph, and sponsored by the leading British and American companies.

In other countries, target shooting assumed patriotic overtones, as for example in Italy, where the Società Nazionale di Tiro a Segno (National Target Shooting Association) supplied instructors and administrative support for Garibaldi's volunteers; in France and Germany, target shooting was part and parcel of the general training of military reservists.

The recognition of several target shooting specialities at the Olympic Games, the involvement of growing numbers of women and youngsters in the numerous competitions which take place every day in every corner of the world, and the very degree of specialization of the materials used to manufacture modern target weapons have all helped to reduce the military overtones of this fascinating sport, encouraging it to be seen purely in terms of competition, with the result that, despite the sometimes over-zealous legislation, the numbers of enthusiasts practicing this sport is constantly on the increase.

Walther Model Olympia automatic pistol (West Germany)

Ruger Model Mark I Target automatic pistol (U.S.A.).

BIBLIOGRAPHICAL NOTES

[1] H. W. L. Hime, *Gunpowder and Ammunition, their Origin and Progress*. London, 1904.

[2] Roger Bacon, *Opus Tertium* in *Opera quaedam hactenus inedita*, edited by J. S. Brewer, London, 1859, and quoted in H. L. Blackmore, *Guns and Rifles of the World*, London, 1965.

[3] Cf. J. von Wlassaty, "Combat anno 1399. Welche Schussleistung besass die Tannenberg Büchse?" in *Deutsches Waffen – Journal* 6, 1977.

[4] Described and illustrated in W. Reid, *Weapons through the Ages*, London, 1984.

[5] Photo and description in Blackmore, op. cit.

[6] This theory is advanced by H. L. Peterson, *The Treasury of the Gun*, New York, 1962, and reiterated in a more recent short article by B. Humphrey, "The Hussites – Jan Zizka and his Army" in *Strategy and Tactics* 108, 1986.

[7] Codex MS. 3069, Austrian National Library, Vienna, reproduced in Blackmore, op. cit.

[8] Cf. Blackmore, op. cit.

[9] See details of individual weapons and diagrams of firing mechanisms; cf. Blackmore, op. cit.

[10] Ludovico Ariosto, *Orlando Furioso*, canto IX, octave 91.

[11] B. de Monluc, *I Commentari*, Florence, 1630.

[12] The arms and armour of Maximilian I of Hapsburg were illustrated in a great celebratory work, the *Triumphzug*, to which artists like Dürer, Altdorfer and various others contributed; an edition for the public, based on drawings by Jörg Kölderer, came out in 1526.

[13] A few pieces are kept in the Royal Armoury in Madrid; others are dispersed in various museums.

[14] Cf. Blackmore on the subject, op. cit.

[15] Described by C. Blair, *A note on the early history of the wheel-lock*, in "Journal of the Arms and Armour Society" III, 1959–61, pp. 221–56. Blackmore also mentions these weapons, without giving a date, although considering them older than a decree issued by the Duke of Ferrara in 1522.

[16] See G. Rotasso, "L'armamento dell'uomo d'arme dal XV al XVI secolo," in *Studi Storico-Militari – 1985*, Stato Maggiore dell'Esercito, Ufficio Storico (Army General Staff, Historical Office), Rome, 1986.

[17] See the decree issued by Emperor Maximilian I in 1517 in this connection; also that of 1522 by the Duke of Ferrara, reported by A. Angelucci in *Catalogo dell'Armeria Reale di Torino*, Turin, 1890, p. 420.

[18] Matchlock pistols were particularly common in Japan, as a result of a certain conservatism with regard to firearms, plus the fact that Japan cut herself off from other nations for centuries.

[19] Famous sixteenth-century gunsmiths included the Markwart brothers, Augusta, and Peter Pech of Munich; on the Markwart brothers see J. F. Hayward, *The Art of the Gunmaker*, London, 1962–3.

[20] For a detailed history of the masters of the province of Brescia, the town of Gardone Val Trompia and, in particular, the Beretta family, see M. Morin and R. Held, *Beretta – La dinastia industriale più antica del mondo*, Chiasso, 1980.

[21] Cf. Hayward again, op. cit.

[22] There is evidence of another curious ignition system using pyrites, called *Mönchbüchse* or the "Monk's Gun," also described in Blackmore, op. cit.

[23] On the various families of artists and artisans, see Hayward, op. cit.

[24] Hayward, op. cit., discusses this decorator at length; a magnificent example of his work is shown in C. Blair and L. G. Boccia, *Armi e armature*, Milan, 1981.

[25] This type of pistol was called a "puffer."

[26] François de La Noue, *Discours politiques et militaires*, Geneva, 1967, cf. R. Puddu, op. cit.

[27] H. J. C. von Grimmelshausen, *Der Abenteuerliche Simplicissimus Teutsch...*, 1669 (translated as *Simplicius Simplicissimus* by H. Weissenborn and L. Macdonald, London, 1964.)

[28] Hayward, op. cit.

[29] Reported, among others, by Peterson, op. cit.

[30] Discussed in detail in F. Wilkinson, *The World's Great Guns*, London, 1977.

[31] Wilkinson, op. cit.

[32] See for example the magnificent arquebus of the Farnese family, illustrated pp.28–9.

[33] There are however two items: a proclamation issued in Florence in the same year and a passage from *The Life of Benvenuto Cellini* (book I, chapter 99), which could suggest that "flintlock arquebuses" were in existence in Italy. According to Morin, op. cit., the term used in the Florentine proclamation was synonymous with "wheel-lock arquebus." The passage from Cellini: "Mounted on my noble steed, I lowered the stone of my arquebus" could also refer to a wheel-lock weapon.

[34] Blackmore, op. cit., with reference to A. Meyerson, *Vapenindustrierna i Arboga undre äldre Vasatid*, Stockholm, 1939; also quoted in Hayward, op. cit., who includes under the term "Scandinavian" locks which others call "Baltic" type, for instance, Morin, op. cit., who even calls the lock from Stockholm a "Baltic" one.

[35] Op. cit., page 28.

[36] Quoted in A. Angelucci, *Documenti inediti per la storia delle armi da fuoco italiane, raccolti, annotati e pubblicati da A.A.*, Turin, 1869, cited by J. Gelli, *Guida del Raccoglitore e dell'Amatore d'Armi antiche*, Florence, 1900 (reprinted Milan, 1968).

[37] Morin and Held, op. cit., page 66, also refer to this.

[38] Hayward, op. cit.

[39] Photographed and described in Blackmore, op. cit., photo 176, and in Hayward, op. cit., photo 48a.

[40] T. Lenk, *Flintlåset dess uppkomst och utveckling*, Stockholm 1939.

[41] There are differences of opinion between scholars on this subject too. The term "Baltic" is used by Morin, op. cit., while in J. Durdik, M. Mudra and M. Šáda, *Firearms – a collector's guide: 1326–1900*, London 1981, reference is made to a "Swedish" lock, and it is considered likely that the device described above is a

"uniquely Swedish improvement on the first flintlock." On the other hand, similar types of frizzen have been found on weapons of other nations, also for military use, like the Model 1814 musket for the Bodyguard of His Majesty, the King of Sardinia (see historical and technical section).

[42] Blackmore, op. cit., page 26.

[43] Peterson, op. cit.

[44] For this list of artists and artisans we are largely indebted to Hayward, op. cit.

[45] C. Jacquinet, *Plusieurs Models de plus nouvelles manières qui sont en usage en l'art d'Arquebuzerie*, Paris, c.1660.

[46] M. Morin, R. Held, op. cit.

[47] M. Morin, R. Held, op. cit.

[48] Hayward, op. cit.

[49] Peterson, op. cit.

[50] Blackmore, op. cit.

[51] Information taken from S. R. Turnbull, *The Book of the Samurai*, London, 1982. The battle took place in 1575.

[52] P. Pieri, *Il Rinascimento e la crisi militare italiana*, Turin, 1952.

[53] Note, however, that according to some scholars the granulation process had been known since the fifteenth century; cf. Durdik et al., op. cit., who refer to sources from 1421.

[54] W. W. Greener, *The Gun and its Development*, first edition Birmingham, 1881, last reprinting London, 1986.

[55] Morin, Held, op. cit.

[56] See G. Rotasso, "La baionetta nella storia delle guerre," in *Studi Storico-Militari – 1984*, Stato Maggiore dell'Esercito, Ufficio Storico (Army General Staff, Historical Office), Rome, 1985.

[57] E. Fournier, *L'Esprit dans l'histoire*, 1883, quoted in C. Falls et al, *Great military battles*, London, 1964.

[58] Wilkinson, op. cit.

[59] This type of cartridge is illustrated in A. Dolleczec, *Monographie der k.u.k. österr.-ung. Blank-und Handfeuerwaffen*, Vienna, 1896, reprinted Graz, 1970; L. and F. Funcken, *L'uniforme et les armes des soldats de la guerre en dentelle*, Tournai, 1975; Durdik et al, op. cit.

[60] H. R. Peterson, R. Elman, *The Great Guns*, London, 1971.

[61] J. Macdonald, *Great Battlefields of the World*, London, 1984.

[62] See also G. Rotasso, "L'armamento portatile dell'Armata Sarda negli anni della Restaurazione," in *Studi Storico-Militari – 1986*, Stato Maggiore dell'Esercito – Ufficio Storico (Army General Staff, Historical Office), Rome, 1987.

[63] B. P. Hughes, *Firepower – Weapons' Effectiveness on the Battlefield 1630–1850*, London, 1974.

[64] Quoted in P. Haythornthwaite, *Weapons and Equipment of the Napoleonic Wars*, Poole, Dorset, 1979.

[65] John Forsyth had also thought of the inconvenience of this and, in response to an idea of his, Edward Maynard patented a feed system in the United States in 1845, using a roll of paper tape containing a number of tablets of fulminate. The tape was mechanically unwound from a container near the firing mechanism, the tablets being placed on the nipple, one after the other, each time the hammer was cocked. This system was quite successful at the beginning of the American Civil War, until the danger of unexploded tablets if the tape got caught up was appreciated. A similar system had already been used in the Kingdom of Sardinia for a few carbines of the *Bersaglieri* (light infantry). (See historical and technical section).

[66] Peterson, Elman, op. cit.

[67] M. Lespart, *Messieurs Smith & Wesson*, Paris, 1971.

[68] Peterson, Elman, op. cit.

[69] C. F. Waterman, *The Treasury of Sporting Guns*, New York, 1979.

[70] Peterson, Elman, op. cit.

[71] The Remington was however adopted by various armies: the Vatican bought quantities of this rifle in 1868 for its troops, largely made up of foreign volunteers, and so did Denmark in 1867, Norway and Sweden in 1868, Spain in 1869 and Egypt and Argentina in 1873 (cf. historical and technical section).

[72] The real name of this capable industrialist, who was active in Philadelphia, was Henry Deringer Jnr; his pocket pistols appeared around 1830 and were percussion-type. The introduction of metal cartridges increased the use of this type of weapon.

ARMS

from the mid eighteenth
century to the present day

HISTORICAL AND
TECHNICAL SURVEY

FROM MATCHLOCK TO FLINTLOCK

From the first half of the eighteenth century to the first decades of the nineteenth, a constant process took place in various European countries as far as the use of individual firearms was concerned. On the one hand, the models issued to troops tended to become more uniform and standardized; on the other, the weapons became comparatively specialized to cater for different operational needs.

The following section illustrates some of the most significant types of (long and short) weapon during this period, subdivided by country, not merely geographically, and taking into account the historical significance of certain models, their use in contexts different from those for which they were originally intended, and the influence they had on countries without a creative military industry of their own.

Germany and Italy were still politically divided during this period. The former consisted, up to 1806, of a few medium-sized states, foremost of which was Prussia, and numerous small principalities or duchies. The latter was divided into the Kingdom of Sardinia, the Papal State, the Kingdom of the Two Sicilies and other minor states. The Napoleonic Wars temporarily disrupted the political situation in continental Europe and Italy (for example, by the creation first of the Republic and then of The Kingdom of Italy in 1805) and led in the armaments sector to an enormous increase in production by the great powers, with Britain and Russia in the lead.

After the Congress of Vienna (1815) and the restoration of the Bourbon monarchy, in a situation of relative peace, individual arms technology began to take the first basic steps towards the generalized use of percussion systems.

MECHANISMS

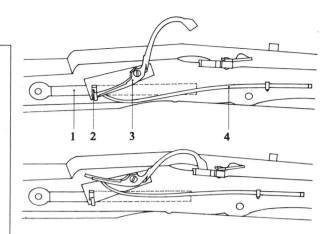

Snap-matchlock mechanism, late fifteenth century

This particular type of matchlock mechanism used a tubular support into which linen, hemp or cotton twine which had been boiled in a saturated solution of saltpeter was inserted; the lighted end projected from the support in the direction of the priming pan. The support was in fact the top end of the serpentine, the opposite end of which (the foot) pressed down on a spring, while at the same time it was held by a stud projecting through a hole in the lock plate. The stud was part of the sear lever. When the trigger, often in the form of a button, was pressed, the stud withdrew into the lock, freeing the spring which pushed up the foot of the serpentine, sending the match-holder down towards the priming pan.

1 trigger button; 2 sear; 3 serpentine; 4 spring.

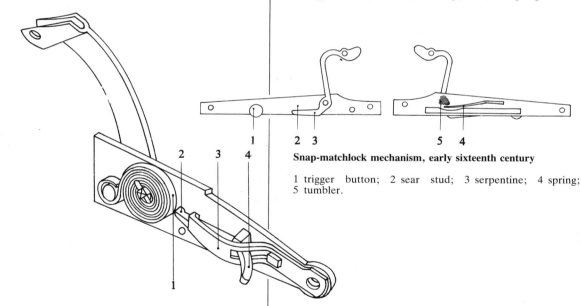

Snap-matchlock mechanism, early sixteenth century

1 trigger button; 2 sear stud; 3 serpentine; 4 spring; 5 tumbler.

Japanese snap-matchlock mechanism, late eighteenth century

In this mechanism, the axle of the serpentine is connected to the inner end of a spiral spring, the outer end of which is fixed to the inside of the lock plate. The serpentine is held in the firing position by the stud of the sear lever, which passes through the plate. These plates were usually made of copper or bronze, while the springs were of brass.

1 spiral spring; 2 sear; 3 sear spring; 4 sear.

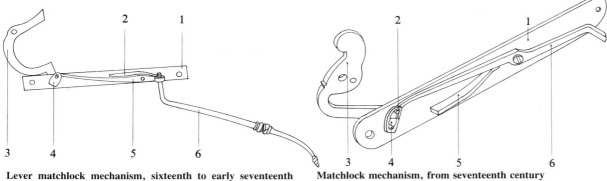

Lever matchlock mechanism, sixteenth to early seventeenth century

When the end of the trigger lever is pushed up towards the butt, the other end, which fits into a slot in the tumbler, forces the latter downwards. This movement is transferred to the serpentine, which is fixed to the outside of the tumbler and causes it to turn towards the priming pan in the direction of the firer. The lighted fuse, inserted in the serpentine, ignites the powder in the pan.

1 lock plate; 2 lever spring; 3 serpentine; 4 tumbler; 5 serpentine lever; 6 trigger lever.

Wheel-lock, sixteenth to seventeenth century

1 lock plate; 2 cock; 3 sear; 4 sear spring; 5 bridle; 6 wheel axle with transmission chain ending in a swivel; 7 mainspring; 8 trigger lever; 9 wheel; 10 wheel protection ring; 11 priming pan; 12 sliding pan cover; 13 cock spring; 14 pan cover arm; 15 pan cover spring; 16 safety lever; 17 safety lever spring. ▼

Matchlock mechanism, from seventeenth century

1 lock plate; 2 tumbler; 3 serpentine; 4 flattened end of axle of serpentine; 5 spring; 6 serpentine lever operated by a proper trigger.

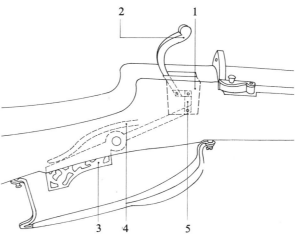

Oriental matchlock mechanism (Indian)

The match-holder projects through a characteristic recess just behind the barrel. The rest of the mechanism is hidden inside the stock. Indian arquebuses have no lock plate. The trigger lever is held by an iron pin inside the stock. The bottom end of the lever, which is sometimes flat, projects below the neck of the stock. Trigger lever and match-holder are connected by a mobile joint, which transfers the movement of the trigger to the serpentine when the base of the trigger is pressed up towards the stock.

1 recess cut into stock to house mechanism; 2 serpentine match-holder; 3 trigger; 4 spring; 5 connection between trigger lever and serpentine.

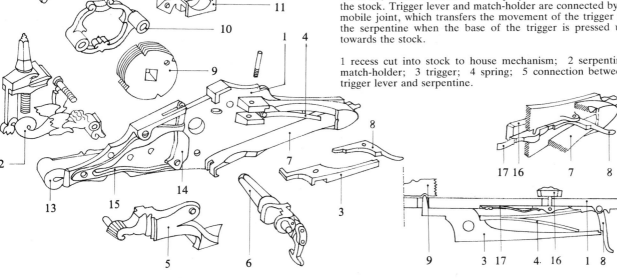

99

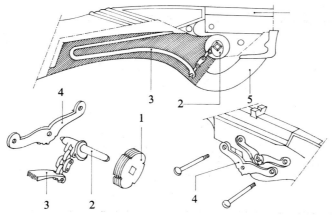

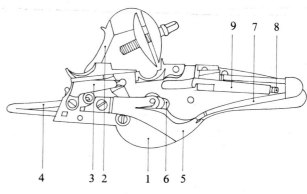

French-style wheel-lock

In these types of lock, the upper arm of the main spring is fixed in a cavity inside the stock; the lower arm is connected to the wheel axle by a swivel and chain. Furthermore, the end of the wheel axle opposite the one to which the key is fitted is held by a side-plate on the other side of the gun, instead of being secured by a bridle inside the lock itself. These technical details made it possible to use bigger, more reliable springs and, at the same time, meant that arquebuses and pistols could be given thinner, lighter stocks.

1 wheel; 2 wheel axle and transmission chain with swivel; 3 main spring; 4 side-plate; 5 stock.

Wheel-lock, seventeenth century

1 lock plate; 2 cock; 3 spring of sliding pan; 4 cock spring; 5 bridle supporting wheel axle; 6 wheel axle with transmission chain and swivel; 7 main spring; 8 trigger lever; 9 sear lever.

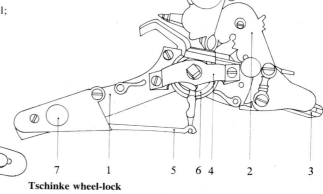

Tschinke wheel-lock

1 lock plate; 2 cock; 3 cock spring; 4 bridle; 5 main spring; 6 wheel; 7 trigger button.

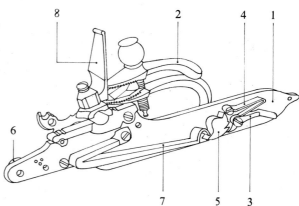

Combined matchlock and wheel-lock, mid seventeenth century

1 bridle supporting wheel axle; 2 lock plate; 3 match-holder spring; 4 sear lever for match-holder; 5 match-holder; 6 pan cover spring; 7 cock; 8 sear lever for wheel-lock mechanism; 9 trigger lever for wheel-lock mechanism; 10 main spring.

Baltic lock, second half of seventeenth century

1 lock plate; 2 cock; 3 sear; 4 sear spring; 5 tumbler; 6 steel spring; 7 main spring; 8 steel.

100

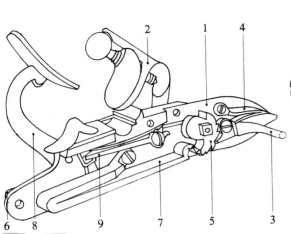

Snaphance type lock, late seventeenth century

1 lock plate; 2 cock; 3 sear; 4 sear spring; 5 tumbler; 6 steel spring; 7 main spring; 8 steel; 9 pan cover spring.

Catalan-style, Patilla or Miquelet lock

A further transformation of this mechanism produced the Spanish miquelet lock.

1 lock plate; 2 cock; 3 half-cock sear; 4 full-cock sear; 5 bridle of cock; 6 priming pan; 7 main spring; 8 bridle of frizzen; 9 steel of frizzen.

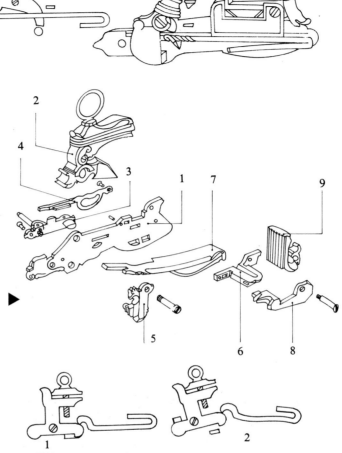

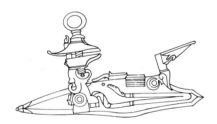

Operation of cock in a Roman-style lock

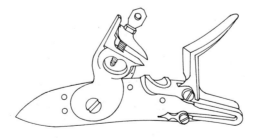

1 half-cock position; to fire the gun, the cock is pulled back until its toe is held by the sear (2) in the full-cock position.

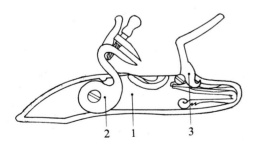

French-style or modern-style lock, eighteenth century

An efficient mechanism, but with some delicate parts, such as the "swan's neck" cock and unsupported frizzen screw.

1 lock plate; 2 cock; 3 frizzen.

Lock from late eighteenth to early nineteenth century

This is characterized by a strong "heart-shaped" cock and a reinforcement between the priming pan and frizzen screw.

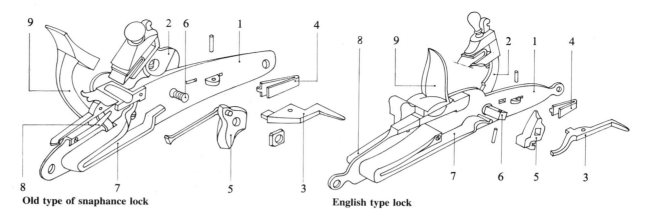

Old type of snaphance lock

1 lock plate; 2 cock; 3 sear with stud for holding cock in the "fully-cocked" position; 4 sear spring; 5 tumbler with arm to open the pan cover as the cock falls; 6 screw of cock; 7 main spring; 8 pan cover spring; 9 steel.

English type lock

1 lock plate; 2 cock; 3 sear with studs for half- and full-cock positions; 4 sear spring; 5 tumbler; 6 axle of cock; 7 main spring; 8 steel spring; 9 steel.

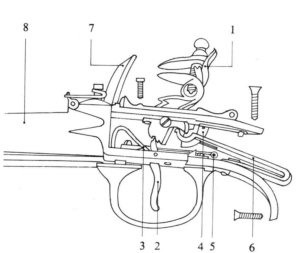

Box lock, from 1750 to the beginning of the nineteenth century

1 cock; 2 trigger; 3 trigger spring; 4 cock safety catch; 5 trigger safety catch; 6 main spring; 7 steel; 8 barrel.

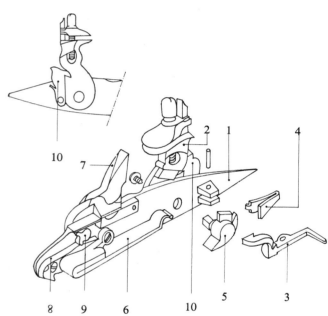

English dog-lock, from 1650 to the beginning of the nineteenth century

1 lock plate; 2 cock; 3 sear; 4 sear spring; 5 tumbler; 6 main spring; 7 steel; 8 internal steel spring; 9 tumbler connected to axle of frizzen; 10 manual safety catch (dog catch).

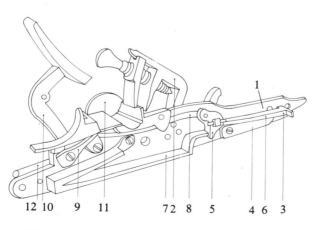

Dutch lock, from the end of the sixteenth century

Often found on North African (Algerian, Kabyle) weapons of a later period.

1 lock plate; 2 cock; 3 arm of sear; 4 sear spring; 5 tumbler; 6 sear; 7 main spring; 8 arm to open the pan cover as the cock falls; 9 pan cover spring; 10 steel; 11 pan cover "button"; 12 steel spring.

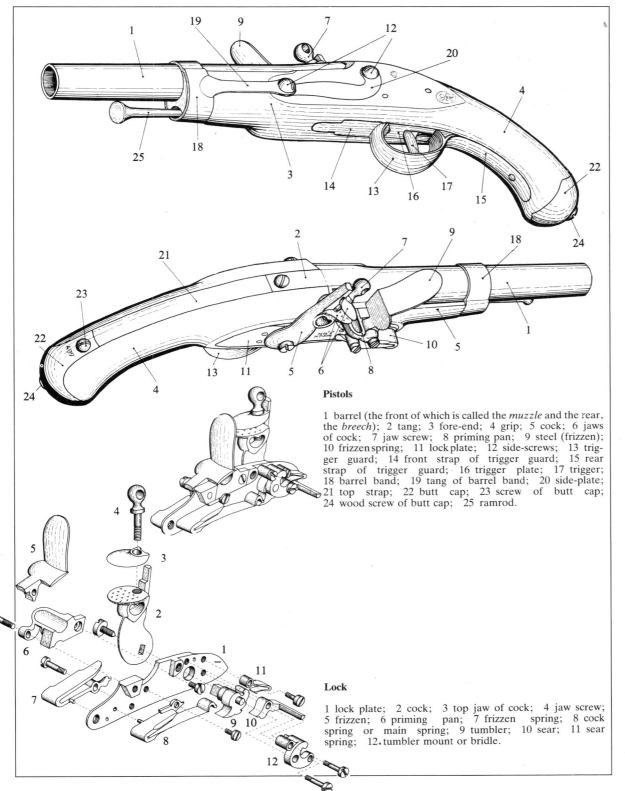

Pistols

1 barrel (the front of which is called the *muzzle* and the rear, the *breech*); 2 tang; 3 fore-end; 4 grip; 5 cock; 6 jaws of cock; 7 jaw screw; 8 priming pan; 9 steel (frizzen); 10 frizzen spring; 11 lock plate; 12 side-screws; 13 trigger guard; 14 front strap of trigger guard; 15 rear strap of trigger guard; 16 trigger plate; 17 trigger; 18 barrel band; 19 tang of barrel band; 20 side-plate; 21 top strap; 22 butt cap; 23 screw of butt cap; 24 wood screw of butt cap; 25 ramrod.

Lock

1 lock plate; 2 cock; 3 top jaw of cock; 4 jaw screw; 5 frizzen; 6 priming pan; 7 frizzen spring; 8 cock spring or main spring; 9 tumbler; 10 sear; 11 sear spring; 12 tumbler mount or bridle.

PRINCIPALITY OF WÜRZBURG

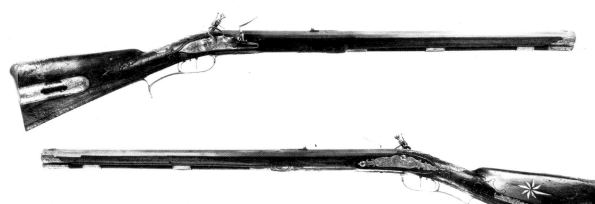

Left side of weapon

Jäger-type Carbine, mid eighteenth century

The weapon has a long stock which accompanies the heavy barrel right up to the muzzle, a feature retained in arms developed overseas, like the famous Kentucky rifles.

The elegance is typical of the Austrian school of Karlsbad. Carbines of this type are also known as "Viennese style," probably because they were adopted by nobles of the Hapsburg Empire.

The modern style flintlock mechanism has a "swan's neck" cock. The forged iron barrel, signed *Staudinger a Wirtzburg*, has a rifled bore with seven helical grooves.

There is a double trigger mechanism (Stecher system) for greater sensitivity and safety: the first acts as a safety catch to the second while aiming the weapon; the second releases the cock on very slight pressure.

caliber: 14 mm
total length: 42.51 in (108 cm)
length of barrel: 27.56 in (70 cm)
weight: 7.87 lb (3,570 g)

Detail of lock

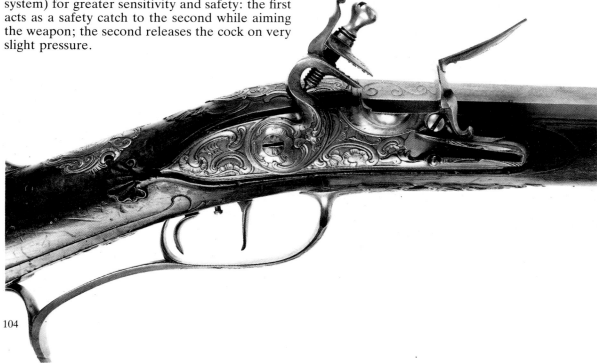

WÜRTTEMBERG

1825 Infantry Rifle
(*Neues Oberndorfer Schützengewehr*)

caliber: 17.64 mm
total length: 57.68 in (146.5 cm)
length of barrel: 42.72 in (108.5 cm)
weight: 9.92 lb (4,500 g)

The lock has a distinctive double-necked cock and a projection in front of the pan to halt the cock.

This is typical of the firearms made at Oberndorf at that period. It has brass furniture.

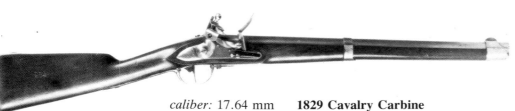

caliber: 17.64 mm
total length: 35.24 in (89.5 cm)
length of barrel: 19.88 in (50.5 cm)
weight: 6.39 lb (2,900 g)

1829 Cavalry Carbine
(*Oberndorfer kurzer karabinier*)

This has brass furniture.

Detail of lock

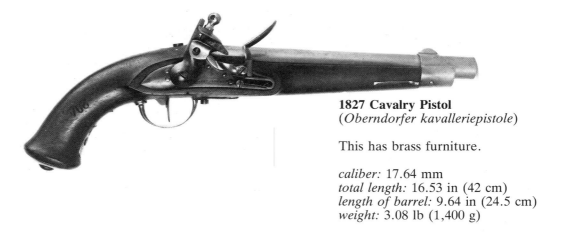

1827 Cavalry Pistol
(*Oberndorfer kavalleriepistole*)

This has brass furniture.

caliber: 17.64 mm
total length: 16.53 in (42 cm)
length of barrel: 9.64 in (24.5 cm)
weight: 3.08 lb (1,400 g)

PRUSSIA

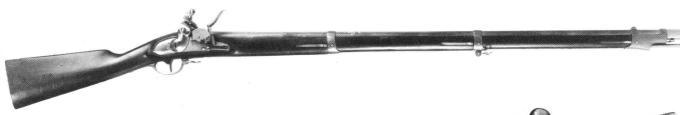

Model 1809 Infantry Rifle
(*Neupreussisches Gewehr*)

This was the new, regulation Prussian rifle built at Potsdam. The lock has a "heart-shaped" cock and the priming pan has a flash shield. The barrel is held to the stock by metal bands fixed by flat springs.
It has brass furniture.

caliber: 18.57 mm
total length: 56.49 in (143.5 cm)
length of barrel: 41.14 in (104.5 cm)
weight: 12.78 lb (5,800 g)

Detail of lock and fixed bayonet

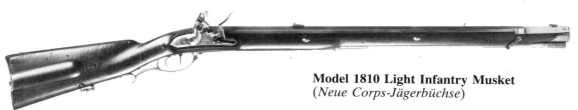

Model 1810 Light Infantry Musket
(*Neue Corps-Jägerbüchse*)

caliber: 14.7 mm
total length: 43.30 in (110 cm)
length of barrel: 28.07 in (71.3 cm)
weight: 10.14 lb (4,600 g)

Also known as *Potsdamer Büchse*, this was the new musket given to the infantry following the reforms of 1809.

There is a double trigger mechanism (Stecher system). The butt has a compartment with a sliding cover (Schuber) for carrying accessories.

It has brass furniture.

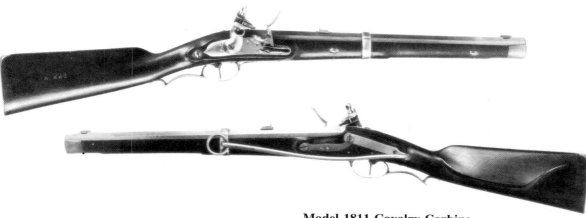

Left side of weapon

Model 1811 Cavalry Carbine
(*Neuepreussischer cavalleriekarabiner*)

caliber: 15.17 mm
total length: 31.88 in (81 cm)
length of barrel: 16.93 in (43 cm)
weight: 6.61 lb (3,000 g)

Apart from the new features introduced with the infantry rifle, this weapon also has a rifled barrel.

It has brass furniture.

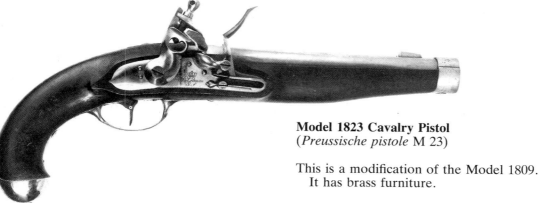

Model 1823 Cavalry Pistol
(*Preussische pistole* M 23)

This is a modification of the Model 1809.
It has brass furniture.

caliber: 15.90 mm
total length: 15.75 in (40 cm)
length of barrel: 9.25 in (23.5 cm)
weight: 3.30 lb (1,500 g)

HANOVER

Pistol with shoulder stock
(*Kolbenpistole*)

caliber: 16 mm
total length of pistol: 17.72 in (45 cm)
length of barrel: 11.22 in (28.5 cm)
length of pistol with butt: 27.56 in (70 cm)
weight: 2.86 lb (1,300 g)
weight of pistol with butt: 4.29 lb (1,950 g)

Weapon in use with the cavalry in the first half of the nineteenth century.
The shoulder stock is fixed to the pistol grip by a sleeve which fits into a special slot.
It has brass furniture.

REPUBLIC OF VENICE

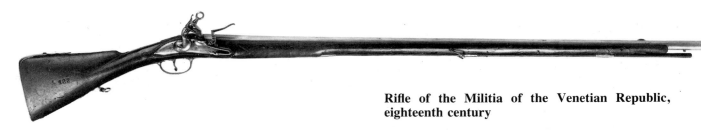

Rifle of the Militia of the Venetian Republic, eighteenth century

Manufactured in Brescia. It has iron furniture.

caliber: 18.5 mm
total length: 60.62 in (154 cm)
length of barrel: 44.88 in (114 cm)
weight: 9.25 lb (4,200 g)

KINGDOM OF ITALY

caliber: 18 mm
total length: 59.84 in (152 cm)
length of barrel: 44.68 in (113.5 cm)
weight: 9.48 lb (4,300 g)

French style Infantry Rifle of 1812

Made by the Royal Arms Factory in Brescia. It has brass furniture.

KINGDOM OF SARDINIA

Model 1814 Infantry Rifle

caliber: 17.5 mm
total length: 59.45 in (151 cm)
length of barrel: 43.82 in (111.3 cm)
weight: 9.70 lb (4,400 g)

This is similar to the French Model Anno IX, from which it was derived.

This was the standard rifle of the Sardinian Army after the fall of the Napoleonic empire which, with a few changes, remained in use until the unification of Italy.

It has iron furniture.

caliber: 17.1 mm
total length: 45.04 in (114.4 cm)
length of barrel: 29.92 in (76 cm)
weight: 7.50 lb (3,400 g)

Model 1814 Musket of Royal Carabineers

Similar to the French Anno IX cavalry model.

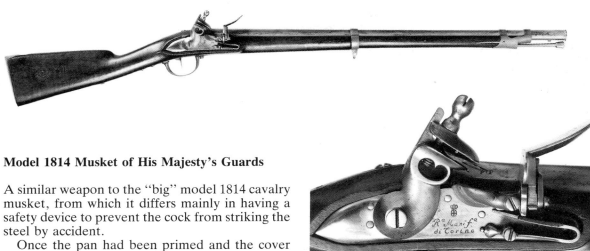

Model 1814 Musket of His Majesty's Guards

A similar weapon to the "big" model 1814 cavalry musket, from which it differs mainly in having a safety device to prevent the cock from striking the steel by accident.

Once the pan had been primed and the cover closed, the steel was turned sideways to avoid accidental firing.

caliber: 17.1 mm
total length: 42.52 in (108 cm)
length of barrel: 27.80 in (70.6 cm)
weight: 7.10 lb (3,220 g)

Detail of lock.

Detail of lock with safety mechanism engaged.

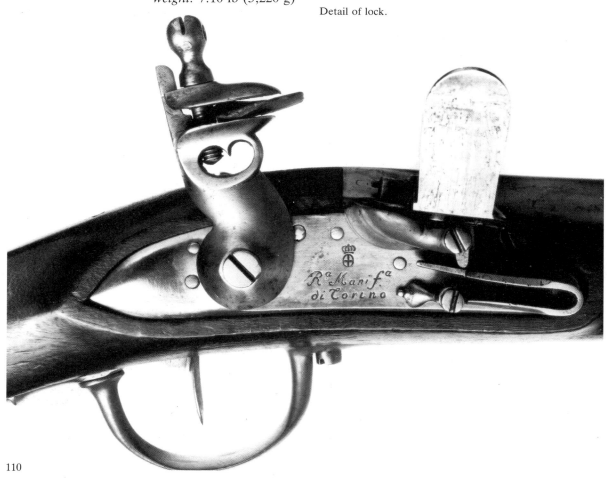

caliber: 17.1 mm
total length: 33.27 in (84.5 cm)
length of barrel: 18.50 in (47 cm)
weight: 5.51 lb (2,500 g)

Model 1833 Cavalry Musket

This has iron furniture.

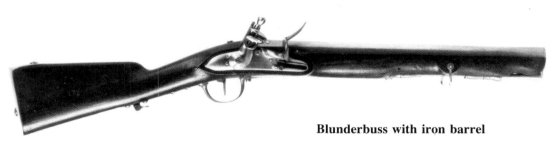

Blunderbuss with iron barrel

caliber: 22.6 mm
total length: 33.46 in (85 cm)
length of barrel: 18.11 in (46 cm)
weight: 10.03 lb (4,550 g)

Weapon used by the army in the first half of the nineteenth century.
It has brass furniture.

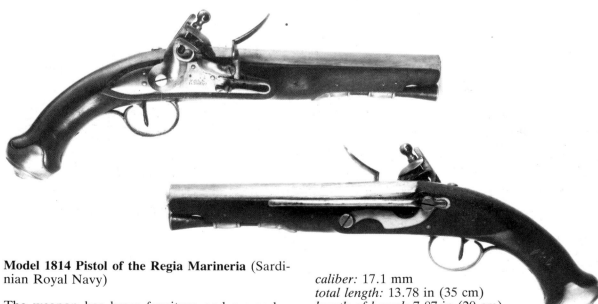

Left side of weapon.

Model 1814 Pistol of the Regia Marineria (Sardinian Royal Navy)

The weapon has brass furniture and a wooden ramrod.

caliber: 17.1 mm
total length: 13.78 in (35 cm)
length of barrel: 7.87 in (20 cm)
weight: 2.42 lb (1,100 g)

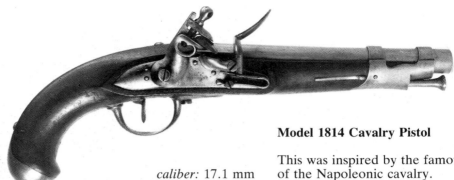

Model 1814 Cavalry Pistol

caliber: 17.1 mm
total length: 14.37 in (36.5 cm)
length of barrel: 8.38 in (21.3 cm)
weight: 2.75 lb (1,250 g)

This was inspired by the famous Model Anno IX of the Napoleonic cavalry.

It has iron furniture. The same pistol, but with brass furniture, was supplied to His Majesty's Guards.

Pistol-carbine

length with butt: 22.83 in (58 cm)
weight with butt: 5.40 lb (2,450 g)

This was the Model 1814 cavalry pistol with the addition of a detachable shoulder stock.

KINGDOM OF THE TWO SICILIES

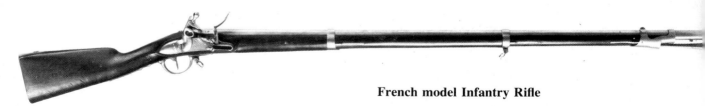

French model Infantry Rifle

caliber: 18 mm
total length: 57.87 in (147 cm)
length of barrel: 42.52 in (108 cm)
weight: 9.92 lb (4,500 g)

This weapon was made in the first years of the restoration of the monarchy after the fall of the Napoleonic empire. It was derived from the French Anno IX model.

It has iron furniture.

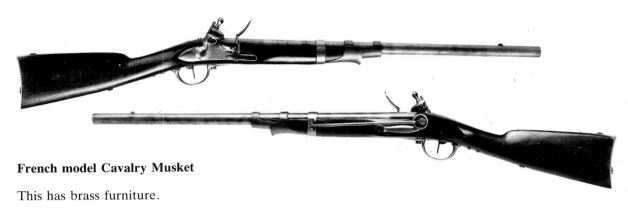

Left side of weapon.

French model Cavalry Musket

This has brass furniture.

caliber: 18 mm
total length: 37.40 in (95 cm)
length of barrel: 23.42 in (59.5 cm)
weight: 6.17 lb (2,800 g)

Semi-breech-loading rifle of 1831

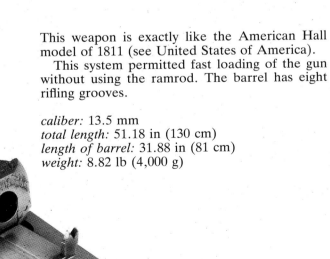

Detail of breech with inscription.

This weapon is exactly like the American Hall model of 1811 (see United States of America).
   This system permitted fast loading of the gun without using the ramrod. The barrel has eight rifling grooves.

caliber: 13.5 mm
total length: 51.18 in (130 cm)
length of barrel: 31.88 in (81 cm)
weight: 8.82 lb (4,000 g)

Detail with mobile breech raised.

AUSTRIA

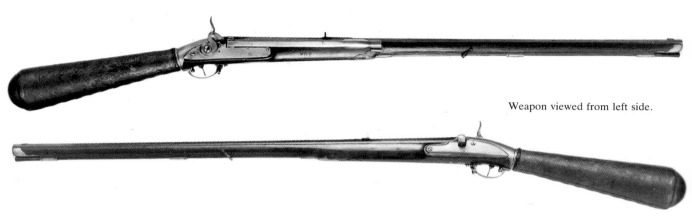

Weapon viewed from left side.

Model 1780 compressed-air repeating rifle
(*Repetierwindbüchse* M 1780)

This extraordinary rifle, designed by Bartolomeo Girardoni (born at Cortina d'Ampezzo according to some sources), works on compressed air contained in special, interchangeable cylinders which also serve as a butt.

The bullets (up to twenty) are housed in a magazine at the side of the barrel and fed into the barrel by the transverse-sliding breech-block.

The hammer is only used to cock the weapon.

At the moment of firing, the tumbler operates a valve-opening pin, releasing a quantity of compressed air which drives the bullet out of the barrel.

Despite its mechanical fragility, the *Repetierwindbüchse* was quite extensively employed for military purposes, as demonstrated by the use Austria made of it during the war of the First Coalition against France.

The weapon was accompanied by a leather bag containing two spare cylinders and various accessories for recharging the cylinders and casting bullets.

caliber: 10.5 mm
total length: 48.03 in (122 cm)
length of barrel: 32.68 in (83 cm)
weight: 9.92 lb (4,500 g)

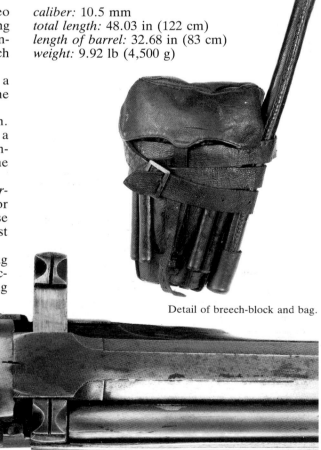

Detail of breech-block and bag.

114

Model 1768 Musket with superimposed barrels
(*Doppelstutzen*)

This military combination weapon with a double lock permitted two different types of fire, the top barrel being rifled (seven helical grooves) and the bottom smooth-bore.

For more accurate firing, the musket was leant on a mobile hook fitted to the shaft of a special lance (*Hacken-Lanze*), which thus served as a rest.

The lance was 5.5 ft (2.5 m) long and was used against enemies on foot or horseback when the ammunition ran out.

caliber: 14.8 mm
total length: 41.34 in (105 cm)
length of barrel: 25.98 in (66 cm)
weight: 12.12 lb (5,500 g)

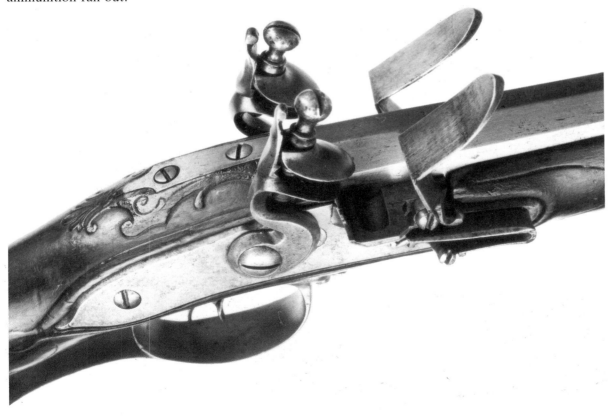

Detail of locks.

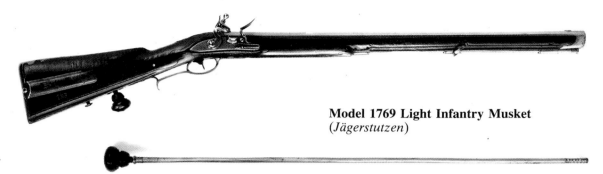

Model 1769 Light Infantry Musket
(*Jägerstutzen*)

Detail of ramrod.

caliber: 14.8 mm
total length: 41.14 in (104.5 cm)
length of barrel: 26.38 in (67 cm)
weight: 10.80 lb (4,900 g)

This was the typical Austrian light infantry weapon with a heavy barrel and a long stock extending to the muzzle. The barrel has seven rifling grooves.

The sliding cover (Schuber) of the container for the accessories projects from the butt.

Below the butt, near the screw for holding the sling, is the pommel which fits on to the ramrod for loading the gun and cleaning the barrel.

The weapon has brass furniture.

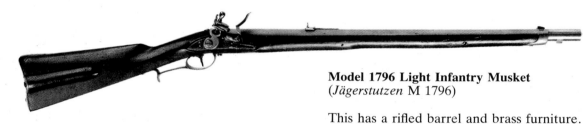

Model 1796 Light Infantry Musket
(*Jägerstutzen* M 1796)

This has a rifled barrel and brass furniture.

caliber: 14.8 mm
total length: 41.14 in (104.5 cm)
length of barrel: 26.18 in (66.5 cm)
weight: 7.27 lb (3,300 g)

Model 1798 Hussars' Carbine
(*Karabiner für Husaren* M 1798)

caliber: 17.58 mm
total length: 33.54 in (85.2 cm)
length of barrel: 18.50 in (47 cm)
weight: 5.51 lb (2,500 g)

The lock of this weapon has a safety catch for the cock.

The furniture is made of brass.

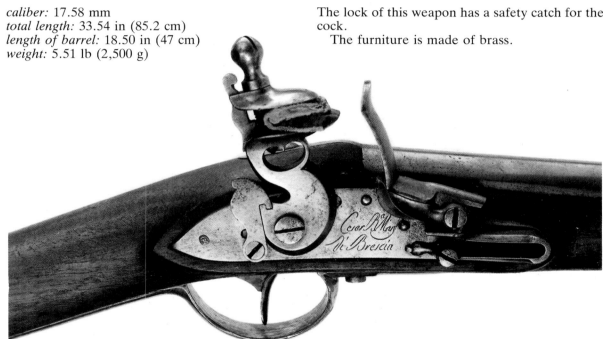

Detail of lock with the safety catch in position.

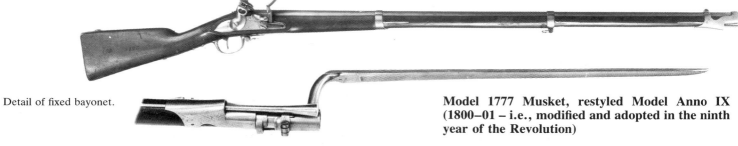

Detail of fixed bayonet.

Model 1777 Musket, restyled Model Anno IX (1800–01 – i.e., modified and adopted in the ninth year of the Revolution)

This was the basic weapon of Napoleon's infantry and may be regarded as the most sturdy and functional model of that period. It has a lock with a heart-shaped (double-necked) cock and a flange extending from the priming pan to support the frizzen screw.

The smooth-bore barrel is held to the stock by metal bands.

The furniture is made of iron, except for the sight, which is brass.

After the fall of the Napoleonic empire, many European armies adopted weapons of similar design to the Model Anno IX.

caliber: 17.5 mm
total length: 59.64 in (151.5 cm)
length of barrel: 44.76 in (113.7 cm)
weight: 9.64 lb (4,375 g)

Detail of lock.

118

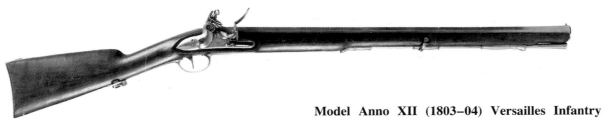

Model Anno XII (1803–04) Versailles Infantry Carbine

caliber: 13.5 mm
total length: 40.94 in (104 cm)
length of barrel: 25.59 in (65 cm)
weight: 7.60 lb (3,450 g)

This is a modification of the Model 1793 carbine which was the French answer to the *Jägers* of the states of central Europe.

It has a rifled barrel and brass furniture.

caliber: 17.5 mm
total length: 60.20 in (152.9 cm)
length of barrel: 44.76 in (113.7 cm)
weight: 9.63 lb (4,370 g)

Model 1822 Infantry Weapon

This was derived from the Model Anno IX.
It has iron furniture.

caliber: 17.5 mm
total length: 57.91 in (147.1 cm)
length of barrel: 42.64 in (108.3 cm)
weight: 9.60 lb (4,355 g)

Model 1822 Grenadier Rifle

This has brass furniture.

caliber: 17.1 mm
total length: 37.72 in (95.8 cm)
length of barrel: 23.62 in (60 cm)
weight: 5.73 lb (2,600 g)

Model 1829 Artillery Musket

This has brass furniture.

119

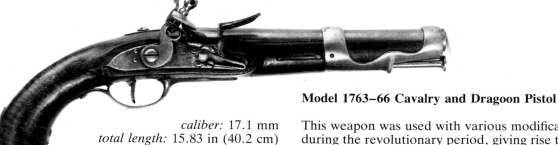

Model 1763–66 Cavalry and Dragoon Pistol

caliber: 17.1 mm
total length: 15.83 in (40.2 cm)
length of barrel: 9.05 in (23 cm)
weight: 2.71 lb (1,230 g)

This weapon was used with various modifications during the revolutionary period, giving rise to the Model Anno IX.

It has brass furniture.

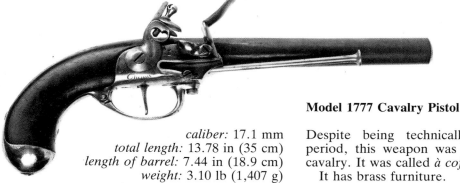

Model 1777 Cavalry Pistol

caliber: 17.1 mm
total length: 13.78 in (35 cm)
length of barrel: 7.44 in (18.9 cm)
weight: 3.10 lb (1,407 g)

Despite being technically advanced for the period, this weapon was not popular with the cavalry. It was called *à coffre*.

It has brass furniture.

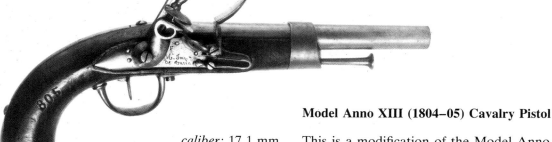

Model Anno XIII (1804–05) Cavalry Pistol

caliber: 17.1 mm
total length: 13.86 in (35.2 cm)
weight: 2.80 lb (1,269 g)

This is a modification of the Model Anno IX. It was made easier to handle by replacing the muzzle with two half rings by a simpler one and shortening the stock. Strong and reliable like the model from which it was derived, it has a "heart-shaped" cock and a flange extending from the priming pan to support the frizzen screw.

After the fall of the Napoleonic empire, various armies produced imitations of this model.

It has brass furniture.

BRITAIN

Musket of the East India Company (India Pattern Musket)

caliber: 0.75 in
total length: 55.11 in (140 cm)
weight: 9.03 lb (4,100 g)

Commonly known as Brown Bess, this is a classic eighteenth-century weapon with a "fin-shaped" butt and a barrel that was pinned to the stock, features which it retained even after being transformed from flintlock to percussion lock. Models prior to 1809 have locks with "swan's neck" cocks, despite the fact that similar weapons of the French adversary had been fitted with strong, "heart-shaped" cocks for years and had the barrels fixed to the stocks by metal bands.

The India Pattern musket was used by the British Army during the campaign against Napoleon to make up for the shortage of Land Pattern muskets, from which it differed only in having a lower standard of finish.

It has brass furniture.

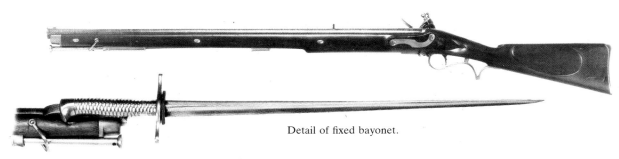

Left side of weapon.

Detail of fixed bayonet.

Baker Rifle adopted in 1823

This short German-style (*Jäger* type) rifle was the best British flintlock weapon produced.

It has brass furniture.

caliber: 0.625 in
total length: 45.67 in (116 cm)
length of barrel: 29.92 in (76 cm)

The first types of Baker rifle were distributed to crack troops of the British Army at the time of the Napoleonic campaigns.

121

DENMARK

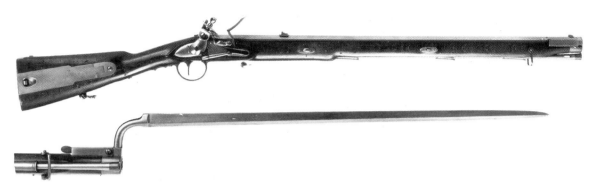

Detail of fixed bayonet.

Model 1829 Carbine

caliber: 15.5 mm
total length: 44.09 in (112 cm)
length of barrel: 28.86 in (73.3 cm)
weight: 9.92 lb (4,500 g)

Weapon with rifled barrel and a special safety device which immobilizes the cock, similar to the one fitted to the locks of Württemberg Schützen carbines.

It has brass furniture.

Detail of lock with safety catch engaged.

Cavalry Pistol, first half of the nineteenth century

This has brass furniture.

caliber: 17.7 mm
total length: 18.11 in (46 cm)
length of barrel: 10.83 in (27.5 cm)
weight: 3.30 lb (1,500 g)

RUSSIA

caliber: 18.5 mm
total length: 47.83 in (121.5 cm)
length of barrel: 33.27 in (84.5 cm)
weight: 5.73 lb (2,600 g)

Cossack Musket of 1851

The unusual stock shape distinguishes this from the regulation weapons of the Tsarist army.

123

FROM PERCUSSION TO BREECH-LOADING

The middle decades of the nineteenth century marked a series of very important steps in the development of individual firearms. New ideas and technological innovations abounded during this period, and not just in Europe. The United States of America was now a force to be reckoned with in the field of technological developments and its products were becoming familiar in the Old World as well. In Europe, the process of unification of nation states was completed between 1860 and 1870. First Italy, then Germany achieved national and political unity, while France and Britain completed their program of colonial conquests.

This section also follows a chronological and/or technological order, starting with the development of muzzle-loading weapons with percussion lock ignition systems and progressing to breech-loading systems, the development and diffusion of which began from roughly the 1840s. This period was also characterized by a more "modern" approach to the manufacture of weapons. Mass production became a clearly defined economic and industrial reality, and the idea of the "patent" linked to a single engineer or inventor was introduced.

Various types of weapon were reproduced and manufactured outside their country of origin, the original model being adapted to suit the requirements of individual states and their respective armies. What often happened, for reasons of economy, was that old weapons were updated by new breech-block systems. German, Austrian, French, British and American products dominated the European scene in terms of quality and progressive features.

MECHANISMS

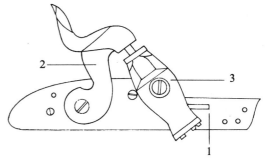

Forsyth percussion lock

1 lock plate; 2 hammer; 3 rotating container of primer dubbed the "scent bottle."

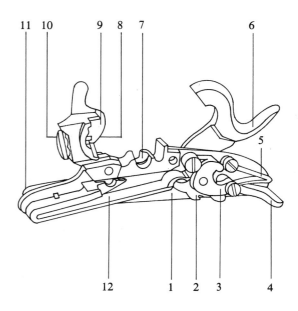

Augustin system percussion lock

In both this lock and the Console system type, invented by the Italian Giuseppe Console, the explosive charge is ignited by a short copper tube of fulminate. The hammer does not strike the tube directly in either case, but detonates it by hitting a metal lid in the Console system, or a firing pin in the Augustin system. Both lid and firing pin transfer the energy of the blow to the top of the tube, thereby detonating the fulminate inside it. Various flintlock weapons of the Austrian Imperial Army were converted to the Console and Augustin systems, but the results proved unsatisfactory.

1 lock plate; 2 tumbler; 3 mount; 4 sear lever; 5 sear spring; 6 hammer; 7 cavity for explosive tube; 8 tip of percussion pin; 9 lid protecting cavity for explosive tube; 10 head of percussion pin; 11 spring of lid protecting explosive tube; 12 main spring.

La Chaumette-Ferguson system

With big vertical screw for breech-loading (open).

1 gun barrel; 2 breech-loading screw with trigger-guard lever.

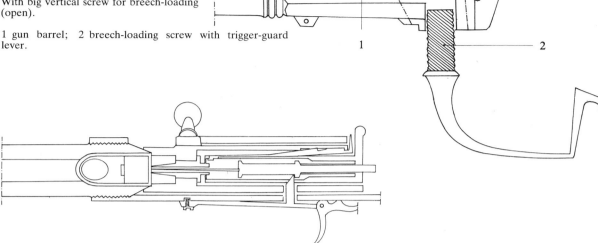

Dreyse system single-shot breech-loading needle gun

The action of the percussion (needle in this case) is clearly visible: passing through the base of the cartridge filled with gunpowder, it strikes the cap of primer, detonating the explosive compound contained in it. By pulling back the bolt, visible at the top, the user can feed a new cartridge directly into the chamber after firing. The needle meanwhile, operated by the bolt, has gone back with the breech-block. Having inserted the new cartridge, the firer pushes the bolt forward again, closing the breech-block. Pulling the trigger causes the needle to shoot forward, thus firing another round.

Peabody system falling-block single-shot breech-loading rifle

This weapon was patented by the American Henry O. Peabody in 1862. The breech-block is lowered by means of a lever below the trigger (which also acts as the trigger guard), allowing the cartridge to be inserted; when the lever is returned, the base of the cartridge is held in position by a cam which serves as an extractor.

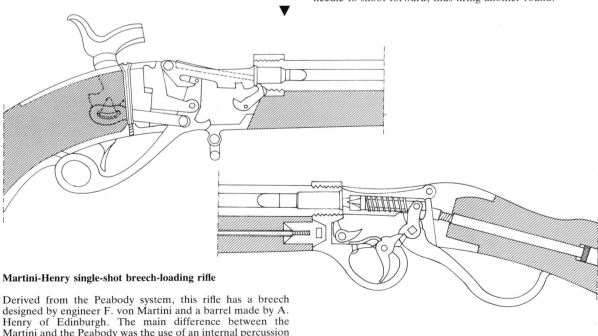

Martini-Henry single-shot breech-loading rifle

Derived from the Peabody system, this rifle has a breech designed by engineer F. von Martini and a barrel made by A. Henry of Edinburgh. The main difference between the Martini and the Peabody was the use of an internal percussion system, instead of an external hammer. The Martini-Henry was adopted by the British Army in 1871 and was the standard weapon used in various colonial wars.

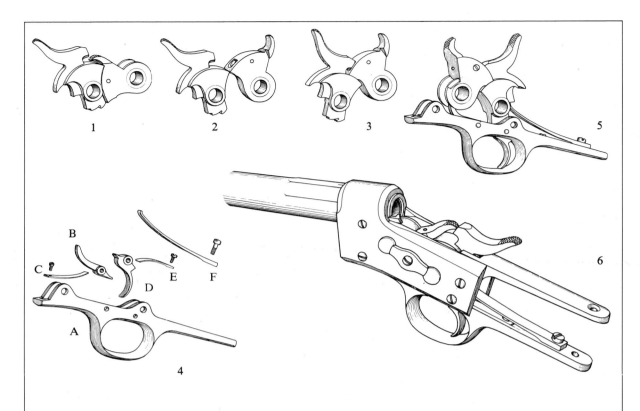

Rolling Block system used on Remington weapons – mechanical details

1 This illustration, and the following, show the principle of operation of Remington guns, based on two rotating parts. Here, the one which serves as a breech-block is turned right back. The chamber is thus open and the cartridge case can be extracted and a new cartridge introduced.
2 The breech-block is turned right forward so that its flat front surface closes the chamber. The hammer is cocked and is held only by the sear of the trigger which is engaged in the firing notch. The weapon is thus ready for firing.
3 The hammer has fallen forward, firing the shot by striking the percussion pin let into the breech-block. To open the chamber and reload the weapon, the hammer must be recocked by repeating the process described above in reverse order.

4 Trigger guard and parts connected to it: A trigger guard; B breech-block lever; C lever spring; D trigger; E trigger spring; F hammer spring.
5 Trigger guard reassembled shown together with breech-block and hammer. Below the breech-block is the lever which, when pushed by its spring, slows rotation of the block enough to keep it stable. When the breech-block is closed, the top end of the lever fits into a recess, thus preventing accidental opening of the chamber when the hammer is cocked and therefore offers no resistance.
6 Parts reassembled. The breech-block is open, opening the chamber and causing the extractor to move back. On the right of the mount the heads of two pins project, on which the breech-block and hammer turn. Between them is a plate to hold them in place. The screw visible at the side of the breech-block restricts movement of the extractor.

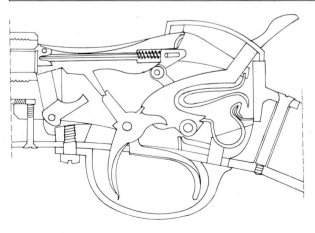

Bayerisch Blitz (Bavarian Lightning), invented by J. L. Werder

Cross-section of the breech-loading rifle adopted by the Bavarian Army. This operates by a falling-block system similar to the one invented by the American H. O. Peabody in 1862 and perfected by Westley Richards and Friedrich von Martini. The Werder has a more complex structure than the Martini-Henry used by the British Army. The cartridge fits into a cavity at the top of the breech-block, which is lowered by pushing forward the first of the two triggers; the cartridge is slid into the chamber on pressure from the finger, and the breech-block is returned to the original position, thereby cocking the hammer. Pulling the second trigger causes the hammer to strike the percussion pin against the base of the cartridge, thus firing the shot. Further pressure on the first trigger causes the breech-block to swing downwards, so that the cartridge can be expelled and a new round chambered.

Trap-door breech-block system

This was used in the American rifle, designed by E. S. Allin, adopted by the United States Army and in use up to the end of the last century. It was one of the most common ways of converting old muzzle-loading weapons to breech-loading. The breech-block is hinged to a support screwed to the front part of the barrel and closed by a cam on the opposite side.

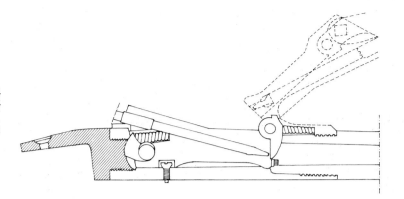

TERMINOLOGY

Percussion lock (nipple type)

Exploded view of lock.

1 lock plate; 2 hammer and screw of tumbler; 3 steel main spring; 4 iron tumbler, tempered with its screw; 5 sear; 6 steel sear spring; 7 tumbler mount (or bridle) with mount screw and sear screw.

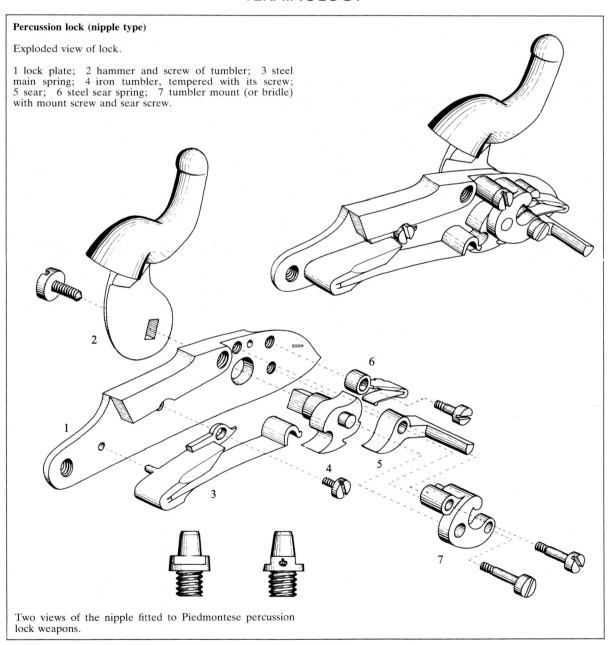

Two views of the nipple fitted to Piedmontese percussion lock weapons.

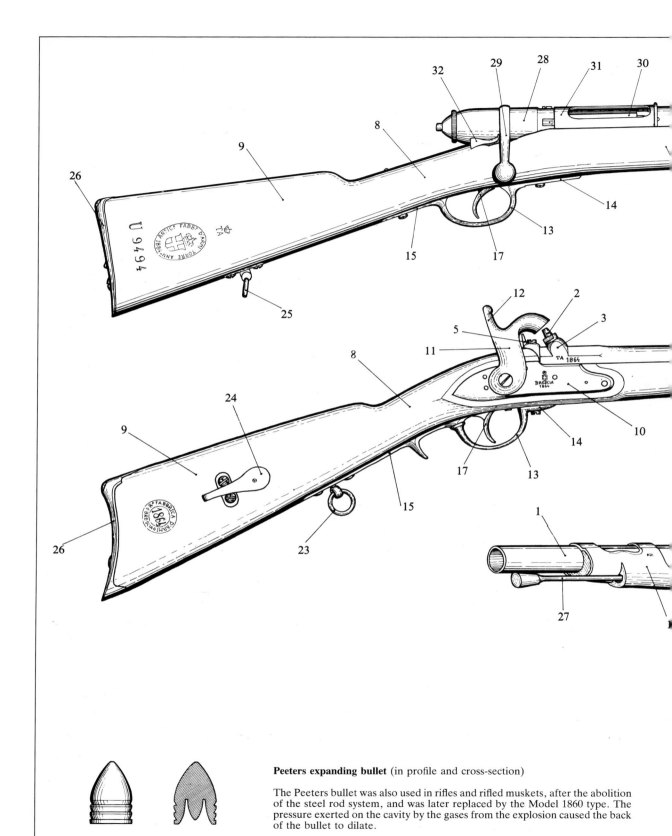

Peeters expanding bullet (in profile and cross-section)

The Peeters bullet was also used in rifles and rifled muskets, after the abolition of the steel rod system, and was later replaced by the Model 1860 type. The pressure exerted on the cavity by the gases from the explosion caused the back of the bullet to dilate.

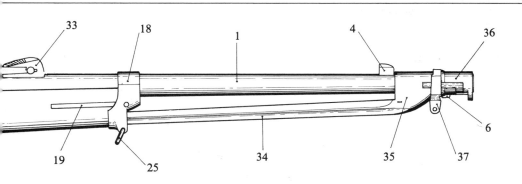

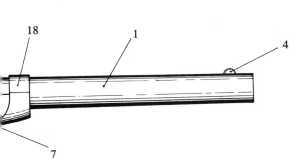

1 barrel (the front of which is called the muzzle and the rear, the breech); 2 nipple; 3 nipple holder; 4 foresight; 5 back sight notch; 6 bayonet lug; 7 fore-end; 8 grip; 9 butt; 10 lock plate; 11 hammer; 12 spur of hammer; 13 trigger guard; 14 front strap of trigger guard; 15 rear strap of trigger guard; 16 trigger plate; 17 trigger; 18 first barrel band; 19 spring holding latter; 20 second barrel band; 21 sideplate; 22 carrier; 23 ring; 24 belt hook; 22 sling swivel; 26 butt-plate; 27 ramrod; 28 bolt-action breech-block; 29 bolt handle; 30 extractor; 31 breech cover; 32 safety catch; 33 backsight; 34 blade; 35 arm; 36 sleeve; 37 socket.

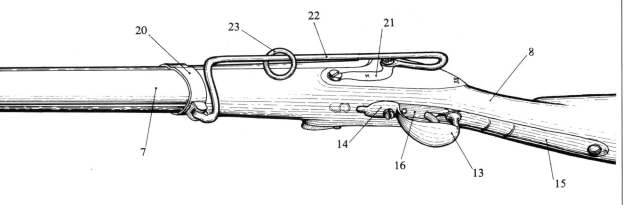

Model 1860 17.2 mm triangular cavity expanding bullet. This was used for all Model 1860 weapons, new or reduced, the powder charge varying according to the type of weapon (seen in profile, from below, and in cross-section).

Square cavity bullet

This replaced the above in 1867 (seen in profile, from below, and in cross-section).

WÜRTTEMBERG

1819 Infantry Rifle converted to percussion lock

caliber: 17.64 mm
total length: 57.87 in (147 cm)
length of barrel: 42.72 in (108.5 cm)
weight: 9.59 lb (4,350 g)

BADEN

Cavalry Carbine converted to percussion lock
(*Kurzer-Karabiner*)

caliber: 17.5 mm
total length: 33.66 in (85.5 cm)
length of barrel: 18.58 in (47.2 cm)
weight: 5.95 lb (2,700 g)

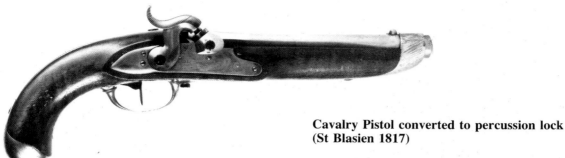

Cavalry Pistol converted to percussion lock (St Blasien 1817)

This has brass furniture.

caliber: 17.5 mm
total length: 14.57 in (37 cm)
length of barrel: 8.19 in (20.8 cm)
weight: 2.86 lb (1,300 g)

PRUSSIA

caliber: 18.57 mm
total length: 56.49 in (143.5 cm)
length of barrel: 41.14 in (104.5 cm)
weight: 12.78 lb (5,800 g)

Model 1809 Infantry Rifle converted to percussion lock

This is the old *Neupreussisches Gewehr* converted to the new nipple ignition system (see Model 1809 rifle).

caliber: 15.43 mm
total length: 51.57 in (131 cm)
length of barrel: 30.90 in (78.5 cm)
weight: 9.81 lb (4,450 g)

Model 1860 Dreyse Gun for "Füsilier-Regimenter" (*Zündnadel-Füsiliergewehr* M 60)

This has brass furniture.

Detail with bayonet fixed.

Dreyse Model 1862 Infantry Rifle
(*Zündnadel-Infanteriegewehr* M 62)

caliber: 15.43 mm
total length: 52.75 in (134 cm)
length of barrel: 33.46 in (85 cm)
weight: 10.47 lb (4,750 g)

This was derived from the famous Model 1841 issued in 1848. This weapon with a "needle-type" breech-block for firing ready-primed paper cartridges was invented by Johann Nikolaus von Dreyse of Sommerda. It was the first (turn-bolt) bolt-action breech-block to be used on a regulation weapon at a time when the most up-to-date armies had only just switched from the flintlock mechanism.

This system, with various modifications, was imitated in many countries; later converted to take metal cartridges, it is still used today.

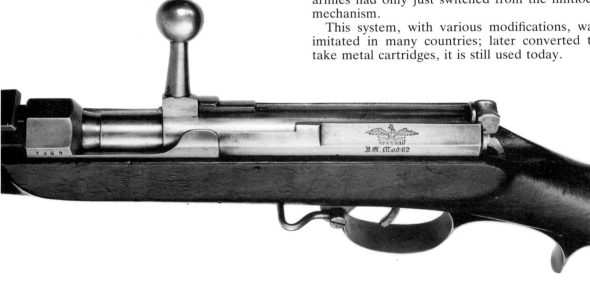

Detail with breech-block closed, and open with needle projecting.

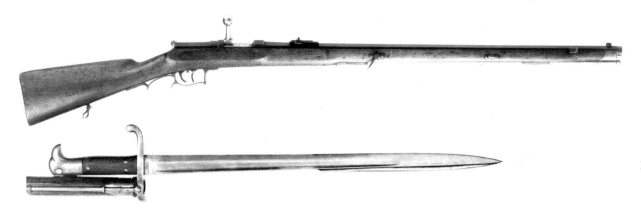

Detail with bayonet fixed.

Dreyse Model 1865 Light Infantry Rifle
(*Zündnadel-Jägerbüchse* M 65)

caliber: 15.43 mm
total length: 48.82 in (124 cm)
length of barrel: 30.31 in (77 cm)
weight: 9.92 lb (4,500 g)

This has a double (hair) trigger mechanism (Stecher system).
It has brass furniture.

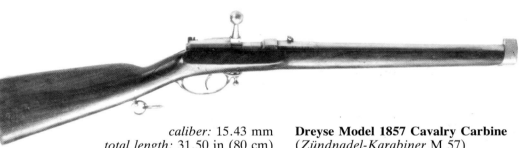

caliber: 15.43 mm
total length: 31.50 in (80 cm)
length of barrel: 15.16 in (38.5 cm)
weight: 6.28 lb (2,850 g)

Dreyse Model 1857 Cavalry Carbine
(*Zündnadel-Karabiner* M 57)

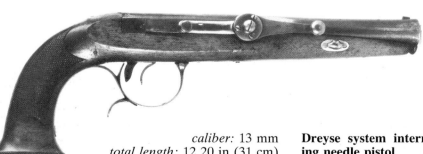

caliber: 13 mm
total length: 12.20 in (31 cm)
length of barrel: 8.46 in (21.5 cm)
weight: 1.21 lb (550 g)

Dreyse system internal-percussion, muzzle-loading needle pistol
(*Zündnadel* System)

BAVARIA

Model 1842/58 Podewils Musket

caliber: 17.8 mm
total length: 56.69 in (144 cm)
length of barrel: 41.22 in (104.7 cm)
weight: 9.70 lb (4,400 g)

This is the old Musketen M 42, which has been fitted with a rifled barrel for expanding bullets developed by the Bavarian General Philipp von Podewils.

Detail of fixed bayonet.

Werder Model 1869 Infantry Rifle

caliber: 11 mm
total length: 51.97 in (132 cm)
length of barrel: 35.03 in (89 cm)
weight: 9.70 lb (4,400 g)

This rifle, called *Bayerisch Blitz* (Bavarian lightning), was quite popular with European armies on account of its fast-loading system. The breech-block is opened by pushing forward the front trigger; having inserted the cartridge, cocking the hammer closes the breech-block.

The weapon is then ready for firing.

Detail with breech-block open.

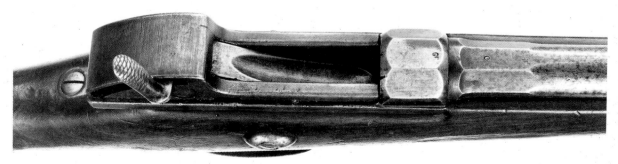

SCHAUMBURG-LIPPE

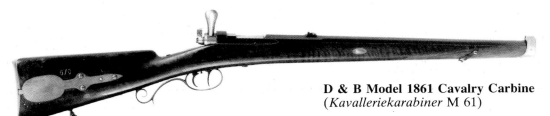

D & B Model 1861 Cavalry Carbine
(*Kavalleriekarabiner* M 61)

caliber: 15 mm
total length: 36.22 in (92 cm)
length of barrel: 18.50 in (47 cm)
weight: 6.17 lb (2,800 g)

Needle gun adopted by the army of Schaumburg-Lippe in 1861. This system was developed by Joseph Carl Doersch and Cramer von Baumgarten, by converting a Dreyse gun.

GERMANY

Mauser Model 1871 Rifle
(*Infanteriegewehr* M 71)

This was the first Mauser regulation weapon of the German Imperial Army.

Interesting features included a bolt-action breech-block, which cocked the firing pin automatically when it was opened.

This device obviated any risk of accidentally firing the weapon when the breech-block was closed, as well as simplifying operation of the gun.

This rifle was the first of many successful projects by the brilliant inventor and gunsmith from Oberndorf.

After the battles of Plevna in 1877, profiting from the success of the Turks armed with Winchesters, he transformed his 71s into repeaters, by fitting them with tubular magazines.

Detail with breech-block closed.

caliber: 11 mm
total length: 52.95 in (134.5 cm)
length of barrel: 33.66 in (85.5 cm)

Mauser Model 1871 Carbine
(*Karabiner* M 71)

caliber: 11 mm
total length: 39.37 in (100 cm)
length of barrel: 20.16 in (51.2 cm)

KINGDOM OF SARDINIA

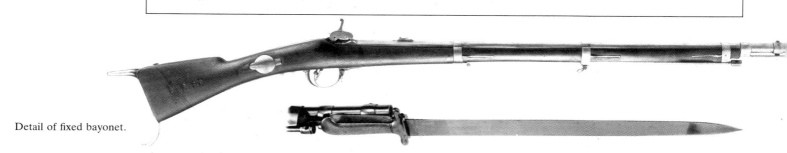

Detail of fixed bayonet.

La Marmora System Light Infantry (*Bersaglieri*) Carbine

This weapon was part of an experimental series given to the *Bersaglieri* in 1839.

It has a rifled barrel and uses the Delvigne chambered breech system.

An unusual feature is the self-priming (or successive primer) percussion lock to speed up the loading process.

caliber: 16 mm
total length: 52.75 in (134 cm)
length of barrel: 35.35 in (89.8 cm)
weight: 8.60 lb (3,900 g)

This system used primers incorporated into a copper strip rolled into a circular housing in the butt. Cocking the hammer wound the strip on, placing the primer over the nipple each time. Ingenious as it was, this system was not used for long as the tape proved too fragile.

An almost identical system was later used in the United States of America on Springfield Model 1855 rifles.

The weapon has iron furniture.

Detail of self-priming lock.

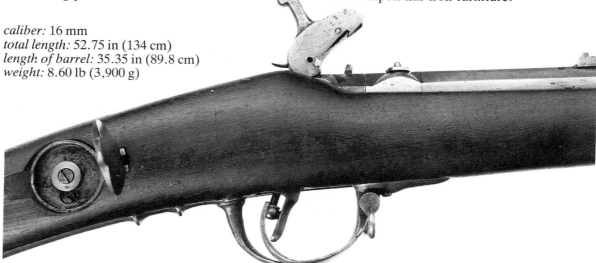

Model 1848 Light Infantry (*Bersaglieri*) Carbine

This is the new model carbine with a simple lock which uses loose caps. Derived from the Model 1844, it was the first regulation carbine of the *Bersaglieri*.

caliber: 16.9 mm
total length: 46.38 in (117.8 cm)
length of barrel: 29.92 in (76 cm)
weight: 8.60 lb (3,900 g)

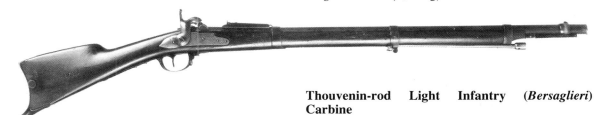

Thouvenin-rod Light Infantry (*Bersaglieri*) Carbine

This was the only *Bersagliere* carbine to use the Thouvenin system.

It is the same shape as the Model 1848, but has a musket lock which was to be used on the subsequent Model 1856.

Detail of fixed bayonet.

caliber: 17.5 mm
total length: 48.23 in (122.5 cm)
length of barrel: 31.89 in (81 cm)
weight: 10.14 lb (4,600 g)

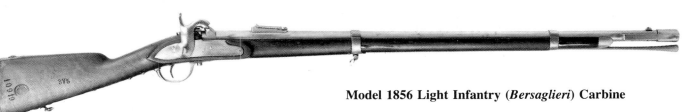

Model 1856 Light Infantry (*Bersaglieri*) Carbine

This model, which is similar to the infantry rifles and muskets, has a rifled barrel and a normal type of breech-block which used expanding bullets made by Peeters.

caliber: 17.5 mm
total length: 49.92 in (126.8 cm)
length of barrel: 34.64 in (88 cm)
weight: 9.94 lb (4,510 g)

Model 1860 Infantry Carbine

caliber: 17.5 mm
total length: 55.67 in (141.4 cm)
length of barrel: 40.43 in (102.7 cm)
weight: 9.48 lb (4,300 g)

Derived from the Model 1844 which was a descendant of the old Model 1814 (see Model 1814 Infantry Rifle).

With the Model 1860, rifling and expanding bullets were introduced into the individual armament of the Sardinian Army.

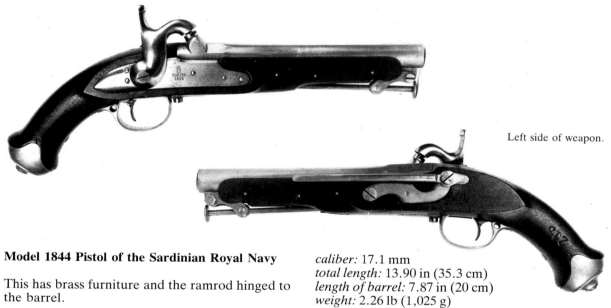

Left side of weapon.

Model 1844 Pistol of the Sardinian Royal Navy

This has brass furniture and the ramrod hinged to the barrel.

caliber: 17.1 mm
total length: 13.90 in (35.3 cm)
length of barrel: 7.87 in (20 cm)
weight: 2.26 lb (1,025 g)

Cavalry Officer's Pistol adopted in 1848

The barrel has no fewer than forty right-handed, triangular-section rifling grooves and a Delvigne system chambered breech.

The weapon has brass furniture.

caliber: 16.7 mm
total length: 13.38 in (34 cm)
length of barrel: 7.99 in (20.3 çm)
weight: 2.42 lb (1,100 g)

Detail of ramrod carried separately from the gun.

PAPAL STATES

Remington Model 1868 Infantry Rifle

This is a version of the American Remington rolling-block rifle, made in Liège by Emile & Leon Nagant for the Pope's army.

caliber: 12.7 mm
total length: 51.18 in (130 cm)
length of barrel: 34.64 in (88 cm)
weight: 9.21 lb (4,180 g)

Remington Model 1868 Artillery Musket

caliber: 12.7 mm
total length: 40.03 in (101.7 cm)
length of barrel: 23.03 in (58.5 cm)
weight: 7.80 lb (3,540 g)

Remington Model 1868 Gendarmerie Carbine

caliber: 12.7 mm
total length: 44.88 in (114 cm)
length of barrel: 28.35 in (72 cm)
weight: 8.46 lb (3,840 g)

141

KINGDOM OF THE TWO SICILIES

caliber: 17.5 mm
total length: 56.10 in (142.5 cm)
length of barrel: 40.47 in (102.8 cm)
weight: 8.82 lb (4,000 g)

Mounted Light Infantry (*Cacciatori a cavallo*) Rifle with 38-in barrel*

A weapon with a short stock adopted in 1848. It has brass furniture.

Carbine for Light Infantry (*Cacciatori*) battalions with 32-in barrel* (of 1849)

caliber: 17.5 mm
total length: 49.60 in (126 cm)
weight: 10.25 lb (4,650 g)

Weapon with rifled barrel and Delvigne system chambered breech.
Brass furniture.

*(1 inch = 27.07 mm according to the Neapolitan system).

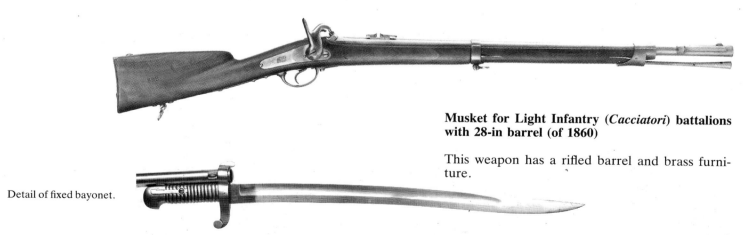

Musket for Light Infantry (*Cacciatori*) battalions with 28-in barrel (of 1860)

This weapon has a rifled barrel and brass furniture.

Detail of fixed bayonet.

caliber: 17.5 mm
total length: 45.07 in (114.5 cm)
weight: 8.60 lb (3,900 g)

142

ITALY

Doersch-Baumgarten Rifle

caliber: 17.5 mm
total length: 55.51 in (141 cm)
length of barrel: 36.22 in (92 cm)
weight: 9.70 lb (4,400 g)

Weapon presented to the committee responsible for the conversion of weapons from muzzle to breech-loading in 1867.

It uses the needle system of the Schaumburg-Lippe gun invented by Doersch and Baumgarten.

Detail of open breech-block.

Terssen Rifle

Weapon presented to the committee responsible for the conversion of weapons from muzzle to breech-loading in 1867.

This uses the trap-door system invented by Colonel Terssen, in charge of the arms factory at Liège.

caliber: 17.5 mm
total length: 55.51 in (141 cm)
length of barrel: 37.79 in (96 cm)
weight: 9.92 lb (4,500 g)

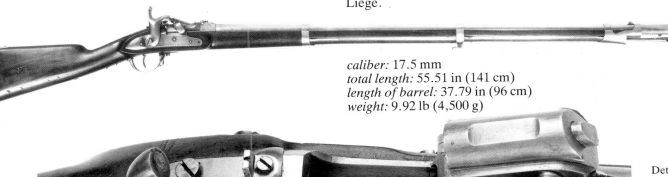

Detail of open breech-block.

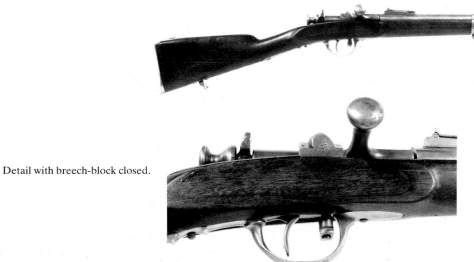

Detail with breech-block closed.

Model 1856 Light Infantry (*Bersaglieri*) Carbine converted to breech-loading using the Carcano system

This was the first Italian muzzle-loading weapon to be converted to breech-loading in 1867, using a needle-type breech-block. It has kept the old stock, the hole which housed the lock being stopped with wood.

caliber: 17.5 mm
total length: 49.92 in (126.8 cm)
weight: 9.59 lb (4,350 g)

Carcano Rifle adopted in 1867

caliber: 17.5 mm
total length: 55.67 in (141.4 cm)
weight: 9.48 lb (4,300 g)

This uses a needle-type breech-block produced by Salvatore Carcano in 1867 and inspired by the Prussian Dreyse gun, the Doersch-Baumgarten of Schaumburg-Lippe and the French Chassepot, to turn the old muzzle-loading rifles into breech-loaders. The breech-block, which works like an ordinary door-bolt, was fitted into the breech of the barrel, which was milled to receive it.

The nipple holder has been partially flattened and the touch-hole blocked up.

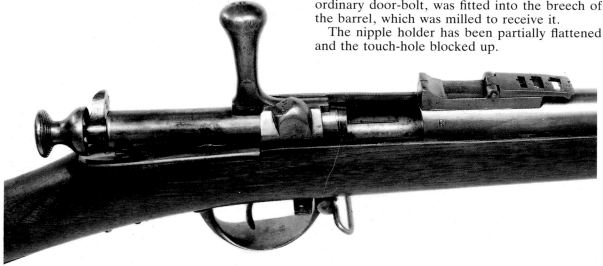

Detail with breech-block open and needle protruding.

Albini Model 1868 Carbine for the Italian Royal Navy

caliber: 14.5 mm
total length: 48.03 in (122 cm)
length of barrel: 30.31 in (77 cm)
weight: 9.92 lb (4,500 g)

The system invented by Albini to convert the Naval Rifle Pattern 1858 adopted by the Italian Royal Navy in 1863 is similar to the Wänzel mechanism adopted in Austria.

Detail of open breech-block and fixed bayonet.

Vetterli Model 1870 Infantry Rifle (first type)

caliber: 10.35 mm
total length: 53.11 in (134.9 cm)
length of barrel: 33.94 in (86.2 cm)
weight: 9.37 lb (4,250 g)

In Italy, the Vetterli rifle was produced to begin with in a successive loading version, because the repeater mechanism with the tubular magazine of the Swiss model was regarded as too fragile, and costly, to be entrusted to the soldiers of the day. It fired cartridges with a center-fire metal case, lead bullet and gunpowder charge.

After 1890, the charge consisted of Nobel ballistite and the bullet was coated with an alloy of copper and zinc.

Detail with breech-block open and bayonet fixed.

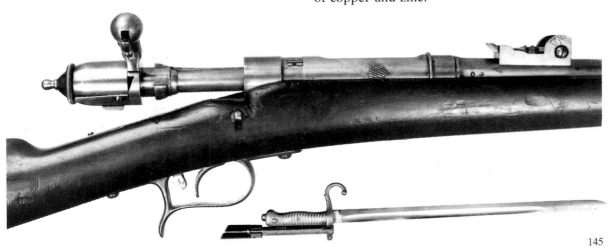

145

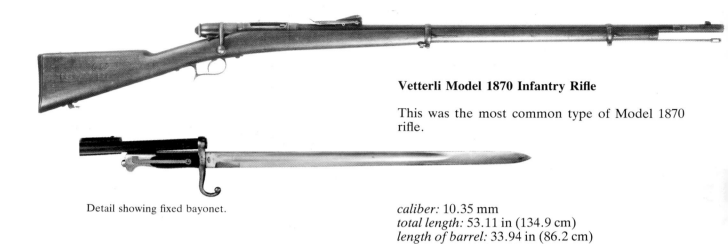

Vetterli Model 1870 Infantry Rifle

This was the most common type of Model 1870 rifle.

Detail showing fixed bayonet.

caliber: 10.35 mm
total length: 53.11 in (134.9 cm)
length of barrel: 33.94 in (86.2 cm)
weight: 9.04 lb (4,100 g)

Vetterli Model 1870 Royal Carabineer Musket

caliber: 10.35 mm
total length: 42.91 in (109 cm)
length of barrel: 24.01 in (61 cm)

Detail showing fixed bayonet.

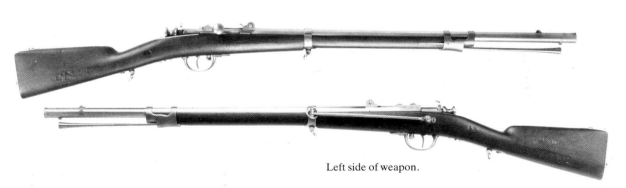

Left side of weapon.

Mounted RRCC (Royal Carabineer) Musket converted to breech-loading using the Carcano system

This has retained the brass furniture.

caliber: 17.4 mm
total length: 45.16 in (114.7 cm)
weight: 7.72 lb (3,500 g)

Detail of breech-block removed from weapon.

Hall Rifle
(J. H. Hall, Harper's Ferry, United States, 1834)

This weapon, the first flintlock version of which appeared in 1811, represents one of many semi-breech-loading systems which had already aroused some interest in previous centuries, to the extent that some had even been tested for military use, despite their high cost and mechanical complexity.

These include the Crespi system carbine of 1770 issued to some Austrian Army Dragoons.

A similar mechanism to that of John Hall, dated 1831, was produced in Naples (see Kingdom of the Two Sicilies).

Another distinctive feature of the Hall rifle was the breech-block which, apart from the chamber, contained the percussion and trigger mechanisms, and could therefore be removed from the gun and used as a pistol.

caliber: 0.54 in
total length: 52.75 in (134 cm)
length of barrel: 32.68 in (83 cm)
weight: 10.25 lb (4,650 g)

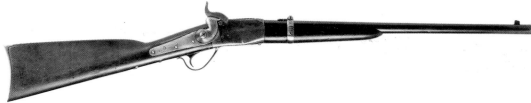

Peabody Cavalry Carbine

This breech-loading weapon, using rim-fire cartridges with metal cases, was patented at Boston (Massachusetts) in 1862 by Henry Peabody.

Its closure mechanism is of the falling block type and is operated by the trigger guard as in the Sharps.

By pushing the trigger-guard lever forwards and downwards, the breech-block is lowered and the cartridge can be fed in.

Although this system was simple, sturdy and permitted a rapid rate of fire, it was not successful in America; it did, however, realize its potential in Europe, where it was adopted by various armies after a few modifications.

caliber: 0.50 in
total length: 38.19 in (97 cm)
length of barrel: 19.88 in (50.5 cm)
weight: 6.72 lb (3,050 g)

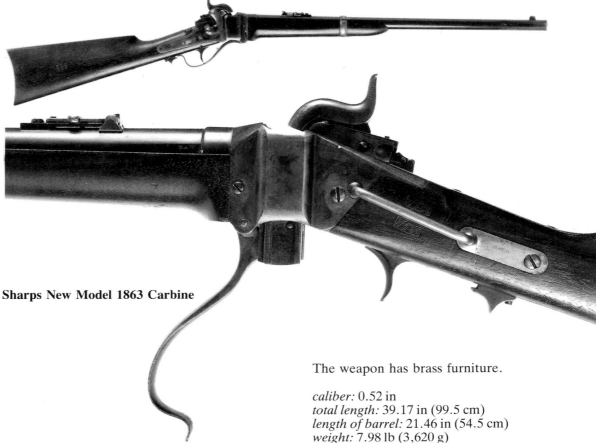

Detail of open breech-block.

Sharps New Model 1863 Carbine

The weapon has brass furniture.

caliber: 0.52 in
total length: 39.17 in (99.5 cm)
length of barrel: 21.46 in (54.5 cm)
weight: 7.98 lb (3,620 g)

This is one of the variants of the strong, vertically-sliding (dropping-block) mechanism using paper cartridges with a separate primer and invented by Christian Sharps. This mechanism, which was patented by Sharps at Cincinnati (Ohio) back in 1848, consists of a breech-block which is opened and closed perpendicular to the axis of the barrel, by maneuvering the trigger-guard lever. Having chambered the cartridge, the end of it was cut through by the closure of the breech-block, bringing the black powder into contact with the touch-hole of the nipple. To speed up loading, these rifles were also fitted with self-priming systems.

Because of their precision and power, Sharps weapons were used not only for military purposes, but also for shooting bison.

caliber: 0.58 in
total length: 55.90 in (142 cm)
length of barrel: 39.76 in (101 cm)
weight: 9.26 lb (4,200 g)

Model 1863 Infantry Rifle

Muzzle-loader with a rifled barrel.

Also known as the Springfield musket, this was the product of modifications to the earlier Model 1861 during the American Civil War.

It has iron furniture.

Allin Model 1866 Infantry Rifle

caliber: 0.50 in
total length: 51.57 in (131 cm)
length of barrel: 36.61 in (93 cm)
weight: 9.15 lb (4,150 g)

This is the Springfield musket converted to breech-loading by the trap-door system with cam closure invented by E. S. Allin. Smaller caliber guns with this type of breech-block were regulation weapons of the United States Army up to 1892, when the first Krag-Jorgensen repeating rifles were issued, but they remained in use until after the Hispano-American war.

Detail with breech-block closed, and open.

Remington Naval Rifle adopted in 1867

caliber: 0.50 in
total length: 51.18 in (130 cm)
length of barrel: 34.64 in (88 cm)
weight: 9.21 lb (4,180 g)

A distinctive feature of this weapon is the rolling-block type breech-block.

This system was patented by Leonard Geiger, an inventor from Vermont, and bought by the Ilion Remington factory (New York), where it was perfected by Joseph Rider in 1866.

The sturdiness and simplicity of this mechanism, which was inspired by that of Flobert, was such that Remington rolling-block weapons were adopted by a number of different armies.

Detail with breech-block open.

150

BRITAIN

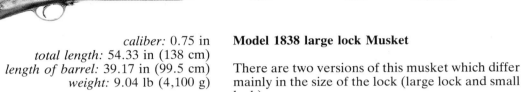

Model 1838 large lock Musket

caliber: 0.75 in
total length: 54.33 in (138 cm)
length of barrel: 39.17 in (99.5 cm)
weight: 9.04 lb (4,100 g)

There are two versions of this musket which differ mainly in the size of the lock (large lock and small lock).

The weapon has brass furniture.

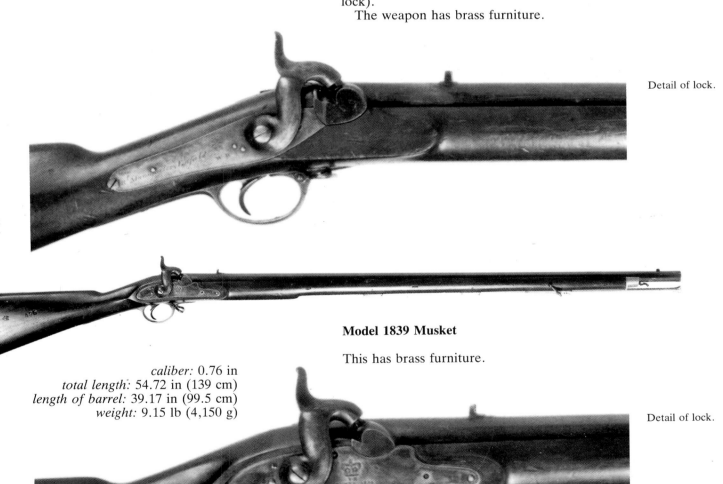

Detail of lock.

Model 1839 Musket

This has brass furniture.

caliber: 0.76 in
total length: 54.72 in (139 cm)
length of barrel: 39.17 in (99.5 cm)
weight: 9.15 lb (4,150 g)

Detail of lock.

151

caliber: 0.577 in
total length: 54.92 in (139.5 cm)
length of barrel: 38.97 in (99 cm)
weight: 10.36 lb (4,700 g)

Enfield Model 1853 Rifle

This weapon has a rifled barrel and iron furniture.

Detail of lock.

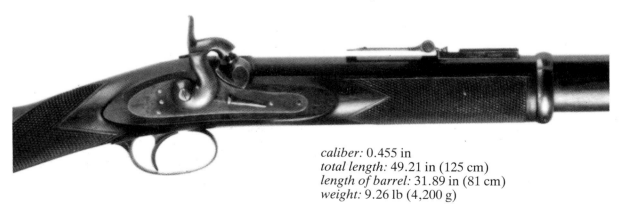

Whitworth Carbine, *c*.1860

An excellent target weapon, with elegant lines and a high standard of finish.

Detail of lock.

caliber: 0.455 in
total length: 49.21 in (125 cm)
length of barrel: 31.89 in (81 cm)
weight: 9.26 lb (4,200 g)

Snider Model 1853/66 Rifle

This is the Enfield Model 1853 rifle converted to breech-loading using the snuff box system invented by the American Jacob Snider.

caliber: 0.577 in
total length: 54.92 in (139.5 cm)
length of barrel: 35.43 in (90 cm)
weight: 10.47 lb (4,750 g)

Detail with breech-block closed, and open.

Model 1837 Tirailleur Carbine

A rifled weapon with a Delvigne system chambered breech, and a backward-spring *à la Pontcharra* type of lock.

The gun is also known as the *Carabine Pontcharra* (Pontcharra Carbine).

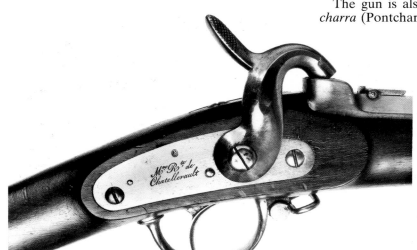

Detail of lock.

caliber: 17 mm
total length: 51.57 in (131 cm)
length of barrel: 34.25 in (87 cm)
weight: 8.82 lb (4,000 g)

Model 1846 Carbine

caliber: 17.8 mm
total length: 49.68 in (126.2 cm)
length of barrel: 34.17 in (86.8 cm)
weight: 9.83 lb (4,460 g)

This carbine with a rifled bore uses the steel rod type of breech-block like the subsequent Model 1853.

This steel-rod system, devised by Thouvenin, gave good results but made the weapons hard to clean and slow-loading. After the expanding bullet invented by Minié was introduced, the steel rod was eliminated and the weapons thus transformed were denominated Model 1846 T and Model 1853 T.

It has iron furniture.

154

Model 1840 Infantry Rifle

This was the first French Army rifle with a backward-spring lock. When the new nipple-type weapons were introduced, this type of lock was also adopted by other European armies.

caliber: 18 mm
total length: 58.03 in (147.4 cm)
length of barrel: 41.61 in (105.7 cm)
weight: 9.61 lb (4,360 g)

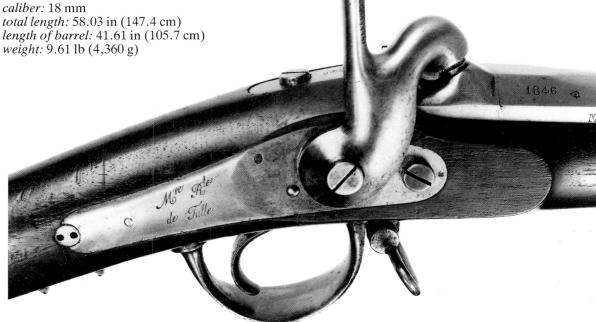

Detail of lock.

caliber: 17.8 mm
total length: 58.07 in (147.5 cm)
length of barrel: 42.64 in (108.3 cm)
weight: 9.68 lb (4,390 g)

Model 1853 Infantry Weapon

This firearm derived from the Model 1842, with a few modifications, became the basic French infantry weapon of the mid nineteenth century. The subsequent Models 1853 T (with rifled barrel) and 1857 (with cast steel barrel) were converted to breech-loading in 1867 using the Schneider snuff box system.

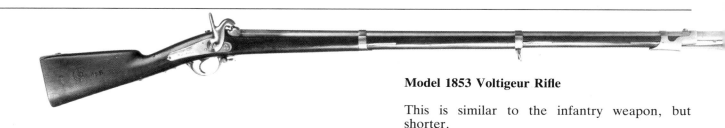

Model 1853 Voltigeur Rifle

This is similar to the infantry weapon, but shorter.

caliber: 17.8 mm
total length: 55.94 in (142.1 cm)
length of barrel: 40.51 in (102.9 cm)
weight: 9.57 lb (4,340 g)

Model 1866 Chassepot Rifle

Several years after Prussia adopted the Dreyse needle gun, a weapon with a similar system was developed in France by Antoine-Alphonse Chassepot. However, the system arrived on the scene too late, partly because it was not a means of converting muzzle-loaders to breech-loaders, as in other countries.

This would have been useful until a more modern weapon was available, if only to cut costs, as the gun would not have had to be manufactured in its entirety. The Chassepot became famous after the Battle of Mentana (1867), although victory over Garibaldi's men was due more to the numerical superiority of the Franco-Papal troops than to this "modern" weapon.

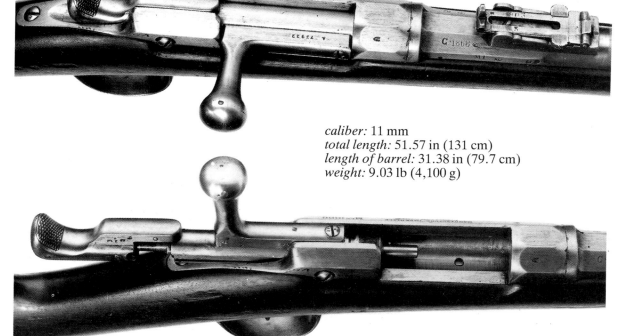

Detail with breech-block closed, and open.

caliber: 11 mm
total length: 51.57 in (131 cm)
length of barrel: 31.38 in (79.7 cm)
weight: 9.03 lb (4,100 g)

Chassepot Model 1866 Musket

caliber: 11 mm
total length: 39.37 in (100 cm)
length of barrel: 20.27 in (51.5 cm)
weight: 8.16 lb (3,700 g)

Model 1867 Infantry Rifle *à tabatière*

caliber: 17.8 mm
total length: 55.94 in (142.1 cm)
length of barrel: 37.72 in (95.8 cm)
weight: 9.81 lb (4,450 g)

This system for converting muzzle-loaders to breech-loaders (Model 1853 T and Model 1857), known as the snuff-box system, and similar to the Snider method (see p.153), was invented by the French gunsmith Schneider.

Detail with breech-block closed, and open.

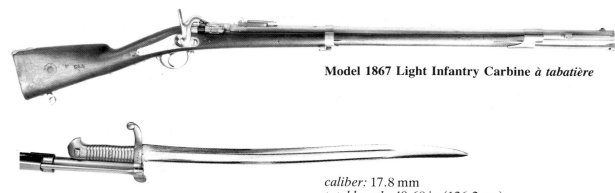

Model 1867 Light Infantry Carbine *à tabatière*

Detail of fixed bayonet.

caliber: 17.8 mm
total length: 49.68 in (126.2 cm)
length of barrel: 31.30 in (79.5 cm)
weight: 9.92 lb (4,500 g)

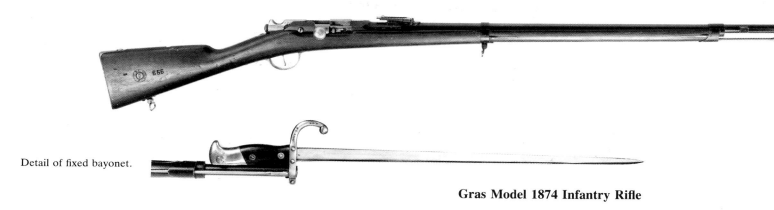

Detail of fixed bayonet.

Gras Model 1874 Infantry Rifle

This successive loading weapon, using cartridges with metal cases, was developed by Captain Gras and directly derived from the Chassepot, thus enabling the old weapons with needle breech-blocks to be reused.

Detail of closed breech-block.

caliber: 11 mm
total length: 51.57 in (131 cm)
length of barrel: 31.38 in (79.7 cm)
weight: 9.21 lb (4,180 g)

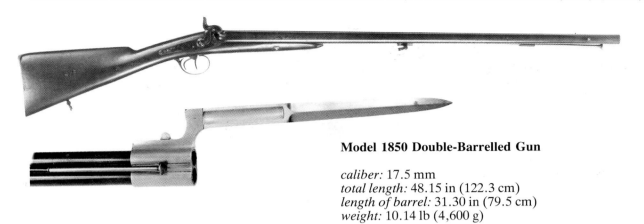

Detail of fixed bayonet.

Model 1850 Double-Barrelled Gun

caliber: 17.5 mm
total length: 48.15 in (122.3 cm)
length of barrel: 31.30 in (79.5 cm)
weight: 10.14 lb (4,600 g)

Model 1829 T Artillery Musket

This rifled weapon has a rod-type breech-block.

Detail of fixed bayonet.

caliber: 17.6 mm
total length: 37.72 in (95.8 cm)
length of barrel: 23.62 in (60 cm)
weight: 5.63 lb (2,555 g)

Model 1822 T Cavalry Pistol

This is derived from the Model 1816 which was a
direct descendant of the Anno XIII.
   Originally a flintlock weapon, it was converted
to percussion (Model 1822 T).
   It has brass furniture.

caliber: 17.6 mm
total length: 13.70 in (34.8 cm)
length of barrel: 7.87 in (20 cm)
weight: 2.71 lb (1,230 g)

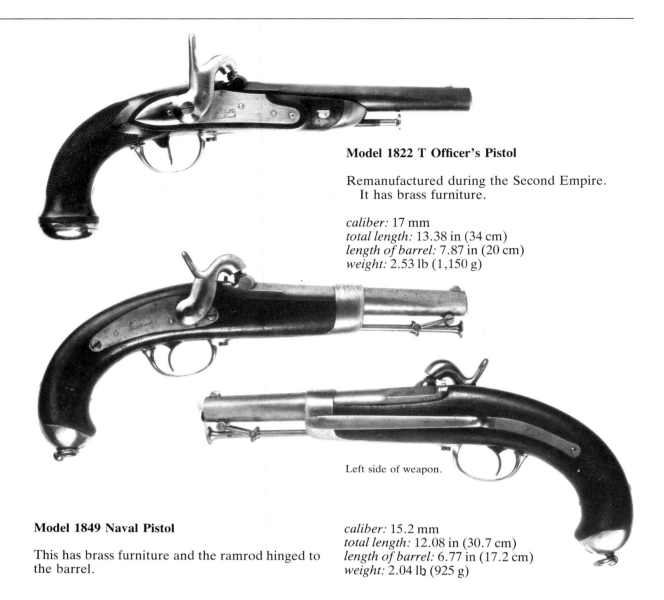

Model 1822 T Officer's Pistol

Remanufactured during the Second Empire. It has brass furniture.

caliber: 17 mm
total length: 13.38 in (34 cm)
length of barrel: 7.87 in (20 cm)
weight: 2.53 lb (1,150 g)

Left side of weapon.

Model 1849 Naval Pistol

This has brass furniture and the ramrod hinged to the barrel.

caliber: 15.2 mm
total length: 12.08 in (30.7 cm)
length of barrel: 6.77 in (17.2 cm)
weight: 2.04 lb (925 g)

Model 1855 Staff Officer's Pistol

This weapon has two superimposed rifled barrels and the ramrod is attached to the right-hand side by a chain.

caliber: 17.1 mm
total length: 13.58 in (34.5 cm)
length of barrel: 7.08 in (18 cm)
weight: 2.90 lb (1,315 g)

AUSTRIA

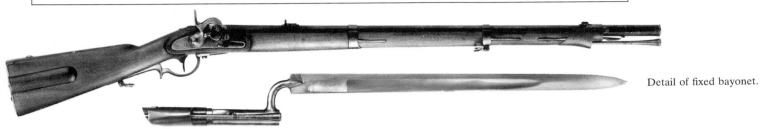

Detail of fixed bayonet.

Model 1842 Rifle with chambered breech
(*Kammerbüchse* M 1842)

This weapon has an Augustin system lock of the explosive tube (Zünder) type, which totally replaced the Console system in the armament of the imperial army.

The system is named after Baron von Augustin, a native of Pest and the officer in charge of Austrian artillery at that time, who was keenly interested in weapon design, although it was probably invented by other, anonymous engineers.

The *Kammerbüchse* M 1842 has a barrel with 12 rifling grooves and a Delvigne system chambered breech.

caliber: 18.1 mm
total length: 48.35 in (122.8 cm)
length of barrel: 34.01 in (86.4 cm)
weight: 10.14 lb (4,600 g)

Model 1842 Light Infantry Musket
(*Jägerstutzen* M 1842)

This weapon uses the Augustin ignition system.

It is derived from the *Jägerstutzen* M 1835 which had a Console lock.

It has brass furniture.

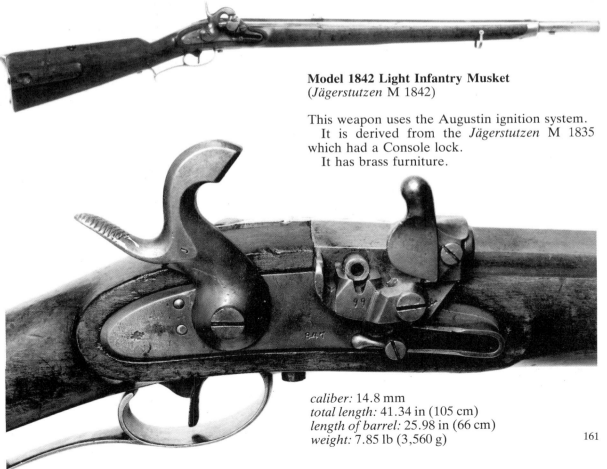

Detail of lock.

caliber: 14.8 mm
total length: 41.34 in (105 cm)
length of barrel: 25.98 in (66 cm)
weight: 7.85 lb (3,560 g)

161

Detail of fixed bayonet.

Lorenz Model 1854 Infantry Rifle
(*Infanteriegewehr* M 1854)

Although the Augustin system lock was quite successful in Austria, the nipple system was undeniably simpler and more practical.

Accordingly, in the fifties it was decided to convert all weapons from the Zünder system and all newly-manufactured ones were given nipples.

The *Infanteriegewehr* M 1854 was the first Austrian gun to use the nipple system and was also one of the most accurate muzzle-loading infantry rifles in its day.

Lorenz was a lieutenant in the army when he produced the compression bullet, the idea for which probably came from research by Wilkinson in Britain.

This system gave such good results that the large calibers then in use were immediately reduced, a caliber of 13.90 mm being adopted with rifling and the projectile invented by Lorenz.

The weapon has iron furniture.

total length: 52.56 in (133.5 cm)
length of barrel: 37.40 in (95 cm)
weight: 9.08 lb (4,120 g)

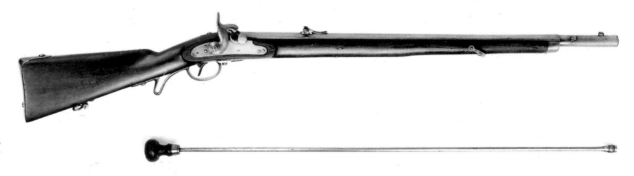

Detail of ramrod (carried separately from gun).

Model 1854 Light Infantry Musket
(*Jägerstutzen* M 1854)

This has iron furniture.

Detail of fixed bayonet.

caliber: 13.9 mm
total length: 43.15 in (109.6 cm)
length of barrel: 27.95 in (71 cm)
weight: 9.03 lb (4,100 g)

Lindner Experimental Rifle

This is the *Infanteriegewehr* M 1862 converted to breech-loading using the Lindner system.
It uses cartridges with a metal case.

caliber: 13.9 mm
total length: 52.48 in (133.3 cm)
weight: 9.08 lb (4,120 g)

Detail with breech-block open.

Wänzel Model 1867 Infantry Rifle
(*Infanteriegewehr* M 1867)

This is the old *Infanteriegewehr* Model 1854 converted to breech-loading using the Wänzel system.
The breech-block is of the trap-door type and rim-fire cartridges are used.

caliber: 13.9 mm
total length: 52.36 in (133 cm)
length of barrel: 34.80 in (88.4 cm)
weight: 9.81 lb (4,450 g)

163

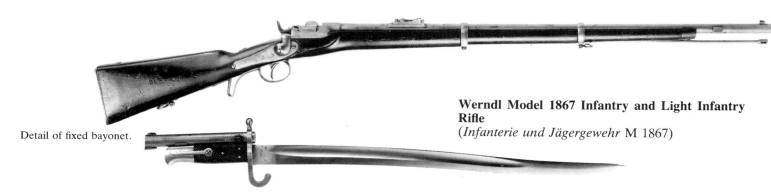

Werndl Model 1867 Infantry and Light Infantry Rifle
(*Infanterie und Jägergewehr* M 1867)

Detail of fixed bayonet.

In view of the clear superiority of the Prussian Dreyse guns at the Battle of Sadowa, Austria decided to adopt a small caliber breech-loading rifle with center-fire cartridges, as well as transforming her weapons from muzzle- to breech-loading.

The weapon chosen was by Josef Werndl. It had a barrel-shaped system of closure and had given better results than the already famous Remington rolling block system during trials at the Vienna Arsenal polygon.

caliber: 11 mm
total length: 50.39 in (128 cm)
length of barrel: 33.19 in (84.3 cm)
weight: 9.88 lb (4,480 g)

Detail with breech-block open.

Werndl Model 1867 Carbine
(*Karabiner* M 1867)

caliber: 11 mm
total length: 38.86 in (98.7 cm)
length of barrel: 22.28 in (56.6 cm)
weight: 7.40 lb (3,360 g)

Wänzel Model 1867 Light Infantry Musket
(*Jägerstutzen* M 1867)

caliber: 13.9 mm
total length: 43.31 in (110 cm)
length of barrel: 25.47 in (64.7 cm)
weight: 9.92 lb (4,500 g)

Detail with breech-block open.

caliber: 11 mm
total length: 50.43 in (128.1 cm)
length of barrel: 33.19 in (84.3 cm)
weight: 9.26 lb (4,200 g)

Model 1873 Infantry and Light Infantry Rifle
(*Infanterie und Jägergewehr* M 1873)

This is a variant of the Model 1867.

caliber: 16.9 mm
total length: 16.53 in (42 cm)
length of barrel: 9.84 in (25 cm)
weight: 3.30 lb (1,500 g)

Model 1844 Cavalry Pistol
(*Kavalleriepistole* M 1844)

This is similar to the Model 1798 flintlock, but has an Augustin system lock with explosive tube primer (Zünder). As with the old model, the ramrod is carried separately and the furniture is made of brass.

Detail with lock ready for priming.

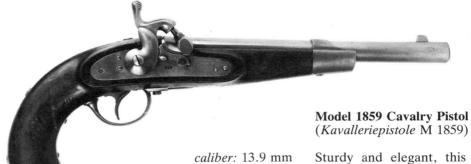

Model 1859 Cavalry Pistol
(*Kavalleriepistole* M 1859)

caliber: 13.9 mm
total length: 18.50 in (40 cm)
weight: 3.30 lb (1,500 g)

Sturdy and elegant, this was one of the best percussion lock military pistols.

It used the Lorenz type of rifling and compression bullet. The external safety catch enabled the weapon to be carried loaded and primed with the hammer down.

It has iron furniture.

SWITZERLAND

Model 1842 Infantry Rifle
(*Infanteriegewehr*, model 1842)

caliber: 18 mm
total length: 57.87 in (147 cm)
length of barrel: 42.56 in (108.1 cm)
weight: 10.47 lb (4,750 g)

Detail of lock.

166

Milbank-Amsler Model 1859/67 Infantry Rifle

This was the old Model 1859 infantry rifle converted to breech-loading using the Milbank-Amsler system. The breech-block was of the trap-door type and it used rim-fire cartridges.

caliber: 18 mm
total length: 57.87 in (147 cm)
length of barrel: 39.84 in (101.2 cm)
weight: 9.92 lb (4,500 g)

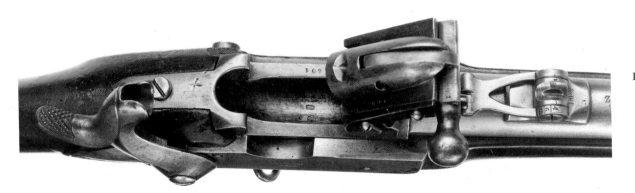

Detail with breech-block open.

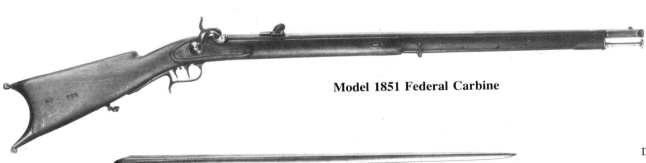

Model 1851 Federal Carbine

Detail of fixed bayonet.

This is the most famous Swiss carbine, which was used by various volunteer corps in a number of states in the mid nineteenth century.

caliber: 10.5 mm
total length: 49.60 in (126 cm)
length of barrel: 32 in (81.3 cm)
weight: 9.92 lb (4,500 g)

BELGIUM

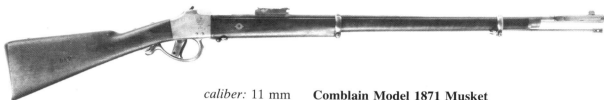

caliber: 11 mm
total length: 47.64 in (121 cm)
length of barrel: 32.87 in (83.5 cm)
weight: 9.26 lb (4,200 g)

Comblain Model 1871 Musket

A successive-loading weapon in which the breech-block is operated by the trigger guard lever.

Detail with breech-block open.

SPAIN

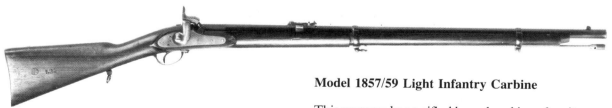

Model 1857/59 Light Infantry Carbine

This weapon has a rifled barrel and iron furniture.

caliber: 14.4 mm
total length: 48.46 in (123.1 cm)
length of barrel: 33.11 in (84.1 cm)
weight: 8.49 lb (3,850 g)

RUSSIA

caliber: 18.4 mm
total length: 47.83 in (121.5 cm)
length of barrel: 33.35 in (84.7 cm)
weight: 6.61 lb (3,000 g)

Cossack Rifle of 1852

This has the same distinctive stock shape as the old flintlock models.

Cossack Carbine

A weapon with a rifled barrel built in Belgium in 1861.

It has no trigger guard and the hammer has a ring-shaped crest.

caliber: 15.5 mm
total length: 48.62 in (123.5 cm)
length of barrel: 33.38 in (84.8 cm)
weight: 6.61 lb (3,000 g)

Left side of weapon.

caliber: 18.5 mm
total length: 32.08 in (81.5 cm)
length of barrel: 16.53 in (42 cm)
weight: 5.73 lb (2,600 g)

Cavalry Musket of 1851

This weapon has a rifled barrel.

Berdan II Model 1871 Rifle

This used the first cartridge of the center-fire type with Berdan primer and a bottle-shaped cartridge case. The American Colonel Hiram Berdan is remembered as the inventor not just of a few breech-blocks for rifles, but also of the type of primer for cartridges which is still used today throughout the world, except in the United States of America, where the type invented by the British Colonel Boxer is preferred.

caliber: 10.66 mm
total length: 52.99 in (134.6 cm)
length of barrel: 32.68 in (83 cm)
weight: 9.26 lb (4,200 g)

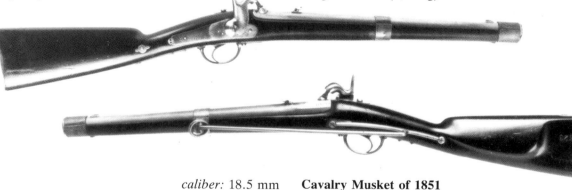

Detail of fixed bayonet.

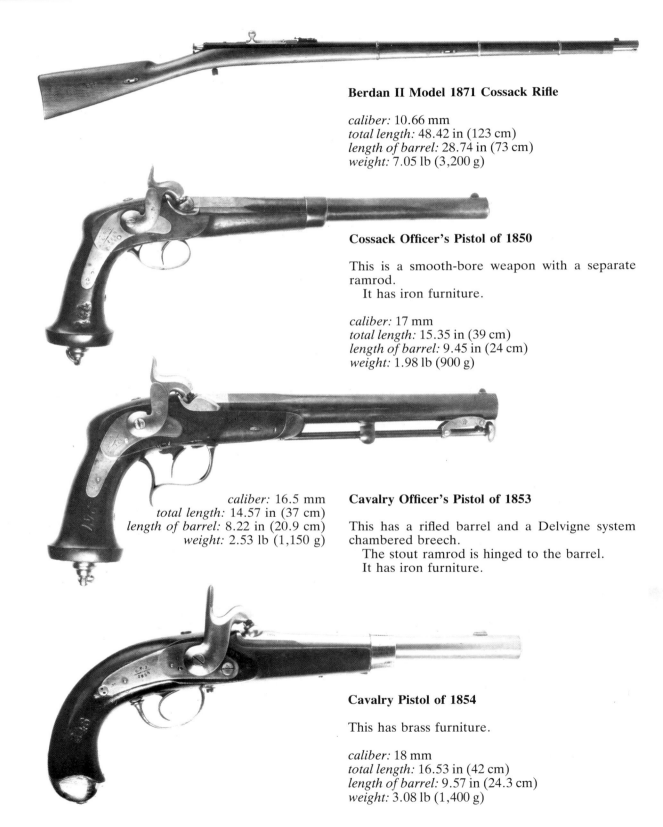

Berdan II Model 1871 Cossack Rifle

caliber: 10.66 mm
total length: 48.42 in (123 cm)
length of barrel: 28.74 in (73 cm)
weight: 7.05 lb (3,200 g)

Cossack Officer's Pistol of 1850

This is a smooth-bore weapon with a separate ramrod.
 It has iron furniture.

caliber: 17 mm
total length: 15.35 in (39 cm)
length of barrel: 9.45 in (24 cm)
weight: 1.98 lb (900 g)

caliber: 16.5 mm
total length: 14.57 in (37 cm)
length of barrel: 8.22 in (20.9 cm)
weight: 2.53 lb (1,150 g)

Cavalry Officer's Pistol of 1853

This has a rifled barrel and a Delvigne system chambered breech.
 The stout ramrod is hinged to the barrel.
 It has iron furniture.

Cavalry Pistol of 1854

This has brass furniture.

caliber: 18 mm
total length: 16.53 in (42 cm)
length of barrel: 9.57 in (24.3 cm)
weight: 3.08 lb (1,400 g)

American-built Peabody and Martini Rifle
(Providence Tool Co., U.S.A.)

caliber: 7.65 mm
total length: 45.07 in (114.5 cm)
length of barrel: 29.13 in (74 cm)
weight: 8.81 lb (4,000 g)

This shows one of the modifications the Peabody underwent in Europe.

The Hungarian engineer Friedrich von Martini elaborated the mechanics of the Peabody, eliminating the external hammer favored by the Americans.

With successive modifications, the old Peabody was used in various calibers up to the Second World War.

JAPAN

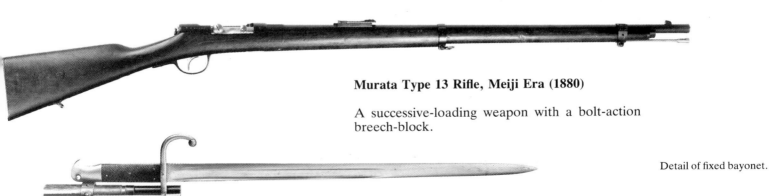

Murata Type 13 Rifle, Meiji Era (1880)

A successive-loading weapon with a bolt-action breech-block.

Detail of fixed bayonet.

caliber: 11 mm
total length: 53.15 in (135 cm)
length of barrel: 33.07 in (84 cm)
weight: 8.82 lb (4,000 g)

REPEATING AND
AUTOMATIC WEAPONS

By the end of the nineteenth century, the transformation of the individual weapon from a more or less hand-crafted item to an industrial product had been a reality for some decades. Technological innovation was constant. From breech-loading systems, manufacturers progressed to repeaters, and, before long, to automatic fire.

The social life of continental and Balkan Europe was disrupted by the First World War. Weapons factories were constantly producing new models which were better, more reliable and, needless to say, more lethal than the last.

Progress was made on improving materials and ammunition for greater fire power and maximum simplicity of operation. Automatic fire had been a reality since the final decade of the nineteenth century.

The period between the two World Wars saw the widespread adoption of the sub-machine gun, which was to have a profound effect on individual fighting techniques.

Once again, a few weapons (and thus a few nations) played a leading role in production as a whole. Here, too, the material is therefore presented in a way that takes account of technical aspects and the spread of the various types of weapon, as well as noting the changes made to them in both chronological and geographical terms.

The different states are not always represented by particularly good models from a technical point of view; in some cases, economic necessity and/or errors of choice led to instruments of war becoming famous which were not equal to the tasks for which they were intended. They have been included here for the sake of completeness, even if they were not as good as their reputation might suggest.

MECHANISMS

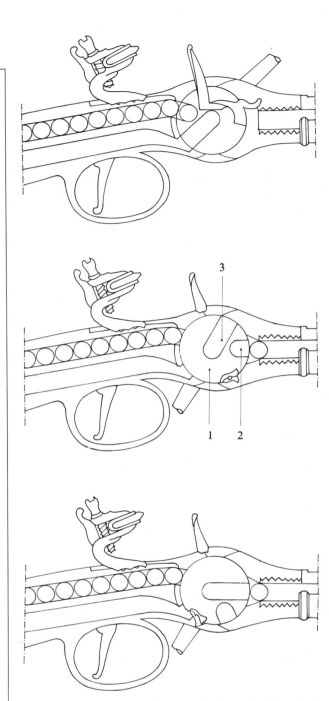

Lorenzoni repeater system (last quarter of seventeenth century)

The transverse breech-block turns in a cylindrical chamber rotated by a lever. The muzzle of the gun is turned downwards in such a way that a bullet and gunpowder charge drop from two tubular compartments in the butt into special recesses in the breech-block. At this point, the block is rotated by means of an external lever so that the ball and charge are transferred to the barrel. Moving the lever also cocks the gun and causes priming powder to be tipped into the pan from another compartment. This loading system is also found in weapons made by the Englishman Cookson, and is therefore also known as the Cookson or Lorenzoni-Cookson system.

1 cylindrical breech-block with lever; 2 bullet cavity; 3 chamber.

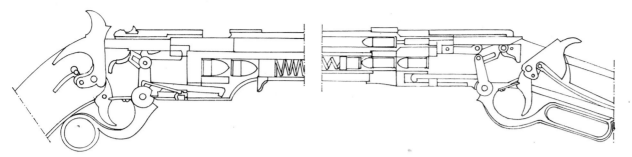

Volcanic repeating rifle

A forerunner of the Henry and Winchester, it used bullets with the charge and primer incorporated.

Henry repeating rifle

With rim-fire cartridges. Moving the trigger-guard lever backwards and forwards extracts the spent cartridge case, cocks the hammer, reloads the weapon and closes the breech.

Mannlicher repeating rifle, with packet magazine (1882)

One of the first weapons of decidedly modern design, even if the position of the magazine was undoubtedly awkward. It was in any case an experimental model developed before the Austrian regulation model (Mannlicher Model '86).

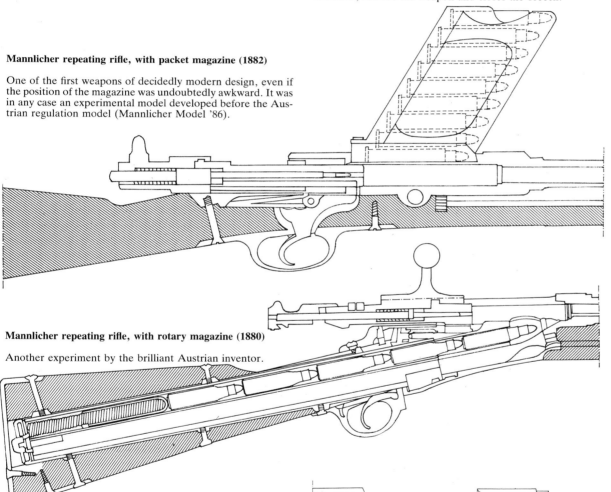

Mannlicher repeating rifle, with rotary magazine (1880)

Another experiment by the brilliant Austrian inventor.

Mauser Model '88 repeating rifle

This is loaded by lifting and pulling back the bolt-handle. The packet magazine, containing five cartridges, is inserted from above; a spring pushes the group of cartridges from the bottom upwards.

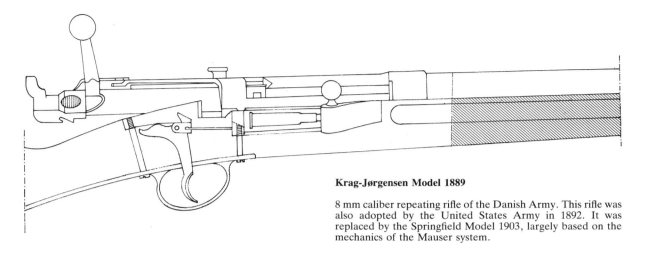

Krag-Jørgensen Model 1889

8 mm caliber repeating rifle of the Danish Army. This rifle was also adopted by the United States Army in 1892. It was replaced by the Springfield Model 1903, largely based on the mechanics of the Mauser system.

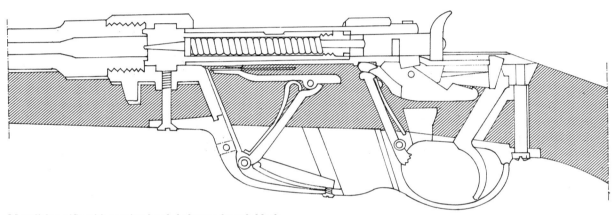

Mannlicher rifle with turning-head, bolt-type breech-block

Cross-section of the von Mannlicher rifle adopted by Austria as Model 1895.

Mosin-Nagant rifle (3-lineaya vintovka obr 1891)

Adopted by the Russian Army. A combination of the feed system produced by the Belgian company Nagant and the mechanism designed by Colonel Mosin of the Tsarist army. The Mosin-Nagant rifle was loaded with a charger of five cartridges inserted from above.

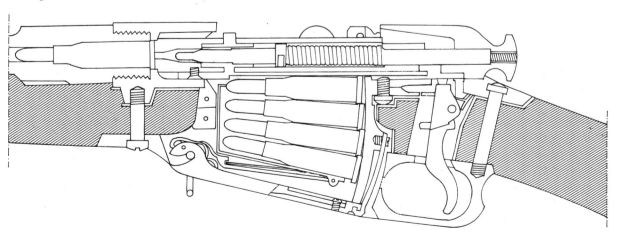

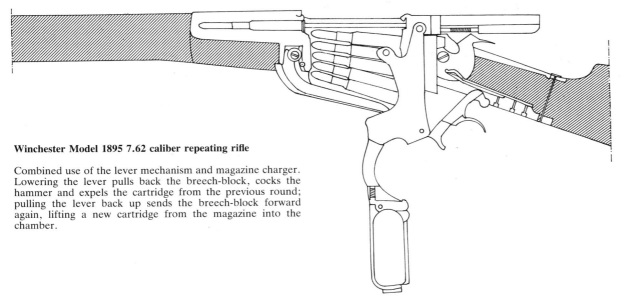

Winchester Model 1895 7.62 caliber repeating rifle

Combined use of the lever mechanism and magazine charger.
Lowering the lever pulls back the breech-block, cocks the
hammer and expels the cartridge from the previous round;
pulling the lever back up sends the breech-block forward
again, lifting a new cartridge from the magazine into the
chamber.

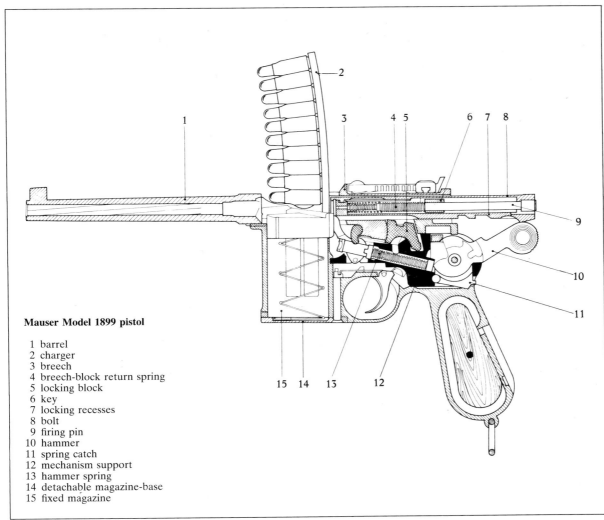

Mauser Model 1899 pistol

  1 barrel
  2 charger
  3 breech
  4 breech-block return spring
  5 locking block
  6 key
  7 locking recesses
  8 bolt
  9 firing pin
10 hammer
11 spring catch
12 mechanism support
13 hammer spring
14 detachable magazine-base
15 fixed magazine

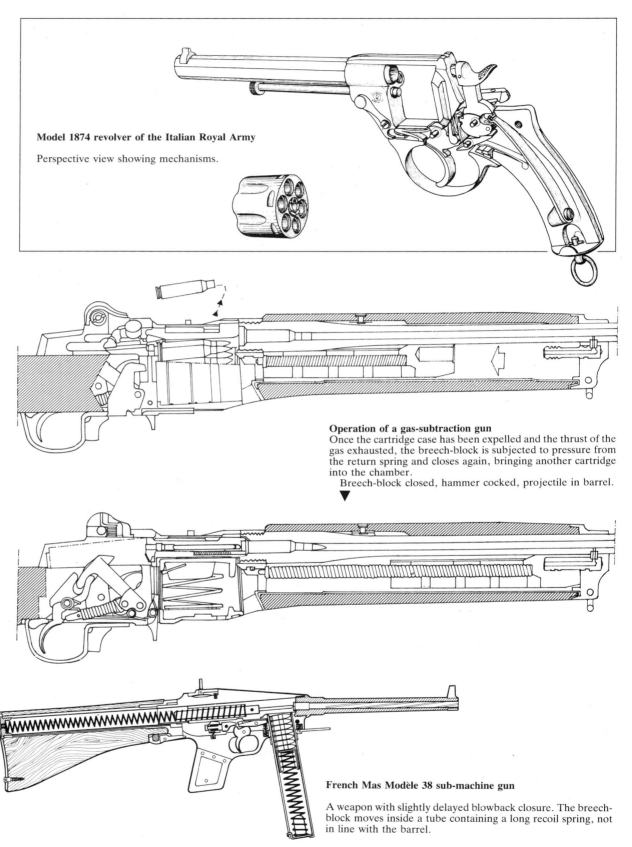

Model 1874 revolver of the Italian Royal Army

Perspective view showing mechanisms.

Operation of a gas-subtraction gun
Once the cartridge case has been expelled and the thrust of the gas exhausted, the breech-block is subjected to pressure from the return spring and closes again, bringing another cartridge into the chamber.

Breech-block closed, hammer cocked, projectile in barrel.

French Mas Modèle 38 sub-machine gun

A weapon with slightly delayed blowback closure. The breech-block moves inside a tube containing a long recoil spring, not in line with the barrel.

178

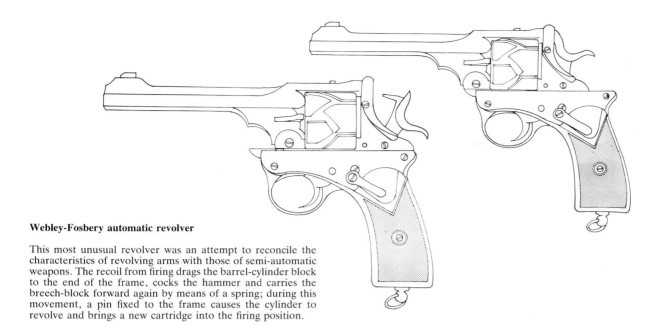

Webley-Fosbery automatic revolver

This most unusual revolver was an attempt to reconcile the characteristics of revolving arms with those of semi-automatic weapons. The recoil from firing drags the barrel-cylinder block to the end of the frame, cocks the hammer and carries the breech-block forward again by means of a spring; during this movement, a pin fixed to the frame causes the cylinder to revolve and brings a new cartridge into the firing position.

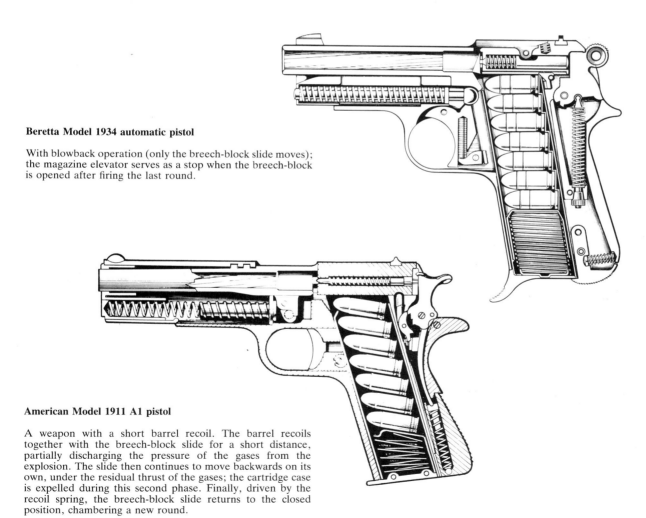

Beretta Model 1934 automatic pistol

With blowback operation (only the breech-block slide moves); the magazine elevator serves as a stop when the breech-block is opened after firing the last round.

American Model 1911 A1 pistol

A weapon with a short barrel recoil. The barrel recoils together with the breech-block slide for a short distance, partially discharging the pressure of the gases from the explosion. The slide then continues to move backwards on its own, under the residual thrust of the gases; the cartridge case is expelled during this second phase. Finally, driven by the recoil spring, the breech-block slide returns to the closed position, chambering a new round.

REPEATING WEAPONS

GERMANY

Mauser Model 1871/84 Rifle
(*Infanteriegewehr* M 71/84)

This is the old *Infanteriegewehr* M 71 turned into a repeater by fitting a tubular magazine under the barrel.

caliber: 11 mm
total length: 50.94 in (129.4 cm)
length of barrel: 31.69 in (80.5 cm)
weight: 9.35 lb (4,240 g)
feed system: 8-round tubular magazine

Detail with breech-block open.

Model 1888 Rifle
(*Infanteriegewehr* M 1888)

caliber: 7.92 × 57 mm
total length: 49.01 in (124.5 cm)
length of barrel: 30.43 in (77.3 cm)
weight: 8.60 lb (3,900 g)
feed system: fixed external box magazine for pack of 5 cartridges

This rifle was developed by the German Army Commission (*Gewehrprüfungskommission Spandau*) and produced using the Mannlicher five-round packet-magazine feed system.

The famous 7.92 × 57 caliber cartridge was adopted with the *Gewehr* 88.

Detail with breech-block closed.

180

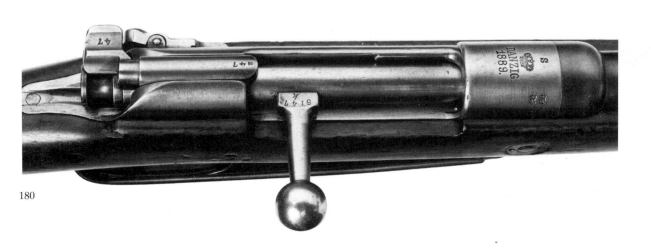

Model 1888 Carbine
(*Karabiner* M 1888)

caliber: 7.92 × 57 mm
total length: 37.40 in (95 cm)
length of barrel: 18.90 in (48 cm)
weight: 6.88 lb (3,120 g)
feed system: fixed external box magazine for pack of 5 cartridges

Mauser Model 1898 Rifle
(*Gew.* 98)

This was the best repeating rifle ever produced.

Its system of closure was adopted by most countries in the world. The bolt-action breech-block has two blocking lugs at the front and one at the back.

The box magazine can be fed by charger or loose cartridges.

It was the standard rifle of the German Army during the First World War and with slight modifications remained in service until the Second World War.

Its 8 Mauser cartridge was also highly successful. It was modified back in 1905 to take the new Spitzer type (pointed) bullet.

caliber: 7.92 × 57 mm
total length: 49.21 in (125 cm)
length of barrel: 29.13 in (74 cm)
weight: 8.82 lb (4,000 g)
feed system: 5-round double-column internal box magazine

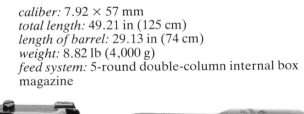

Detail with breech-block open.

Model 1898 Carbine
(*Kar.* 98)

caliber: 7.92 × 57 mm
total length: 37.40 in (95 cm)
length of barrel: 16.93 in (43 cm)
weight: 7.49 lb (3,400 g)
 feed system: 5-round double-column internal box magazine

Model 1898 A Carbine
(*Kar.* 98 A)

caliber: 7.92 × 57 mm
total length: 43.30 in (110 cm)
length of barrel: 23.62 in (60 cm)
weight: 7.98 lb (3,620 g)
 feed system: 5-round double-column internal box magazine

Model 1898 K Carbine
(*Kar.* 98 K)

This carbine was also called the *Wehrmacht* model, because it was adopted in 1935 with the establishment of the armed forces of the Third Reich.

It was basically a shorter version of the *Gewehr* M 1898.

During the War, it was built with a plywood stock and the last batches of 1944–5 had stamped barrel bands and no bayonet attachments.

caliber: 7.92 × 57 mm
total length: 43.82 in (111.3 cm)
length of barrel: 24.72 in (62.8 cm)
weight: 8.60 lb (3,900 g)
feed system: 5-round double-column internal box magazine

Detail with breech-block closed.

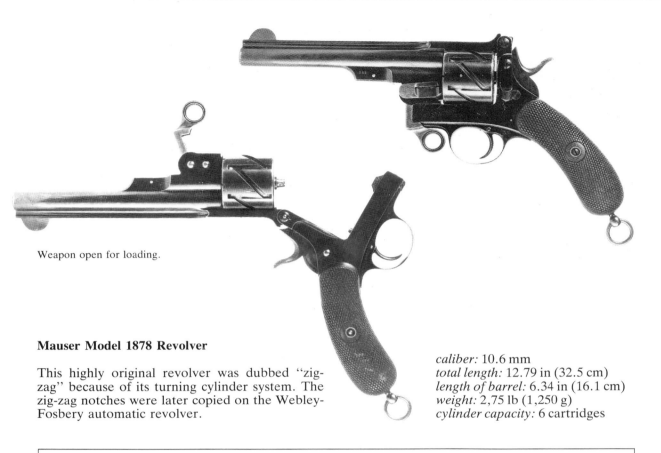

Weapon open for loading.

Mauser Model 1878 Revolver

This highly original revolver was dubbed "zig-zag" because of its turning cylinder system. The zig-zag notches were later copied on the Webley-Fosbery automatic revolver.

caliber: 10.6 mm
total length: 12.79 in (32.5 cm)
length of barrel: 6.34 in (16.1 cm)
weight: 2,75 lb (1,250 g)
cylinder capacity: 6 cartridges

AUTOMATIC WEAPONS

GERMANY

Model 41 semi-automatic Rifle
(*Gew.* 41 W)

This weapon was produced by Walther in 1941 and tested in combat. Subsequently modified for gas operation, it led to the development of the Model 43 rifle.

caliber: 7.92 × 57 mm
total length: 44.29 in (112.5 cm)
length of barrel: 21.38 in (54.3 cm)
weight: 11.02 lb (5,000 g)
feed system: 10-round charger-fed fixed double-column box magazine

183

View of weapon with bipod open. It is shown without the bayonet and diopter.

Model 1942 Paratroop Rifle
(*Fallschirmjäger Gewehr* 42)
(FG 42)

A dual purpose weapon developed by Rheinmetall-Borsig at the request of the *Luftwaffe* to equip paratroops from 1943. This gas-operated, selective fire rifle, chambered for the powerful Mauser 7.92 mm cartridge and equipped with a bipod, was one of the most ingenious weapons of the Second World War. Useful features included a linear stock and muzzle compensator which assisted continuous fire with the weapon resting on the shoulder. For semi-automatic fire the breech-block is left "closed" to increase the stability of fire, while in the automatic mode it fires with the breech-block open, which helps cool the barrel, and avoids the risk of "cook-off," or spontaneous ignition of a cartridge. It also has a small bayonet with a cruciform blade, fitted upside down below the barrel.

The Germans built two versions of the FG 42: one with a pressed steel, and one with a wooden stock.

The Americans used the mechanism of the FG 42 to produce the T 44 sub-machine gun and M 60 machine gun.

total length: 36.61 in (93 cm)
length of barrel: 19.01 in (48.3 cm)
weight: 9.92 lb (4,500 g)
feed system: 20-round double-column removable magazine
rate of fire: 750–800 rpm

Detail of fixed bayonet on woodenstocked FG 42.

Model 1944 *Sturmgewehr* 44 Assault Rifle (StG 44)

This was the first assault rifle to be used in the Second World War and was also, technologically speaking, one of the best light arms produced by Nazi Germany.

Very easy to handle and mechanically perfect, it may still be regarded as one of the most progressive modern assault rifles. Hugo Schmeisser of Haenel designed this weapon in 1943, which was based on the Model MKb 42 which had given excellent results on the Russian Front.

Like the MKb 42, the StG 44 was a gas-operated, selective fire weapon which used the new short, 7.92 mm caliber intermediate cartridge (7.92 × 33 *Infanterie Kurz Patrone*, or 8 Kurz).

Left side of weapon with magazine inserted.

total length: 37 in (94 cm)
length of barrel: 16.50 in (41.9 cm)
weight: 11.46 lb (5,200 g)
feed system: 30-round double-column removable magazine
rate of fire: 500 rpm

Exploded view of weapon.

185

Model 43 semi-automatic Rifle
(G 43)

caliber: 7.92 × 57 mm
total length: 36.61 in (93 cm)
length of barrel: 19.01 in (48.3 cm)
weight: 9.92 lb (4,500 g)
feed system: 20-round double-column removable magazine

This is an improvement on the *Gew.* 41 W, even if the pressures of war meant that the weapon was less carefully finished. The gas operation system is similar to that of the Russian Tokarev Model 40 rifle.

Model 1940 Sub-machine gun
(*Maschinen-Pistole* 1940 MP 40)

caliber: 9 mm Parabellum
total length: 33.70 in (85.6 cm) with butt extended and 24.60 in (62.5 cm) with butt folded
length of barrel: 9.88 in (25.1 cm)
weight: 8.16 lb (3,700 g)
feed system: 32-round double-column removable magazine
rate of fire: 450–540 rpm

This was a modification of the MP 38 produced by ERMA. The MP 38 was a great novelty, given the types of materials used (light alloy frame and plastic breech box) and folding shoulder stock. But high production costs necessitated its redesign. The new model, which also eliminated some technical faults, was designated MP 40. The MP 40 was a blowback, continuous-fire weapon.

Model 1941 Sub-machine gun (MP 41)

caliber: 9 mm Parabellum
total length: 33.98 in (86.3 cm)
length of barrel: 9.88 in (25.1 cm)
weight: 8.16 lb (3,700 g)
feed system: 32-round double-column removable magazine
rate of fire: 450–540 rpm

The MP 41 was produced as a selective fire weapon with the barrel and breech box of the MP 40, and the shoulder stock and firing mechanism of the MP 29/II.

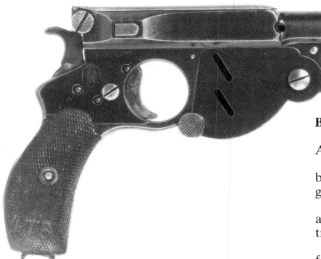

Bergmann no. 3 Automatic Pistol

A blowback pocket gun.

This was one of the first pistols produced by brilliant engineer Theodor Bergmann of Gaggenau.

Bergmann began patenting automatic pistols and distinctive, truncated-conical rimless cartridges from 1893.

These weapons used highly original charger feed systems which, however, proved impractical; the lack of an extractor also created problems over expulsion of the cartridge cases.

caliber: 6.5 mm Bergmann
total length: 10.31 in (26.2 cm)
length of barrel: 4.40 in (11.2 cm)
weight: 1.65 lb (750 g)
feed system: 5-round charger

Mauser Model 1896/12 Automatic Pistol

This is a very famous weapon, like the Luger.

Apart from being one of the first successful automatic pistols, it introduced a cartridge which at a later date, with slight variations, became more famous than the weapon itself, being adopted by the Red Army for pistols and machine guns (Russian 7.62 mm).

About thirty models of Mauser pistol were made, of which one, the Model 1932 or commercial version Model 712, also offering selective fire and with a removable magazine for loading with chargers of ten and twenty cartridges, was used by the German security services during the Second World War.

Apart from the 7.63 Mauser, models chambered for 9 mm Mauser and Parabellum cartridges were produced; there were also 0.45-in Chinese copies.

Given the ballistic performance of the 7.63, it could be used to good effect by fitting the holster-stock and firing with the weapon against the shoulder.

caliber: 7.63 Mauser
total length: 11.81 in (30 cm)
length of barrel: 5.51 in (14 cm)
weight: 2.60 lb (1,180 g)
feed system: fixed 10-round double-column charger-fed box magazine

Model 1908 (P 08) Automatic Pistol

This is undoubtedly the most famous automatic pistol of all time, commonly known as the Luger, from the name of the engineer at Deutsche Waffen-Munitionsfabriken (D.W.M.) in Berlin who produced it by modifying the Borchardt pistol.

The most widely used cartridge for pistols and sub-machine guns in the world was also named after him: the 9 mm Luger or 9 mm Parabellum (from the Latin motto *si vis pacem, para bellum* (if you want peace, prepare for war).

The P 08 (Pistole 1908) is the commonest version of the various models produced, being the one distributed to the German Army during the First World War.

Despite its reputation, however, it failed to satisfy certain military requirements of the Wehr-

caliber: 9 mm Parabellum
total length: 8.78 in (22.3 cm)
length of barrel: 4.01 in (10.2 cm)
weight: 1.87 lb (850 g)
feed system: 8-round removable magazine

Weapon viewed from above.

macht and was therefore replaced by another, less famous automatic weapon in 1938: the Walther P 38.

Walther Model 1938 (P 38) Automatic Pistol

This was the regulation pistol of the German Army during the Second World War.

It was produced by Waffenfabrik Carl Walther of Zella Mehlis. It was much easier to mass produce than the P 08 and had some interesting features for the period such as the double-action trigger.

caliber: 9 mm Parabellum
total length: 8.35 in (21.2 cm)
length of barrel: 5 in (12.7 cm)
weight: 1.85 lb (840 g)
feed system: 8-round removable magazine

Sauer M 38 Automatic Pistol

A blowback double-action weapon with an internal hammer.

An outstanding feature of this pistol, which was one of the best pocket automatics in the world, together with the Walther PP and PPK and Mauser HSc, was the method of cocking and uncocking the hammer in absolute safety by moving an external lever with the thumb.

caliber: 7.65 mm
total length: 6.73 in (17.1 cm)
length of barrel: 3.27 in (8.3 cm)
weight: 1.56 lb (708 g)
feed system: 8-round single-column removable magazine

Walther PPK Automatic Pistol
(*Pistole Polizei Kriminal*)

This is undoubtedly the most famous pocket pistol in the world. Its double-action mechanism strongly influenced pistol manufacture throughout the world in the postwar period.

caliber: 7.65 mm
total length: 5.83 in (14.8 cm)
length of barrel: 3.15 in (8 cm)
weight: 1.25 lb (567 g)
feed system: 7-round single-column removable magazine

189

Mannlicher Model 1888 Rifle
(*Repetiergewehr* M 88)

total length: 50.39 in (128 cm)
length of barrel: 30.12 in (76.5 cm)
weight: 9.92 lb (4,500 g)

This was the first regulation Mannlicher to use the 8 × 50 mm R caliber cartridge, still with gunpowder. The bolt has a sliding movement only, with asymmetric blockage by a hinged block already used on the earlier Model 1886.

It uses the famous 5-round packet magazine feed system (also invented by Mannlicher).

Mannlicher Model 1890 Cavalry Carbine
(*Repetierkarabiner* M 90)

caliber: 8 × 50 mm R (or 8 Mannlicher)
total length: 39.57 in (100.5 cm)
length of barrel: 19.60 in (49.8 cm)
weight: 7.23 lb (3,280 g)
feed system: 5-round packet magazine

Detail of fixed bayonet.

Mannlicher Model 1895 Rifle
(*Repetiergewehr* M 95)

This was the standard rifle of the Austro-Hungarian Army during the First World War.

One of the advantages of this ordinary repeating weapon, for which it was famous at the time, was the breech-block with a sliding (straight-pull) movement only, which enabled it to be loaded by just two movements instead of four. In fact the only part which turned was the head provided with blocking lugs, which was an extension of the internal cylinder of the bolt, operated by the opening and closing movement.

It was one of many brilliant achievements by Ferdinand von Mannlicher.

caliber: 8 × 50 mm R
total length: 50.47 in (128.2 cm)
length of barrel: 30.12 in (76.5 cm)
weight: 8.05 lb (3,650 g)
feed system: 5-round packet magazine

caliber: 8 × 50 mm R
total length: 39.57 in (100.5 cm)
length of barrel: 19.64 in (49.9 cm)
weight: 6.94 lb (3,150 g)
feed system: 5-round packet magazine

Mannlicher Model 1895 Musket
(*Repetierstutzen* M 95)

A weapon distributed to special troops of the Austro-Hungarian Army.

It is shorter than the rifle and has sling swivels fixed to the side of the stock as well.

Mannlicher Model 1895 Carbine with experimental bayonet

This is similar to the musket, but has sling swivels fixed to the side of the stock only.

Detail of fixed bayonet.

Gasser Model 1870 Revolver
(*Armeerevolver* M 70)

A double-action weapon with an open frame. It fired a cartridge similar to that of the M 1867 carbine, but with a lighter charge.

caliber: 11 mm
total length: 12.60 in (32 cm)
length of barrel: 7.24 in (18.4 cm)
weight: 3.02 lb (1,370 g)
cylinder capacity: 6 cartridges

191

Rast-Gasser Model 1898 Revolver
(Armeerevolver M 98)

An interesting feature of this very well finished weapon was the fact that it could be dismantled without any tools.

Having unhooked the trigger guard at the back and turned it downwards, the left-hand lock plate was released, and opened up to reveal the whole mechanism. Another unusual characteristic for a revolver of that time was the fact that the firing pin was fitted in the frame, that is, separate from the hammer.

caliber: 8 mm Gasser
total length: 8.90 in (22.6 cm)
length of barrel: 4.60 in (11.7 cm)
weight: 1.98 lb (900 g)
cylinder capacity: 8 cartridges

View of mechanism.

AUTOMATIC WEAPONS

AUSTRIA

Mannlicher Model 1905 Automatic Pistol

Steyr made this slightly-delayed blowback weapon above all for the South American market, where it became the standard pistol of the Argentinian Army.

caliber: 7.63 mm Mannlicher
total length: 9.84 in (25 cm)
length of barrel: 6.30 in (16 cm)
weight: 2 lb (907 g)
feed system: 8-round charger

Roth-Steyr Model 1907 Automatic Pistol

A weapon produced for the Austro-Hungarian cavalry. Being designed for use from horseback, it was equipped with a special trigger device which made it safer, but less accurate.

Another unusual feature of this pistol is the fact that the breech is blocked by turning the barrel.

The magazine is fixed in the grip and fed by ten-round charger.

caliber: 8 mm Roth-Steyr M 1907
total length: 9.09 in (23.1 cm)
length of barrel: 5.08 in (12.9 cm)
weight: 2.22 lb (1,008 g)

Steyr Model 1912 Automatic Pistol

This was the standard pistol of the Austro-Hungarian Army during the First World War.

It kept the rotating barrel breech-block system and fixed magazine in the grip of the Model 1907.

During the Second World War it was rechambered by the Germans to take 9 mm Parabellum cartridges and the slide was stamped "08." It is also known by the name of "*Steyr-Hahn*" (Steyr with hammer).

caliber: 9 mm Steyr
total length: 8.50 in (21.6 cm)
length of barrel: 5.04 in (12.8 cm)
weight: 2.12 lb (960 g)
feed system: 8-round charger

REPEATING WEAPONS

UNITED STATES OF AMERICA

Spencer Model 1860 Cavalry Carbine

The development of cartridges with metal cases made it easier to produce repeating weapons, with the result that numerous inventors took out patents for a wide variety of mechanisms. Credit is due, above all, to Christopher Spencer for having built the first truly functional repeating rifle.

This extraordinary weapon with a lever mechanism has a removable magazine in the butt.

The semi-circular breech-block, maneuvered by the trigger-guard lever, turns to open the weapon, expelling the spent cartridge case and reloading it with a new cartridge from the tubular magazine.

Spencer's weapons were widely used during the American Civil War and were such powerful competition for the Henry rifle that, after the war, Oliver Winchester bought up the remaining stock of Spencers – which he was to resell many years later – in order to market his new Henry rifle, the Winchester '66.

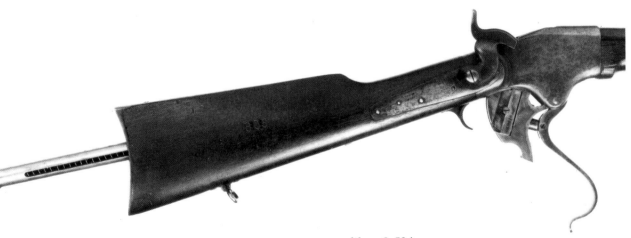

Detail with breech-block open and magazine projecting from the butt.

caliber: 0.52 in
total length: 37.20 in (94.5 cm)
length of barrel: 18.30 in (46.5 cm)
weight: 8.16 lb (3,700 g)

Detail with breech-block open.

Model 1866 Winchester Carbine

This was one of the first long American repeaters with a fairly simple and robust mechanism.

It was produced by making a few improvements to the lever-action Henry rifle.

The tubular magazine for the cartridges is fitted below the barrel. This system was two centuries old and was used on Kalthoff arquebuses, but, by the time of the Winchester (thanks to the use of fulminate of mercury which enabled cartridges to be produced with built-in primers, eliminating the need for complex powder ignition systems), a more functional repeater mechanism could be produced. The cartridges were loaded into the magazine through the opening at the side of the frame; by a simple forward and backward movement of the lever which was an extension of the trigger guard, the breech-block was opened and closed, bringing a new cartridge into the chamber.

It fired .44 caliber rim-fire cartridges.

This weapon also became famous in Europe also after the two victories by the Turks over the Russians at Plevna in 1877, at which 30,000 Winchester '66s were used.

caliber: 0.44–28 in
total length: 38.58 in (98 cm)
length of barrel: 19.68 in (50 cm)
weight: 7.94 lb (3,600 g)
feed system: 13-round tubular magazine

Model 1873 Winchester Carbine

caliber: 0.44–40 in
total length: 38.70 in (98.3 cm)
length of barrel: 19.96 in (50.7 cm)
weight: 7.83 lb (3,550 g)
feed system: 12-round tubular magazine

This is an improvement on the Winchester Model 1866.

With this model, the 44–60 center-fire cartridge was introduced, which had a bigger gunpowder charge than the rim-fire one used for the Model 1866.

The rim-fire cartridge, apart from needing careful handling, could not ensure gas-tightness with large charges, because of the thin metal rim of the case containing the primer.

Also, the frame was no longer of brass, but of steel.

The Winchester 1873 was the most famous lever carbine and by the end of its career was known as "the weapon that won the West."

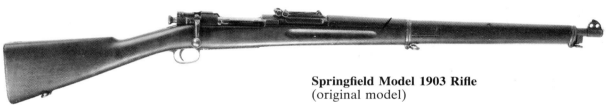

Springfield Model 1903 Rifle
(original model)

caliber: 0.30–03 in (7.62 mm)
total length: 43.19 in (109.7 cm)
length of barrel: 23.98 in (60.9 cm)
weight: 8.70 lb (3,950 g)
feed system: 5-round double-column internal box magazine

This rifle used a variant of the Mauser Model 1898 mechanism.

Originally made in 0.30–03 in caliber, from 1906 it was chambered for the new 0.30–06 in caliber cartridge. It used a ramrod-type bayonet which fitted into the stock beneath the barrel.

With a few modifications it remained in service with the American Army until total issue of the Garand semi-automatic rifle.

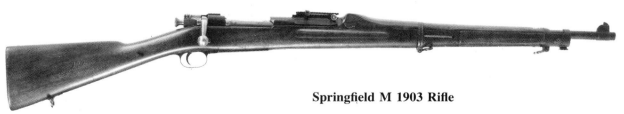

Springfield M 1903 Rifle

caliber: 0.30–06 in (7.62 mm)
total length: 43.19 in (109.7 cm)
length of barrel: 23.98 in (60.9 cm)
weight: 8.70 lb (3,950 g)
feed system: 5-round double-column internal box magazine

Springfield Model 1903 A3 Rifle

This weapon has a back sight with a diopter.

caliber: 0.30–06 in
total length: 43.50 in (110.5 cm)
length of barrel: 23.98 in (60.9 cm)
weight: 8.05 lb (3,650 g)
feed system: 5-round double-column internal box magazine

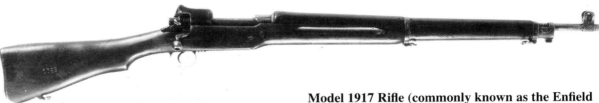

Model 1917 Rifle (commonly known as the Enfield (U.S. Rifle, caliber 0.30 in M 1917)

caliber: 0.30–06 in (7.62 mm)
total length: 46.26 in (117.5 cm)
length of barrel: 25.98 in (66 cm)
weight: 8.16 lb (3,700 g)
feed system: 5-round double-column internal box magazine

This was the 0.303 caliber Pattern 14 built for Britain in the United States and converted to take 0.30–06 cartridges during the Second World War.

This rifle is also a modified Mauser. The breech-block cocks the firing mechanism during forward travel, as in the British Enfield.

It has a combat sight which is more accurate than that of the M 1903.

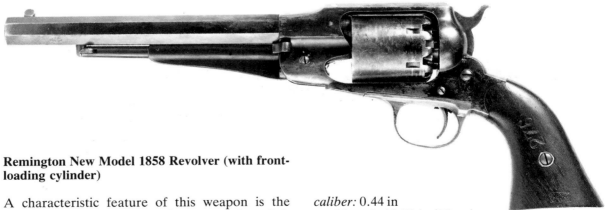

Remington New Model 1858 Revolver (with front-loading cylinder)

A characteristic feature of this weapon is the closed frame, which makes it stronger than Colt revolvers.

Despite this fact, it was less successful than the Colts.

caliber: 0.44 in
total length: 13.78 in (35 cm)
length of barrel: 8 in (20.3 cm)
weight: 2.86 lb (1,300 g)
cylinder capacity: 6 rounds

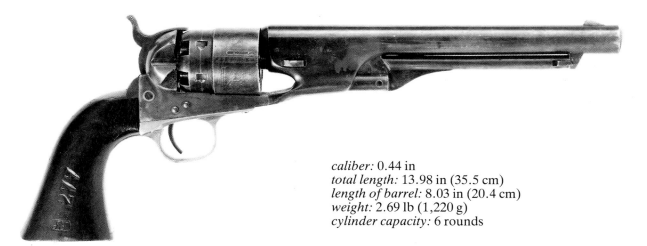

caliber: 0.44 in
total length: 13.98 in (35.5 cm)
length of barrel: 8.03 in (20.4 cm)
weight: 2.69 lb (1,220 g)
cylinder capacity: 6 rounds

Colt Army Model 1860 Revolver (with front-loading cylinder)

The revolver was developed by the American Samuel Colt, at Paterson, New Jersey, in 1835.

Weapons with front-loading cylinders and wheel-lock or flintlock ignition systems had been found in previous centuries, but only with the introduction of percussion caps containing fulminate of mercury, and Colt's simple mechanism which caused the cylinder to rotate automatically when the hammer was cocked, was it possible to fire all the rounds loaded in quick succession.

This mechanism was later called single-action to distinguish it from the continuous-action type which could fire just by pulling the trigger, without cocking the hammer.

Detail of cylinder

Left side of weapon.

199

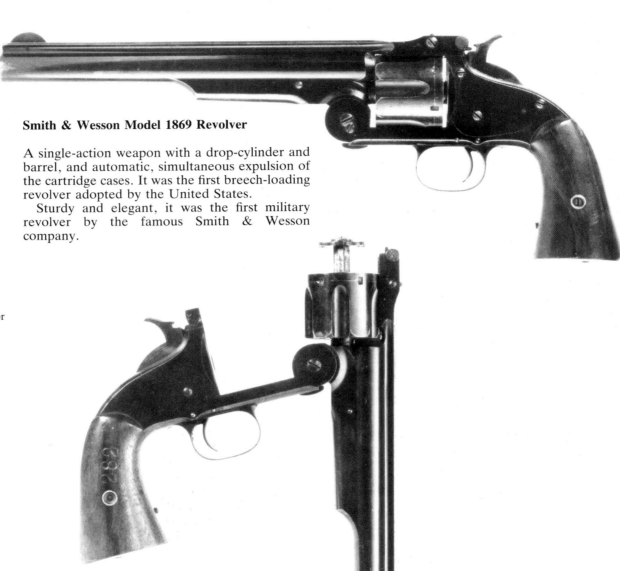

Smith & Wesson Model 1869 Revolver

A single-action weapon with a drop-cylinder and barrel, and automatic, simultaneous expulsion of the cartridge cases. It was the first breech-loading revolver adopted by the United States.

Sturdy and elegant, it was the first military revolver by the famous Smith & Wesson company.

View of weapon open with ejector protruding from cylinder.

caliber: 0.44 in
total length: 12.20 in (31 cm)
length of barrel: 7 in (17.8 cm)
weight: 2.49 lb (1,130 g)
cylinder capacity: 6 rounds

UNITED STATES OF AMERICA

Garand M 1 Rifle
(U.S. Rifle, caliber 0.30 M 1)

A semi-automatic gas-operated weapon.

Adopted by the United States Army in 1936, it gave rise to a number of variants, partly produced during the Second World War. From 1944, it was built as a selective-fire weapon, with a removable magazine and also given a bipod.

caliber: 0.30–06 in (7.62 mm)
total length: 43.58 in (110.7 cm)
length of barrel: 24.01 in (61 cm)
weight: 9.48 lb (4,300 g)
feed system: fixed internal box magazine for pack of 8 cartridges

M 1 Carbine
(U.S. Carbine, caliber 0.30 M 1)

caliber: 7.62 mm (0.30 car. M 1)
total length: 35.63 in (90.5 cm)
length of barrel: 18 in (45.7 cm)
weight: 5.51 lb (2,500 g)
feed system: 15 or 30-round removable double-column magazine

This semi-automatic gas-operated weapon was adopted by the United States Army to replace the pistol in the armament of non-commissioned officers, special troops and subalterns.

It is also known as the Winchester M 1.

It was in fact the Winchester company which won a U.S. Artillery specification of 1940.

It was also made with a folding shoulder stock and fire selector.

201

M1 A1 Carbine

This is similar to the Winchester M1, from which it differs in having a folding metal shoulder stock.

caliber: 7.62 mm (0.30 car. M1)
total length: 30.40 in (90.2 cm) with butt extended; 25.39 in (64.5 cm) with butt folded
weight: 6.17 lb (2,800 g)

Thompson Model 1928 A1 Sub-machine Gun

A delayed blowback, selective fire weapon.

This was a simplified version of the famous Model 1921, produced for the United States Army.

caliber: 0.45 in
total length: 33.85 in (86 cm) with shoulder stock; 25 in (63.5 cm) without shoulder stock
length of barrel: 10.43 in (26.5 cm)
weight: 10.75 lb (4,880 g)
feed system: 20–30 round removable double-column magazine or 50–100 round drum
rate of fire: 600–725 rpm

M3 Grease Gun Sub-machine Gun

A blowback, automatic fire weapon. Adopted at the end of 1942, it was designed to be able to fire Parabellum 9 mm caliber cartridges too by changing the barrel and fitting an adaptor to the magazine.

caliber: 0.45 in
total length: 22.44 in (57 cm); 29.76 in (75.6 cm) with butt extended
length of barrel: 8 in (20.3 cm)
weight: 8.16 lb (3,700 g)
feed system: 30-round double-column removable magazine
rate of fire: 350–450 rpm

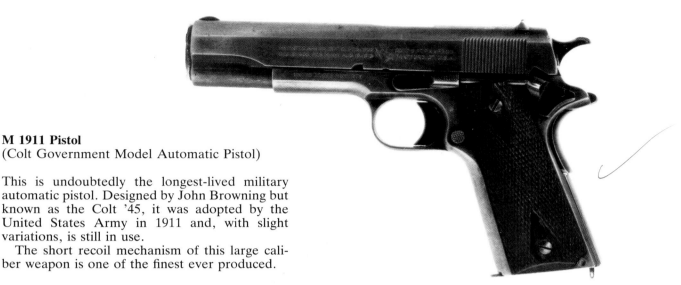

M 1911 Pistol
(Colt Government Model Automatic Pistol)

This is undoubtedly the longest-lived military automatic pistol. Designed by John Browning but known as the Colt '45, it was adopted by the United States Army in 1911 and, with slight variations, is still in use.

The short recoil mechanism of this large caliber weapon is one of the finest ever produced.

caliber: 11.43 mm (0.45 A.C.P.)
total length: 8.66 in (22 cm)
length of barrel: 5 in (12.7 cm)
weight: 2.42 lb (1,100 g)
feed system: 7-round removable magazine

REPEATING WEAPONS

CANADA

Ross Mark III Rifle (also known as the Model 1910)

Although built with high-quality materials, Ross rifles were quite unsuitable for military use, as they had numerous faults. The most serious of these was the fact that incorrect refitting of the breech-block could result in a shot being fired with the breech open.

caliber: 7.7 mm
total length: 50.59 in (128.5 cm)
length of barrel: 31.69 in (80.5 cm)

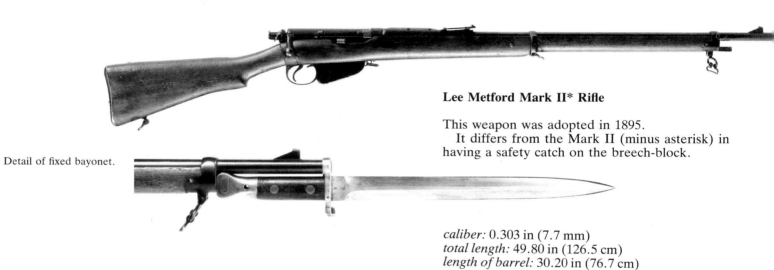

Lee Metford Mark II* Rifle

This weapon was adopted in 1895.

It differs from the Mark II (minus asterisk) in having a safety catch on the breech-block.

Detail of fixed bayonet.

caliber: 0.303 in (7.7 mm)
total length: 49.80 in (126.5 cm)
length of barrel: 30.20 in (76.7 cm)
weight: 10.14 lb (4,600 g)
feed system: 10-round removable magazine with repeater cut-off device.

Lee Enfield no. 1 Mark III Rifle
(N.I.S.M.L.E. Mk III)

caliber: 0.303 in (7.7 mm)
total length: 44.48 in (113 cm)
length of barrel: 25.20 in (64 cm)
weight: 8.60 lb (3,900 g)
feed system: 10-round removable magazine with cut-off device

This was the result of a series of improvements made to various (Lee-Metford and Lee-Enfield) models from 1888 onwards.

Adopted in 1907, it was the basic weapon of the British Army in the First World War and was widely used in the Second also.

Of ordinary repeating rifles with turn-bolt breech-blocks, it was the quickest to maneuver, but the breech-block was not interchangeable.

caliber: 0.303 in (7.7 mm)
total length: 44.48 in (113 cm)
length of barrel: 25.20 in (64 cm)
weight: 9.08 lb (4,120 g)
feed system: 10-round removable magazine

Lee Enfield no. 4 Mark I Rifle

Adopted at the beginning of the Second World War, it remained in use for many years in the Commonwealth and former British colonies.

caliber: 0.303 in (7.7 mm)
total length: 39.37 in (100 cm)
length of barrel: 18.50 in (47 cm)
weight: 7.16 lb (3,250 g)
feed system: 10-round removable magazine

Lee Enfield No. 5 Rifle

This was developed towards the end of the Second World War for use in the Far East.
   Derived from the no. 4, it was called the Jungle Carbine.

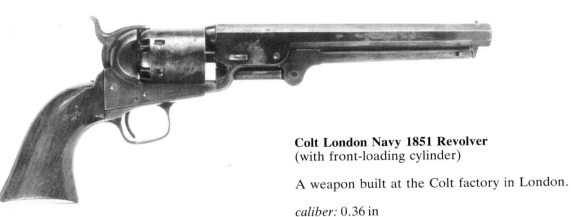

Colt London Navy 1851 Revolver
(with front-loading cylinder)

A weapon built at the Colt factory in London.

caliber: 0.36 in
total length: 13 in (33 cm)
length of barrel: 7.44 in (18.9 cm)
weight: 2.62 lb (1,190 g)
feed system: 6-round cylinder

Adams Double-Action Revolver
(with front-loading cylinder)

The brothers John and Robert Adams were competitors of Colt because they produced a mechanism capable of rotating the cylinder of their revolver simply by pulling the trigger, without cocking the hammer, thereby increasing the rate of fire of the bullets loaded.

Another characteristic of the revolver by the Adams brothers was the closed frame structure, which made the weapon stronger.

Their first revolver was patented in 1851 and manufactured by Deane, Adams & Deane.

caliber: 0.36 in
total length: 11.73 in (29.8 cm)
weight: 1.87 lb (850 g)
cylinder capacity: 5 rounds

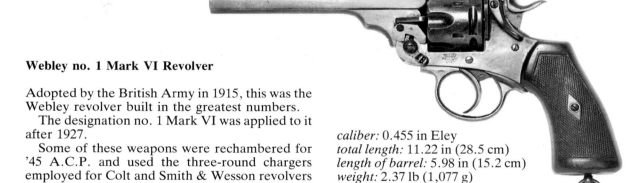

Webley no. 1 Mark VI Revolver

Adopted by the British Army in 1915, this was the Webley revolver built in the greatest numbers.

The designation no. 1 Mark VI was applied to it after 1927.

Some of these weapons were rechambered for '45 A.C.P. and used the three-round chargers employed for Colt and Smith & Wesson revolvers in 1917.

caliber: 0.455 in Eley
total length: 11.22 in (28.5 cm)
length of barrel: 5.98 in (15.2 cm)
weight: 2.37 lb (1,077 g)
cylinder capacity: 6 rounds

Colt Revolver

This is the American Colt New Service revolver chambered for the 0.455 in Eley cartridge issued to the British Army in the First and Second World Wars.

total length: 10.39 in (26.4 cm)
length of barrel: 5.51 in (14 cm)
weight: 2.50 lb (1,135 g)
cylinder capacity: 6 rounds

BRITAIN

Left side of weapon.

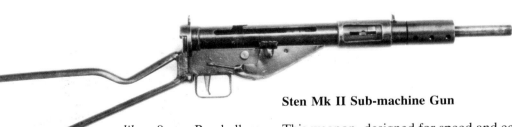

Detail of magazine.

Lanchester Mark I Sub-machine Gun

A blowback, selective fire weapon.

It was developed by George Lanchester of Sterling from the design for the German MP 28 and also given the bayonet attachment of the Enfield rifle.

caliber: 9 mm Parabellum
total length: 33.50 in (85.1 cm)
length of barrel: 7.87 in (20 cm)
weight: 9.66 lb (4,380 g)
feed system: 50-round double-column removable magazine
rate of fire: 575–600 rpm

caliber: 9 mm Parabellum
total length: 30 in (76.2 cm)
length of barrel: 7.75 in (19.7 cm)
weight: 8 lb (3,631 g)
feed system: 32-round removable magazine
rate of fire: 550 rpm

Sten Mk II Sub-machine Gun

This weapon, designed for speed and economy of construction, marked a new era in the manufacture of machine guns.

It was developed by Shepherd and Turpin at Enfield in the middle of the war, its name being derived from the two men's initials plus the first two letters of Enfield.

It was widely imitated by other countries, including Nazi Germany with the MP 3008.

The Sten is a blowback, selective fire weapon.

Sten Mark IV Model B Sub-machine Gun

This is similar in operation, size and weight to the Model A, from which it differs in having the mechanism protection box of the Mark II.

Sten Mark IV Model A Sub-machine Gun

A blowback, selective fire weapon. Very few of these were built as they were intended for special units.

caliber: 9 mm Parabellum
total length: 27.48 in (69.8 cm) with butt extended
length of barrel: 3.85 in (9.8 cm)
weight: 8.85 lb (4,014 g)
feed system: 32-round double-column removable magazine
rate of fire: 475 rpm

Sten Mark VI (S) Sub-machine Gun

This is the Mark V sub-machine gun with the silencer of the Mark II. The weapon was used from 1944, particularly by members of the Resistance.

caliber: 9 mm Parabellum
total length: 35.75 in (90.8 cm)
length of barrel: 7.80 in (19.8 cm)
weight: 9.81 lb (4,450 g)
feed system: 32-round double-column removable magazine
rate of fire: 550 rpm

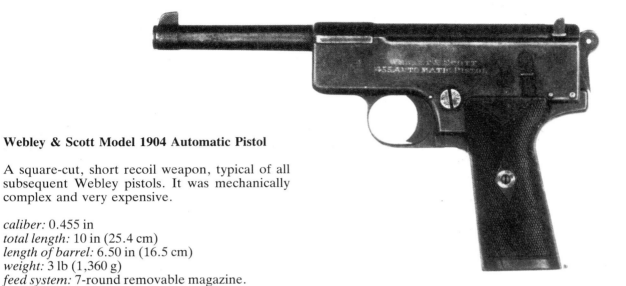

Webley & Scott Model 1904 Automatic Pistol

A square-cut, short recoil weapon, typical of all subsequent Webley pistols. It was mechanically complex and very expensive.

caliber: 0.455 in
total length: 10 in (25.4 cm)
length of barrel: 6.50 in (16.5 cm)
weight: 3 lb (1,360 g)
feed system: 7-round removable magazine.

Webley Mark I Automatic Pistol

This was an improvement of the Model 1904. It was given to the Royal Navy, who used it up to the end of the Second World War. During the First World War, it was also given a butt extension for use on board aircraft.

caliber: 0.455 in
total length: 8.50 in (21.6 cm)
length of barrel: 5 in (12.7 cm)
weight: 2.42 lb (1,100 g)
feed system: 7-round removable magazine

Kropatschek Model 1878 Naval Rifle

The tubular-magazine feed system of this weapon was developed by Kropatschek, Commander of the School of Artillery in Vienna. The same system was used in France for the models 1884, 1885, 1886/93 and 1886/93/35.

All the Model 1878 naval rifles were built at Steyr in Austria.

Detail showing fixed bayonet.

caliber: 11 mm
total length: 48.82 in (124 cm)
length of barrel: 28.35 in (72 cm)
weight: 9.70 lb (4,400 g)
feed system: 7-round tubular magazine

Lebel Model 1866 M 93 Rifle

The French Army was the first to have a small-caliber regulation rifle that used smokeless powder.

The weapon was named after Colonel Lebel, who was a member of the Repeating Arms Commission, while the cartridge was developed by Paul Vieille. The turn-bolt breech-block mechanism was derived from that of the old Gras regulation rifle and the tubular-magazine feed system was that of the Kropatschek rifle used by the French Navy.

Detail showing fixed bayonet.

caliber: 8 × 50 mm R Lebel
total length: 51.18 in (130 cm)
length of barrel: 31.50 in (80 cm)
weight: 9.22 lb (4,180 g)
feed system: 8-round tubular magazine

Mannlicher-Berthier Model 1907/15 Rifle

caliber: 8 × 50 mm R Lebel
total length: 51.42 in (130.6 cm)
length of barrel: 31.61 in (80.3 cm)
weight: 8.40 lb (3,810 g)
feed system: 3-round packet-fed box magazine

This is one of various Berthier models used by the French Army during the First World War. It kept the breech-block of the Model 1886 Lebel, while using a Mannlicher packet-magazine feed system.

These rifles underwent various modifications up to the M 34.

Mannlicher-Berthier Model 1892 Musket

caliber: 8 × 50 mm R Lebel
total length: 37.20 in (94.5 cm)
length of barrel: 17.83 in (45.3 cm)
weight: 6.83 lb (3,100 g)
feed system: 3-round packet-fed box magazine

caliber: 8 × 50 mm R Lebel
total length: 37.20 in (94.5 cm)
length of barrel: 17.83 in (45.3 cm)
weight: 7.16 lb (3,250 g)

Mannlicher-Berthier Model 1892 M 1916 Musket

This differs from the Model 1892 mainly in using a five-cartridge magazine packet instead of a three.

caliber: 7.5 × 54 mm
total length: 40.15 in (102 cm)
length of barrel: 22.24 in (56.5 cm)
weight: 8.27 lb (3,750 g)
feed system: 5-round double-column internal box magazine

M.A.S. Model 1936 Rifle

This uses a modified Mauser magazine. The weapon has no manual safety device; it has a bayonet with a cruciform blade, fitted upside down beneath the barrel.

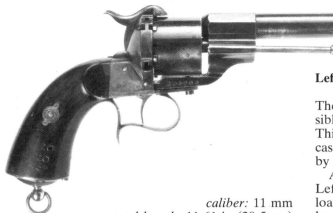

Lefaucheux Commercial Model Revolver

The Frenchman Eugène Lefaucheux was responsible for "speeding up" the loading of revolvers. This was achieved by using cartridges with a metal case and built-in primer and firing pin, developed by Houiller.

At the Exposition Universelle in Paris in 1855, Lefaucheux, inspired by Colt weapons with front-loading cylinders, had already exhibited a breech-loading revolver; this was commonly known as the pin-fire revolver, from the type of cartridge used, which had the top end of the firing pin projecting from the cartridge base.

caliber: 11 mm
total length: 11.61 in (29.5 cm)
length of barrel: 6.20 in (15.75 cm)
weight: 2.31 lb (1,050 g)
cylinder capacity: 6 rounds

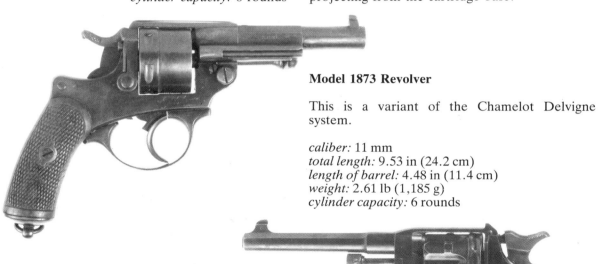

Model 1873 Revolver

This is a variant of the Chamelot Delvigne system.

caliber: 11 mm
total length: 9.53 in (24.2 cm)
length of barrel: 4.48 in (11.4 cm)
weight: 2.61 lb (1,185 g)
cylinder capacity: 6 rounds

View of weapon with cylinder ready for loading.

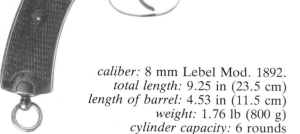

caliber: 8 mm Lebel Mod. 1892.
total length: 9.25 in (23.5 cm)
length of barrel: 4.53 in (11.5 cm)
weight: 1.76 lb (800 g)
cylinder capacity: 6 rounds

Lebel Model 1892 Revolver

This was the standard revolver of the French Army during the two World Wars and was also the first swing-out-cylinder revolver adopted in Europe.

FRANCE

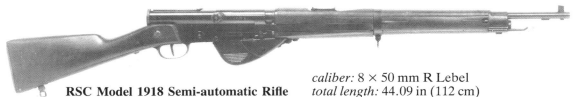

RSC Model 1918 Semi-automatic Rifle

In 1935 this was transformed into an ordinary repeater with a sliding breech-block, abolishing the gas operation system. (Model 1918/35).

caliber: 8 × 50 mm R Lebel
total length: 44.09 in (112 cm)
length of barrel: 21.65 in (55 cm)
weight: 10.47 lb (4,750 g)
feed system: 5-round single-column fixed magazine

caliber: 7.65 mm long
total length: 24.41 in (62 cm)
length of barrel: 8.46 in (21.5 cm)
weight: 6.28 lb (2,850 g)
feed system: 32-round double-column removable magazine
rate of fire: 700 rpm

MAS Model 1938 Sub-machine Gun

A slightly delayed blowback, continuous fire weapon.

The MAS 38 has an unusual safety mechanism: the trigger is pushed forward and folds up; to fire, it has to be returned to the initial position.

REPEATING WEAPONS

BELGIUM

Mauser Model 1889 Carbine

This was the first Mauser to use a single-piece bolt with blocking lugs at the head and a charger feed system.

caliber: 7.65 × 53 mm
total length: 41.14 in (104.5 cm)
length of barrel: 21.61 in (54.9 cm)
weight: 7.75 lb (3,515 g)
feed system: 5-round single-column box magazine

BELGIUM

Bergmann-Bayard Automatic Pistol

This was one of the first 9 mm caliber military pistols.

Initially built in Germany at the Bergmann factory (1903), it was later produced by Pieper of Herstal, where it was commissioned by the Belgian Army.

caliber: 9 mm Bergmann
total length: 9.84 in (25 cm)
length of barrel: 3.94 in (10 cm)
weight: 2.25 lb (1,020 g)
feed system: 6 or 10-round removable magazine (the magazine can be fed by charger with the weapon open)

Browning High-Power Automatic Pistol (1935)

This was the last creation by John Browning and is still one of the most widely used military pistols in the world.

It was first marketed in 1935 in two versions: one with fixed sights and one with a rear sight adjustable up to 500 meters with an attachment for the wooden holster-stock. Its short-recoil system is one of the simplest and most widely used.

It is normally qualified by the initials H.P. (for high power), but is also known as the Pistole 640 (b), given the numbers used by German troops during the last war.

caliber: 9 mm Parabellum
total length: 7.75 in (19.7 cm)
length of barrel: 4.64 in (11.8 cm)
weight: 1.98 lb (900 g) unloaded; 2.31 lb (1,050 g) loaded
feed system: 13-round double-column removable magazine

REPEATING WEAPONS

SWITZERLAND

Vetterli Model 1869 Rifle
(*Repetiergewehr modell* 1869)

caliber: 10.5 mm
total length: 51.18 in (130 cm)
length of barrel: 33.15 in (84.2 cm)
weight: 10.14 lb (4,600 g)
feed system: 11-round tubular magazine

At the end of the 1860s, the Swiss gunsmith Friedrich Vetterli produced the first strong and reliable repeating or rapid fire rifle, as they were known at the time. Its mechanisms were inspired by the Dreyse bolt-action breech-block and Henry-Winchester feed system.

The bolt-handled breech-block was easier for the soldier to operate from the ground than lever weapons.

It used a rim-fire cartridge with a metal case, a lead bullet and gunpowder charge.

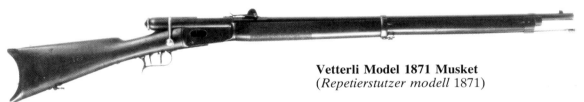

Vetterli Model 1871 Musket
(*Repetierstutzer modell* 1871)

This has a set trigger mechanism (Stecher system).

Detail with breech-block closed.

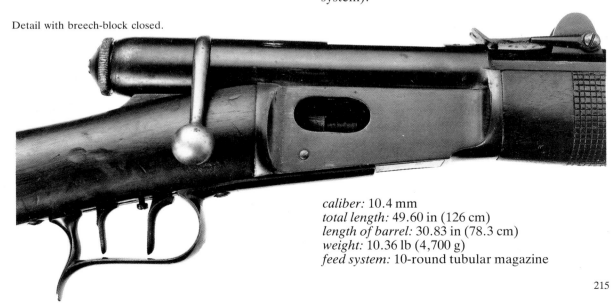

caliber: 10.4 mm
total length: 49.60 in (126 cm)
length of barrel: 30.83 in (78.3 cm)
weight: 10.36 lb (4,700 g)
feed system: 10-round tubular magazine

Vetterli Model 1872 Carbine
(*Repetierkarabiner modell* 1872)

caliber: 10.4 mm
total length: 36.61 in (93 cm)
length of barrel: 18.11 in (46 cm)
weight: 7.72 lb (3,500 g)
feed system: 5-round tubular magazine

Left side of weapon.

Model 1882 (Schmidt system) Standard Revolver

caliber: 7.5 mm
total length: 9.25 in (23.5 cm)
length of barrel: 4.57 in (11.6 cm)
weight: 1.65 lb (750 g)
cylinder capacity: 6 rounds

REPEATING WEAPONS

ITALY

Vetterli-Vitali Model 1870/87 Rifle

caliber: 10.35 mm
total length: 53.11 in (134.9 cm)
length of barrel: 33.94 in (86.2 cm)
weight: 9.63 lb (4,370 g)
feed system: 4-round box magazine with cut-off device

The Model 1870 rifle was converted to a repeater in 1887, by fitting a single-column box magazine designed by Vitali.

The magazine could take four cartridges which were inserted in a pack. This ingenious system solved the serious problem of simultaneous loading of the magazine.

The rifle thus modified was designated Vetterli-Vitali 70/87.

Musket TS Model 1870/87/16

caliber: 6.5 × 52 mm
total length: 43.19 in (109.7 cm)
length of barrel: 24.01 in (61 cm)
weight: 8.64 lb (3,920 g)
feed system: 6-round box magazine

During the First World War the shortage of arms forced the Italians to use Vetterli weapons as well.

To standardize the ammunition, a few batches of these old weapons were chambered for the regulation Model 1891.

A box magazine was then fitted to take a pack of six cartridges.

Mannlicher-Carcano Model 1891 Rifle

This was also called the Mauser-Paravicino after the then President of the Military Commission for Portable Arms and the famous German inventor.

However, the idea of using the breech-block system invented by Mauser was due to Salvatore Carcano, chief technician at the royal factory in Turin; with this improvement and the addition of the Mannlicher feed system, Carcano produced an excellent rifle, which was strong, simple, accurate and low-priced (an important consideration, given Italy's scant financial resources).

The 1891 rifle was used in both World Wars and Italy's colonial enterprises, until the reconstitution of the Italian Republic.

caliber: 6.5 × 52 mm
total length: 50.39 in (128 cm)
length of barrel: 30.70 in (78 cm)
weight: 8.27 lb (3,750 g)
feed system: box magazine for pack of 6 cartridges.

Mannlicher-Carcano Model 1891 Cavalry Musket

caliber: 6.5 × 52 mm
total length: 36.18 in (91.9 cm)
length of barrel: 17.32 in (44 cm)
weight: 6.61 lb (3,000 g)

This was the first variant of the Model 1891 rifle. It was characterized by a triangular section, folding bayonet fixed beneath the barrel.

The weapon was adopted in 1893 and was also given to the *Carabinieri* and cyclist troops.

Detail of sectioned part and fixed bayonet.

Model 1891 Musket for the Royal Carabineers of the King's Guard

This is of similar size to the Model 91 cavalry musket, from which it differs in having a stock extending almost to the muzzle and a socket bayonet similar to that of the Model 1870 cavalry musket.

It has gold furniture.

Detail of fixed bayonet.

Mannlicher-Carcano Model 1891 T.S.* Musket
(*T.S. = special troops)

Detail of fixed bayonet.

caliber: 6.5 × 52 mm
total length: 36.18 in (91.9 cm)
length of barrel: 17.32 in (44 cm)
weight: 6.94 lb (3,150 g)

Mannlicher-Carcano Model 1891/41 Rifle

total length: 46.10 in (117.1 cm)
length of barrel: 27.16 in (69 cm)
weight: 8.20 lb (3,720 g)
feed system: 6-round packet magazine

This was the last descendant of the famous dynasty of 1891s.

Simple and strong like its predecessor, it was built in the middle of the war, still with a 6.5 mm caliber, but with constant pitch rifling.

Mannlicher-Carcano Model 91/38 S T.S. Musket

During the war, a few batches of 91/38 muskets were chambered for the powerful German regulation cartridge, the 7.92 mm Mauser. Apart from a few technical details, these weapons are recognized by the caliber stamped on the sight notch and a big S on the breech-block, which probably stood for spitzer (pointed) or the type of bullet adopted in 1905 for the Mauser Model 1898 rifle.

This transformation may also be regarded as proof of the soundness of the bolt of the 91, discrediting past and present claims about its fragility.

Detail of breech-block.

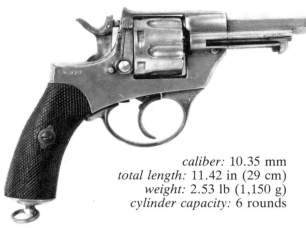

Chamelot-Delvigne Model 1874 Revolving Pistol

caliber: 10.35 mm
total length: 11.42 in (29 cm)
weight: 2.53 lb (1,150 g)
cylinder capacity: 6 rounds

The Italian cavalry passed directly from the Model 1860 muzzle-loading pistol to the Model 1874 center-fire, double-action revolver.

It has been slow in replacing the old weapon, the design of which dated from 1844, but the new one chosen was really progressive for the time.

In fact, the revolving pistols which Chamelot and Delvigne produced at the beginning of the seventies were among the best in Europe.

AUTOMATIC WEAPONS

ITALY

Villar Perosa Model 1915 Sub-machine Gun

weight: approx 15.43 lb (7 kg) with 25-cartridge magazines
feed system: 25 or 50-round double-column removable magazines.

This was the first automatic weapon firing pistol cartridges to be used on board aircraft and therefore the first sub-machine gun (of an unusual shape) to be deployed at the front on a large scale during the First World War.

It was developed by Bethel Abiel Revelli, who granted the patent to the company at Villar Perosa, after which the weapon was named.

The two barrels fired independently, achieving a rate of fire of about 1,500 rounds a minute each and it operated on the delayed blowback system.

The cartridge used was the 9 mm Glisenti. With a few modifications it was used by the infantry and was also mounted on bicycles.

Subsequently produced by Fiat (and therefore also designated Fiat Model 15), it was provided with a shielded support and then a bipod; but because it was awkward to use and the considerable fire power resulted in dispersion of shots, it was withdrawn towards the end of the war and underwent development for use with one barrel only at a lower rate of fire.

Beretta Model 38 A Automatic Musket
(MAB 38 A)

caliber: 9 mm Parabellum
total length: 37.24 in (94.6 cm)
length of barrel: 12.40 in (31.5 cm)
weight: 11 lb (5,000 g)
feed system: 10, 20, 30 or 40-round double-column removable magazine
rate of fire: 600 rpm

This was considered the best Italian weapon of the Second World War and gave rise to a series of very good weapons.

With a few changes it was also adopted by other armies and police forces.

The MAB 38 A is a blowback, selective fire weapon.

Armaguerra Model 39 Semi-automatic Rifle

caliber: 6.5 mm (and 7.35 mm)
total length: 46.06 in (117 cm)
length of barrel: 23.62 in (60 cm)
weight: 8.92 lb (4,045 g)

A short recoil weapon with the packet magazine feed system of the Model 91s.

Also known as the Revelli rifle, it was the only semi-automatic produced in some numbers at the Cremona works of the Genoese company Armaguerra.

It has an unusual cocking device: the breech-block is opened by pulling the weapon sling forward and closed again by pushing the projection at the front of the trigger guard.

caliber: 9 mm Parabellum
total length: 19.68 in (50 cm)
with butt folded;
27.95 in (71 cm)
with butt extended
length of barrel: 7.87 in (20 cm)
weight: 7.27 lb (3,300 g)
feed system: 30–40 round double-column removable magazine
rate of fire: 550 rpm

Beretta Model 38/44 Sub-machine Gun

This weapon was produced for the German armed forces from February 1944.

F.N.A.-B. Model 43 Sub-machine Gun

This weapon, about 7,000 of which were made by the Fabbrica Nazionale d'Armi di Brescia (National Arms Factory, Brescia), was mainly used by the armed forces of the Italian Social Republic.

It has forged steel parts; the butt is folding and the magazine-holder shuts down when not in use.

The F.N.A. 43 is a delayed blowback, selective fire weapon.

caliber: 9 mm Parabellum
total length: 31.10 in (79 cm) with butt extended;
            20.47 in (52 cm) with butt folded
length of barrel: 7.87 in (20 cm)
weight: 7.05 lb (3,200 g)
feed system: 20 and 40-round double-column removable magazine
rate of fire: 400 rpm

Model 1910 Automatic Pistol (commonly known as the Glisenti pistol)

A weapon with an unusual system of closure, which makes it hard to classify.

Because the breech-block stops at the first stage of recoil, fixed to the breech, some people call this pistol a geometric closure weapon.

During recoil, however, the breech-block stops faster than the breech; therefore others classify the Model 1910 as a blowback pistol with delayed opening.

It fires a 9 mm Parabellum cartridge but with a reduced charge.

caliber: 9 mm Glisenti
total length: 8.11 in (20.6 cm)
length of barrel: 3.74 in (9.5 cm)
weight: 1.76 lb (800 g)
feed system: 7-round removable magazine.

Beretta Model 1934 Automatic Pistol

This is the most famous Beretta pistol.

caliber: 9 mm short
total length: 5.90 in (15 cm)
length of barrel: 3.46 in (8.8 cm)
weight: 1.38 lb (625 g)
feed system: 7-round removable magazine

REPEATING AND AUTOMATIC WEAPONS

SPAIN

caliber: 7 × 57 mm
total length: 41.33 in (105 cm)
length of barrel: 21.65 in (55 cm)
weight: 8.31 lb (3,770 g)
feed system: 5-round double-column internal box magazine

Mauser Model 1893 Short Rifle

This is the most famous Spanish Mauser.

The double-column internal box magazine common to all later Mausers was introduced with the Model 1893.

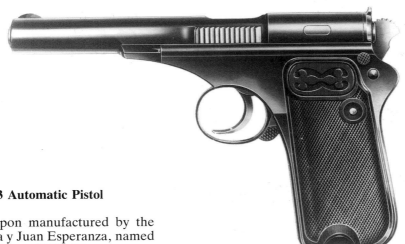

Campogiro Model 1913 Automatic Pistol

A Spanish Army weapon manufactured by the company Pedro Unceta y Juan Esperanza, named Esperanza y Unceta from 1913. The company moved to Guernica in the same year.

Designed by Lieutenant Colonel Venancio Lopez de Caballos y Aguirre, Count of Campo-Giro. It was the first pistol with a fixed barrel adapted for a powerful cartridge like the 9 mm *largo* (wide). The Modelo Campogiro 1913/1916 pistol was derived from it with a few modifications.

caliber: 9 mm Largo (9 mm Bergmann-Bayard)
operation: blowback
total length: 9.25 in (23.5 cm)
length of barrel: 6.50 in (16.5 cm)
weight: 1.98 lb (900 g)
feed system: 8-round removable magazine

Astra Model 400 – 1921 Automatic Pistol
(civil version)

The design for this was based on that of the Campogiro pistol, of which it kept the position of the return spring; but it had many new features, such as the fact that it could be dismantled without tools. Although chambered for 9 mm caliber *largo*, it could also use 9 mm short (380), 9 mm Parabellum, 9 mm Steyr and 9 mm Browning Long cartridges.

It was produced from 1921 to 1945 and was also bought by other countries, such as Germany (which acquired 12,000 in 1941), Colombia, Chile, Ecuador and El Salvador.

During the Spanish Civil War, two copies were produced in the Republican zone: one at Valencia marked RE (*Republica Española*) and the other at Tarrasa (near Barcelona) marked "F. Ascaso" (the name of a famous Anarchist leader).

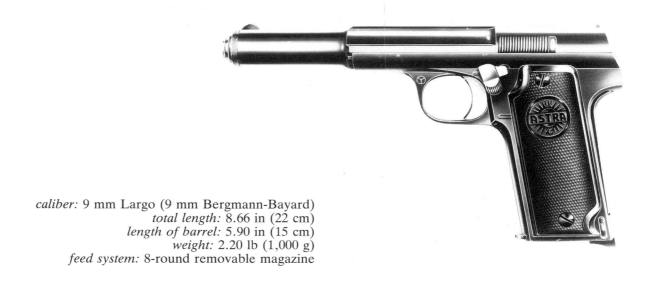

caliber: 9 mm Largo (9 mm Bergmann-Bayard)
total length: 8.66 in (22 cm)
length of barrel: 5.90 in (15 cm)
weight: 2.20 lb (1,000 g)
feed system: 8-round removable magazine

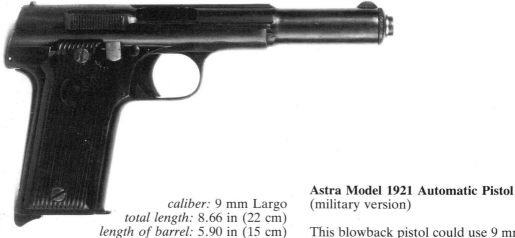

caliber: 9 mm Largo
total length: 8.66 in (22 cm)
length of barrel: 5.90 in (15 cm)
weight: 2 lb (950 g)
feed system: 8-round removable magazine

Astra Model 1921 Automatic Pistol
(military version)

This blowback pistol could use 9 mm *largo*, 9 mm Steyr, 9 mm Browning long, 9 mm Parabellum and 0.38 Super cartridges, equally as well.

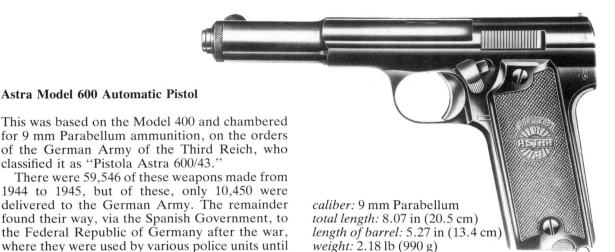

Astra Model 600 Automatic Pistol

This was based on the Model 400 and chambered for 9 mm Parabellum ammunition, on the orders of the German Army of the Third Reich, who classified it as "Pistola Astra 600/43."

There were 59,546 of these weapons made from 1944 to 1945, but of these, only 10,450 were delivered to the German Army. The remainder found their way, via the Spanish Government, to the Federal Republic of Germany after the war, where they were used by various police units until local pistol factories resumed production.

caliber: 9 mm Parabellum
total length: 8.07 in (20.5 cm)
length of barrel: 5.27 in (13.4 cm)
weight: 2.18 lb (990 g)
feed system: 8-round magazine

Astra Model 902 Automatic Pistol

This is one of four models of machine pistol produced between 1928 and 1937 by Unceta y Compania, as the present Astra – Unceta y Compania, S.A. was called from 1926 to 1942.

The Spanish company produced the Model 900 7.63 caliber Mauser with a fixed, 10-round magazine, which was used above all in China, during the long civil war. The Model 902, shown here, differed from it in being larger and above all, in having a fixed, 20-round magazine. The Model 903 could be fitted with a 10- or 20-round magazine and was also chambered for the 9 mm *largo*. The Model F could also take a 10- or 20-round magazine, but was only chambered for the 9 mm *largo*. All four models could be converted to carbines by fitting a wooden holster-stock, like the more famous Mauser pistol, by which it was clearly inspired.

caliber: 7.63 mm Mauser
total length: 13 in (33 cm)
length of barrel: 7.08 in (18 cm)
weight: 3.37 lb (1,530 g)
feed system: fixed 20-round charger-fed magazine

REPEATING WEAPONS

PORTUGAL

Mauser-Vergueiro Model 1904 Rifle

This Mauser has the bolt handle in front of the mobile breech, as in the old *Gew.* 88.

In the thirties, a few of these rifles were converted to take 7.92 × 57 cartridges.

caliber: 6.5 × 58 mm
total length: 48.42 in (123 cm)
length of barrel: 29.13 in (74 cm)
weight: 8.82 lb (4,000 g)
feed system: 5-round double-column internal box magazine

REPEATING WEAPONS

GREECE

Mannlicher Schoenauer Model 1903/14 Rifle

A weapon with a Mannlicher turn-bolt breech-block in two parts and a charger-fed rotary magazine invented by Schoenhauer.

caliber: 6.5 × 54 mm
total length: 48.22 in (122.5 cm)
length of barrel: 28.54 in (72.5 cm)
weight: 8.38 lb (3,800 g)
feed system: 5-round internal magazine

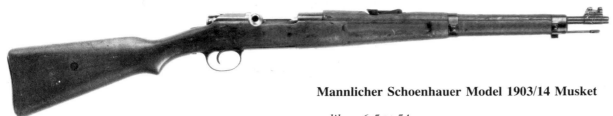

Mannlicher Schoenhauer Model 1903/14 Musket

caliber: 6.5 × 54 mm
total length: 40.35 in (102.5 cm)
length of barrel: 20.47 in (52 cm)
weight: 7.93 lb (3,600 g)
feed system: 5-round internal magazine

REPEATING WEAPONS

RUSSIA/SOVIET UNION

Mosin Nagant Model 1891 Rifle

caliber: 7.62 × 54 R
total length: 51.38 in (130.5 cm)
length of barrel: 31.57 in (80.2 cm)
weight: 9.63 lb (4,370 g)
feed system: 5-round single-column box magazine

This was the last rifle of the Russian Imperial Army and with a few changes became the basic weapon of the Red Army. The mechanism was devised by the Russian colonel Mosin, while the charger feed system was invented by the Belgian Nagant.

The weapon was chambered for a rimmed cartridge.

Despite its long period of use, the rifle has its faults: it has a complex breech-block and the safety catch is stiff to engage and disengage.

caliber: 7.62 × 54 mm R
total length: 48.70 in (123.7 cm)
length of barrel: 28.78 in (73.1 cm)
weight: 8.75 lb (3,970 g)
feed system: 5-round single-column box magazine

Mosin Nagant Dragoon Rifle Model 1891

This is a variant of the Model 1891 designed for the heavy cavalry.

Mosin Nagant Model 1891/30 Rifle

This is an improved version of the Model 1891, produced in 1930.

caliber: 7.62 × 54 R
total length: 48.46 in (123.1 cm)
length of barrel: 28.66 in (72.8 cm)
feed system: 5-round single-column box magazine

Model 1895 Winchester Military Musket

caliber: 7.62 × 54 mm R
total length: 46.46 in (11.8 cm)
length of barrel: 28 in (71.1 cm)
feed system: 5-round box magazine

This excellent lever-action musket with a box magazine, designed for Winchester by John Browning, was chambered for the Russian cartridge during the First World War at the request of the Tsarist government, which purchased a number of them. A Mauser type system was also fitted to speed up the loading of cartridges from the charger into the magazine.

The Winchester 1895s were also used by the Russians in the Second World War.

Mosin Nagant Model 1938 Musket

caliber: 7.62 × 54 mm R
total length: 40 in (101.6 cm)
length of barrel: 20 in (50.8 cm)
weight: 7.60 lb (3,450 g)
feed system: 5-round single-column box magazine

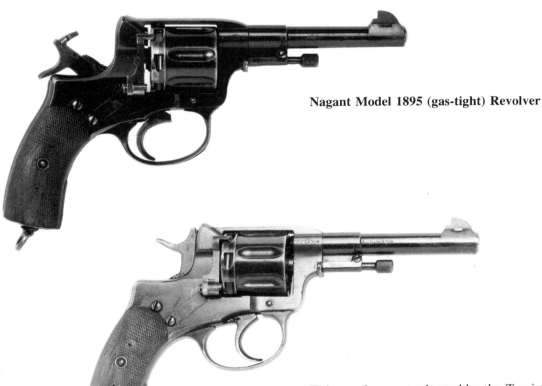

View of weapon with hammer cocked and cylinder forward.

Nagant Model 1895 (gas-tight) Revolver

caliber: 7.62 Nagant
total length: 9.05 in (23 cm)
length of barrel: 4.33 in (11 cm)
weight: 1.65 lb (750 g)
cylinder capacity: 7 rounds

This revolver was adopted by the Tsarist Army in 1895 and remained in service until after the Second World War.

The most interesting feature of this weapon is the unusual mechanism for rotating the cylinder. The latter in fact moves forward before the hammer falls, superimposing one of the chambers on the breech of the barrel at the moment of firing. The cartridge has the bullet fitted right in the neck, to avoid leakage of gas between the chamber and cylinder since the bullet expands as it starts to move, creating an hermetic closure between the chamber and barrel.

AUTOMATIC WEAPONS

SOVIET UNION

Tokarev Model 1938 Semi-automatic Rifle (SVT)

This weapon has a very light structure which makes it unsuitable for military use.
It is gas-operated.

caliber: 7.62 × 54 mm R
total length: 48.11 in (122.2 cm)
length of barrel: 25 in (63.5 cm)
weight: 8.70 lb (3,950 g)
feed system: 10-round double-column removable magazine

Detail with breech-block open.

caliber: 7.62 × 54 mm R
total length: 48.11 in (122.2 cm)
length of barrel: 24.57 in (62.4 cm)
weight: 8.60 lb (3,900 g)
feed system: 10-round double-column removable magazine

Tokarev Model 1940 Semi-automatic Rifle (SVT)

This was an improved version of the Model 1938, which failed to live up to expectations.

230

PPSh M. 1941 Sub-machine Gun
(Pistolet-Pulemyot Shpagina)

An unsophisticated, simply-manufactured, but highly functional weapon.
It is a blowback, selective fire type.

caliber: 7.62 mm (interchangeable with the 7.63 mm Mauser)
total length: 33.11 in (84.1 cm)
length of barrel: 10.59 in (26.9 cm)
weight: 12 lb (5,450 g) (with 71-cartridge drum)
feed system: removable 71-round drum magazine or 30-round packet magazine
rate of fire: 700–900 rpm

TT Model 1933 (Tula Tokarev) Automatic Pistol

This was the standard pistol of the Red Army in the Second World War.
It is based on the Colt-Browning short recoil mechanism.
It uses the 7.62 mm caliber Model 1930 cartridge which is interchangeable with the 7.63 mm Mauser.

total length: 7.68 in (19.5 cm)
length of barrel: 4.49 in (11.4 cm)
weight: 1.87 lb (850 g)
feed system: 8-round removable magazine

REPEATING WEAPONS

TURKEY

caliber: 11 mm
total length: 50.94 in (129.4 cm)
length of barrel: 31.69 in (80.5 cm)
weight: 9.35 lb (4,240 g)
feed system: 8-round tubular magazine

Mauser Model 1871/84 Rifle

This is the *Infanteriegewehr* M 71/84, the first Mauser repeater.
The cartridges are contained in a tubular magazine beneath the barrel.

Mauser Model 1871/84 Carbine

caliber: 11 mm
total length: 39.37 in (100 cm)
length of barrel: 20.16 in (51.2 cm)
weight: 8.60 lb (3,900 g)
feed system: 5-round tubular magazine

REPEATING AND AUTOMATIC WEAPONS

POLAND

caliber: 7.92 × 57 mm
total length: 43.30 in (110 cm)
length of barrel: 23.62 in (60 cm)
weight: 9.04 lb (4,100 g)
feed system: 5-round double-column internal box magazine

Mauser Model 1929 (Wz 29) Rifle

This was derived from the Czech VZ 24, from which it differed in the position of the sling swivels, and the shape of the foresight and bolt handle.

Radom Model 1935 Automatic Pistol
(Fabryka Broni w Radomiu, Radom)

A short recoil weapon based on the Colt-Browning system, with dorsal safety catch only. Also known as the Vis mod. 35 (a war model).

caliber: 9 mm Parabellum
total length: 8.30 in (21.1 cm)
length of barrel: 4.53 in (11.5 cm)
weight: 2.20 lb (1,000 g)
feed system: 8-round removable magazine

CZECHOSLOVAKIA

Mauser Model 1924 (VZ 24) Rifle

This is derived from the German *Gew.* 98 and has a hand guard extending right to the end of the stock and sling swivels on the left of the stock as well.

caliber: 7.92 × 57 mm
total length: 43.30 in (110 cm)
length of barrel: 23.03 in (58.5 cm)
weight: 9.19 lb (4,170 g)
feed system: 5-round double-column internal box magazine

CZ Model 1924 Automatic Pistol
(Českà Zbrojovka)

This is a short recoil weapon despite being chambered for a low power cartridge.

caliber: 9 mm ''short''
total length: 5.98 in (15.2 cm)
length of barrel: 3.54 in (9 cm)
weight: 1.50 lb (680 g)
feed system: 8-round removable magazine

CZ M 38 Automatic Pistol
(Českà Zbrojovka)

A blowback, double-action weapon.
   It is also known as Pistol Model 39(t), a designation given to it by the Germans during the Second World War.

caliber: 9 mm Browning Short
total length: 7.80 in (19.8 cm)
length of barrel: 4.68 in (11.9 cm)
weight: 1.98 lb (900 g)
feed system: 8-round single-column removable magazine

233

REPEATING WEAPONS

ROMANIA

Mannlicher Model 1893 Musket

This is a turn-bolt breech-block Mannlicher.

caliber: 6.5 × 54 mm R
total length: 37.40 in (95 cm)
length of barrel: 17.72 in (45 cm)
weight: 7.27 lb (3,300 g)
feed system: fixed external box magazine for pack of 5 cartridges

REPEATING WEAPONS

HOLLAND

Mannlicher Model 1895 Musket

This uses the breech-block and cartridge of the Romanian Model 1893.

caliber: 6.5 × 54 mm R
total length: 37.40 in (95 cm)
length of barrel: 17.72 in (45 cm)
weight: 7.27 lb (3,300 g)
feed system: fixed external box magazine for pack of 5 cartridges

Arisaka Type 38 Rifle, Meiji Era (1905)

This was the rifle most widely used by the Japanese in the Second World War.

It has a similar type of breech-block to the Mauser, from which it differs in the firing pin safety mechanism.

caliber: 6.5 × 50 mm
total length: 50.20 in (127.5 cm)
length of barrel: 31.50 in (80 cm)
weight: 9.25 lb (4,200 g)
feed system: 5-round double-column internal box magazine

Nambu Type Taisho 14 Automatic Pistol (1925)
(Fourteenth year of Taisho reign, or 1925 according to our calendar)

This short recoil weapon produced in 1925 was the final modification of the Nambu pistol of 1904.

The winter type trigger guard was introduced after the war of 1937 against the Chinese in Manchuria. The official name for this variant was the Kiska model.

caliber: 8 mm Nambu
total length: 8.90 in (22.6 cm)
length of barrel: 4.76 in (12.1 cm)
weight: 2 lb (910 g)
feed system: 8-round removable magazine

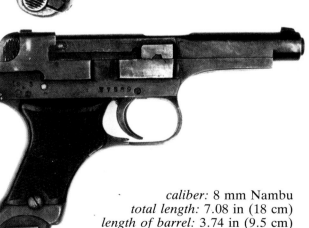

Type 94 Automatic Pistol
(that is, adopted in 2594 according to the Japanese calendar, which corresponds to our 1934)

This weapon did not have a good reputation, being so poorly designed and badly made that its performance was unreliable.

caliber: 8 mm Nambu
total length: 7.08 in (18 cm)
length of barrel: 3.74 in (9.5 cm)
weight: 1.74 lb (790 g)
feed system: 6-round removable magazine

235

Weapons of the street and tavern

Man's inventiveness in the production of defensive weapons has found a rich outlet in the last two centuries, in a public anxious for security and peace and thus susceptible to any form of publicity. Numerous commercial models have been proposed, from pocket pistols (the famous Derringers) to outsize pistols, or even "combination" weapons, many of them of dubious value and impractical, but capable nonetheless of reassuring their owners of their defense.

Two requirements appear to have dominated the market for users whose main aim was to scare off their aggressor, rather than render him completely harmless. The weapon had either to be large and terrifying, or so small that it could be carried in the pocket and pulled out at the right moment. The weapons of the first type had a relatively short season, whereas pocket models are still much in demand and can in fact be lethal at close range, or, at any rate, confound an unwily adversary. But beyond the two localities mentioned in the title – the street and the "dive" – they show all the limitations of instruments of defense with limited accuracy and poor stopping-power.

Pepperbox Pin-fire Revolver

caliber: 7.5 mm
total length: 4.33 in (11 cm)
weight: 0.77 lb (350 g)

Derringer System Pistol

caliber: 5.5 mm
total length: 4.72 in (12 cm)
weight: 0.33 lb (150 g)

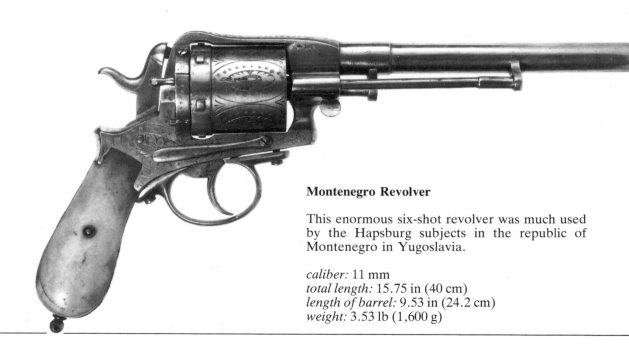

Montenegro Revolver

This enormous six-shot revolver was much used by the Hapsburg subjects in the republic of Montenegro in Yugoslavia.

caliber: 11 mm
total length: 15.75 in (40 cm)
length of barrel: 9.53 in (24.2 cm)
weight: 3.53 lb (1,600 g)

Belgian 20-shot Revolver

This pin-fire revolver with an enormous cylinder was produced by J. Chaineux.

caliber: 7.5 mm
total length: 10.24 in (26 cm)
length of barrel: 5.83 in (14.8 cm)
weight: 2.20 lb (1,000 g)

Baby Browning Pistol

This minute, excellent pocket automatic was produced at the beginning of the twenties and is still in use, despite the fact that its small caliber (6.35 mm) makes it somewhat inadequate for personal defense, given its limited stopping-power.

Cutlass/Revolver

A pin-fire weapon manufactured in Belgium by Dumonthier BSCDC.
   The cartridge case ejector is fitted to the open end of the sheath.

caliber: 9 mm
total length: 13.98 in (35.5 cm)
length of barrel: 5.31 in (13.5 cm)
weight: 1.54 lb (700 g)
cylinder capacity: 6 pin-fire cartridges

CONTEMPORARY WEAPONS

After the Second World War, the division of the world into two opposing blocs which never confronted each other directly on the battlefield led to an internationalization and parcelling out of arms production and commerce. From a structural point of view, the technology of individual firearms has not undergone any major changes comparable with the progress made during the Second World War. On the other hand, important results have been achieved in terms of the development of new materials, designed to make weapons lighter and easier to handle.

The tendency nowadays is to reduce the caliber of weapons and increase the initial velocity of the projectiles in order to enable a larger amount of ammunition to be carried, while still ensuring good stopping-power.

The examples illustrated in this section are particularly well known to the general public, thanks to the widespread reporting and news coverage of both civil and military events. The reader will also find some models featured here which have achieved fame through the media, more for accidental reasons than because of any outstanding technical qualities.

A Red Army lieutenant training Soviet paratroops in the use of the AK 47 rifle.

Guerrillas in the Far East. The man in the foreground is armed with a "Winchester" M1; the man behind is about to fire his "classic" 7.62 mm caliber AK 47. The letters AK stand for *Avtomat Kalashnikova*.

Member of the Moslem Amal Militia, pictured in front of his headquarters after one of the many ephemeral victories of the civil war in the Lebanon. The weapon, adorned by a carnation, is an AKMS of Soviet origin; many weapons used in such conflicts are 'recycled' through illegal arms trafficking channels.

A Russian infantry recruit receives his AK 74 rifle during an official ceremony, at the end of his basic training. The AK 74, a modified version of the AK 47, has completely replaced its predecessor as the regulation weapon of the Soviet Army, in the standard version with a wooden butt and the AK 74S version, for paratroops and special units, with a folding steel butt.

A French "Brigade Mobile" officer on patrol in front of the Paris Law Courts, during the trial of a terrorist. His weapon is a 5.56 × 45 mm caliber *Fusil Automatique* MAS (FAMAS), fitted with a 25-round magazine. Nicknamed "the trumpet" by French soldiers, it should become the standard personal weapon of the whole army by 1990, according to the state factory at St Etienne. In the opinion of many experts, it is an accurate and versatile weapon, capable of serving as a rifle, a carbine or a sub-machine gun.

Above: Sergeant Gary Gavin, of the First Battalion of The Worcestershire and Sherwood Foresters Regiment, pictured with the new British Army 5.56 caliber Royal Ordnance Enfield Individual Weapon, weighing 8.20 lb (3.72 kg), with a 20-round magazine and rate of fire of 650 rounds a minute. Some prototypes of this weapon were apparently tested during the Falklands War.

Interesting features include the bull-pup system magazine behind the pistol grip and the SUIT telescopic sight containing a light source for use in poor visibility. The other weapon shown is the 7.62 × 51 mm L1A1 rifle, which is to be replaced by the new model.

A British soldier armed with a Sterling L2A3 sub-machine gun. This weapon is light and easy to handle and has a 34-round magazine.

An Israeli soldier on patrol in the streets of Ramallah (West Bank). The weapon is the Galil 5.56 mm caliber assault rifle; it can take a 35 or 50-round magazine.

Israeli Army women recruits engaged in their first firing exercises with the UZI sub-machine gun (note the cartridge case just expelled from the weapon in the foreground, suspended in mid air). The initials UZI are from the name of its designer, Major Uziel Gal. It is the standard sub-machine gun of the Israeli Army and has been sold to numerous countries; a semi-automatic version has recently been produced for sale to private individuals, for use as a carbine. The military model shown here has a folding steel butt and is 9 mm Parabellum caliber; it can use 25, 32 or 40-round magazines. This weapon is fairly similar in basic operational principles to the Czech ZK 476 and its derivatives, models 23 and 25.

AUTOMATIC AND SEMI-AUTOMATIC RIFLES

Sectional view of the Model M16.

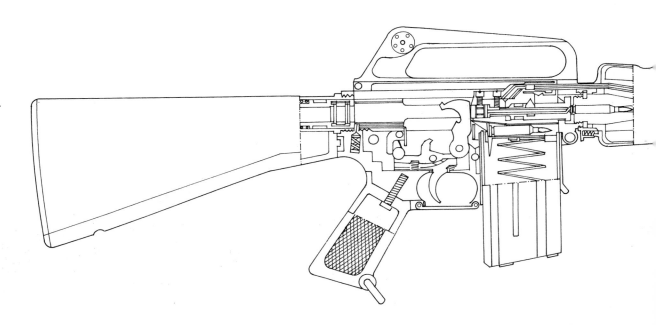

M21 Semi-automatic Rifle

country: U.S.A.
caliber: 7.62 × 51 mm
length: 12.75 in (32.4 cm)
feed system: 20-round double-column magazine
weight: 10 lb (4.55 kg)

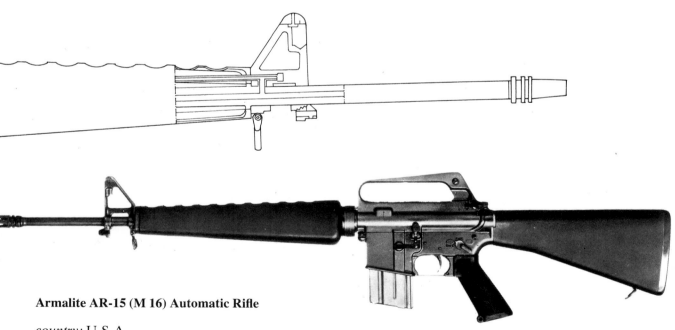

Armalite AR-15 (M 16) Automatic Rifle

country: U.S.A.
action: gas
caliber: 5.56 × 45 mm (.223)
total length: 38.98 in (99 cm)
length of barrel: 20 in (50.8 cm)
feed system: 30-round double-column magazine
weight (without magazine): 6.83 lb (3.1 kg)

Ruger Mini-Thirty Semi-automatic Rifle

country: U.S.A.
caliber: 7.62 × 39 mm Russian Service
total length: 37.25 in (94.6 cm)
length of barrel: 18.50 in (47 cm)

Ruger Mini – 14/5R Semi-automatic Rifle

country: U.S.A.
caliber: 5.56 × 45 mm (.223)
total length: 37.25 in (94.61 cm)
length of barrel: 18.25 in (46.35 cm)
weight: 6.25 lb (2.83 kg)

Ruger K AC-556 F Selective Fire Automatic Rifle

country: U.S.A.
caliber: 5.56 × 45 mm (.223)
total length: 33.46 in (85 cm)
length of barrel: 13 in (33 cm)

In stainless steel with a folding butt.
Control mechanism with a choice of three positions for semi-automatic fire, three-round burst and fully automatic fire.

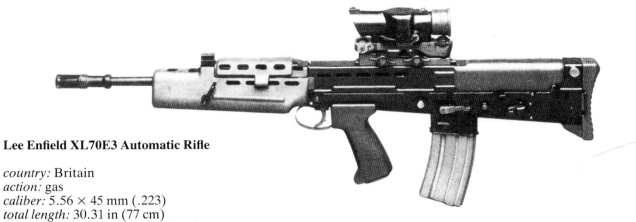

Lee Enfield XL70E3 Automatic Rifle

country: Britain
action: gas
caliber: 5.56 × 45 mm (.223)
total length: 30.31 in (77 cm)
length of barrel: 20.39 in (51.8 cm)
feed system: 30-round double-column magazine
weight (without magazine and telescopic sight):
8.60 lb (3.9 kg)

L1A1 Semi-automatic Rifle

The British version of the Belgian FN FAL (*Fusil Automatique Léger* – Light Automatic Rifle).

country: Britain
action: gas
caliber: 7.62 × 51 mm NATO
total length: 44.48 in (113 cm)
length of barrel: 20.98 in (53.3 cm)
feed system: 20-round magazine
weight (with magazine): 10.47 lb (4.75 kg)

FN FAL Light Automatic Rifle

country: Belgium
action: gas
caliber: 7.62 mm NATO (.308)
total length: 41.46 in (105.3 cm)
length of barrel: 20.98 in (53.3 cm)
feed system: 20-round double-column magazine
weight (without magazine): 9.50 lb (4.31 kg)

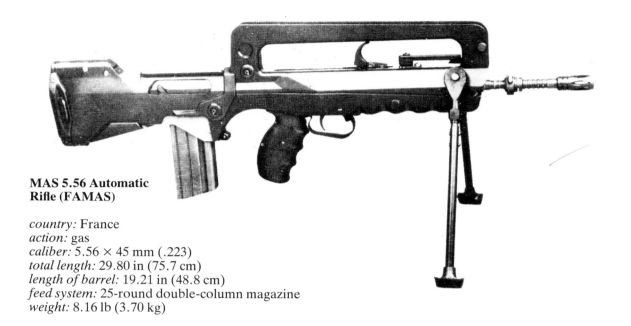

MAS 5.56 Automatic Rifle (FAMAS)

country: France
action: gas
caliber: 5.56 × 45 mm (.223)
total length: 29.80 in (75.7 cm)
length of barrel: 19.21 in (48.8 cm)
feed system: 25-round double-column magazine
weight: 8.16 lb (3.70 kg)

AK 47 Assault Rifle (first version) known as the Kalashnikov (*Avtomat Kalashnikova*)

country: U.S.S.R.
action: gas
caliber: 7.62 × 39 mm M 43
total length: 34.64 in (88 cm)
length of barrel: 16.34 in (41.5 cm)
feed system: 30-round magazine
weight (without magazine): 9.48 lb (4.30 kg)

AK 74 Assault Rifle

This new model has gradually replaced the earlier versions of the AK 47, as the regulation weapon of the Soviet Union.

country: U.S.S.R.
action: gas
caliber: 5.45 × 39 mm
total length: 36.61 in (93 cm)
length of barrel: 15.75 in (40 cm)
feed system: 40-round magazine
weight (without magazine): 7.94 lb (3.60 kg)

**Snayperskaya Vintovka Dragunova (SVD)
Semi-automatic Sniper Rifle**

This model was adopted by the Soviet Army in
1963.

country: U.S.S.R.
action: gas
caliber: 7.62 × 54 mm R
total length: 48.19 in (122.4 cm)
length of barrel: 23.97 in (60.9 cm)
feed system: 10-round magazine
weight (without magazine): 9.50 lb (4.31 kg)

Beretta Model AR 70 Automatic Rifle

country: Italy
action: gas
caliber: 5.56 × 45 mm (.223)
total length: 37.60 in (95.5 cm)
length of barrel: 17.72 in (45 cm)
feed system: 30-round double-column magazine
weight (without magazine): 7.72 lb (3.50 kg)

**Beretta Model SC 70 Automatic Carbine for
Special Troops**

country: Italy
action: gas
caliber: 5.56 × 45 mm (.223)
total length (with butt extended): 37.80 in (96 cm)
length of barrel: 17.72 in (45 cm)
feed system: 30-round double-column magazine
weight (without magazine): 7.83 lb (3.55 kg)

Heckler & Koch G3A3 Automatic Rifle

country: Federal Republic of Germany
action: delayed blowback (with blocking rollers)
caliber: 7.62 × 51 mm NATO
total length: 40 in (101.6 cm)
length of barrel: 17.72 in (45 cm)
feed system: 20-round double-column magazine
weight (without magazine): 9.37 lb (4.25 kg)

**Steyr AUG (Armée Universal-Gewehr) A1
Automatic Rifle**

An unusually light weapon, of the bull-pup type,
that is with the magazine fitted behind the trigger;
telescopic sight with 1.5 magnification and circular reticle; plastic stock.

Produced in four basic versions:
commando (Para) with 13.78 in (35 cm) barrel;
machine carbine with 16.02 in (40.7 cm) barrel;
assault rifle with 20 in (50.8 cm) barrel;
light tactical support weapon with 24.45 in (62.1
cm) barrel.

country: Austria
action: gas
caliber: 5.56 × 45 mm (.223 Remington)
total length: 24.80 in (63 cm); 27.16 in (69 cm);
31.10 in (79 cm); 35.43 in (90 cm)
feed system: 30 or 42-round magazine in
transparent synthetic material
weight (without magazine): 7.05 lb (3.2 kg); 7.27 lb
(3.3 kg); 7.94 lb (3.6 kg); 8.60 lb (3.9 kg)

SG551

SG 551 Assault Rifle

The short version of the SIG (Schweizerische Industrie-Gesellschaft)

country: Switzerland
action: gas
caliber: 5.56 × 45 mm
total length: 32.40 in (82.3 cm)
length of barrel: 23.62 in (60 cm)
feed system: 20 and 30-round magazines
weight (with magazine empty): 7.72 lb (3.5 kg)

SG 550 Assault Rifle

The standard version of the SIG (Schweizerische Industrie-Gesellschaft)

This weapon, under the designation Stgw 90 and Fass 90, will be adopted by the Swiss Army from 1988. A version for sporting associations designated Stgw 90 PE or SIG 90 PE, with 20-round magazines, has also been prepared, the only difference from the military model being that it has no burst-fire capability.

SG 550

Detail of weapon with three magazines side-by-side.

country: Switzerland
action: gas
caliber: 5.56 × 45 mm
total length: 39.37 in (100 cm)
length of barrel: 20.78 in (52.8 cm)
feed system: 20 or 30-round magazines
weight (with empty magazine and bipod): 9.04 lb (4.1 kg)

Galil Assault Rifle

country: Israel
action: gas
caliber: 5.56 × 45 mm (.223)
total length (with butt extended): 38.19 in (97 cm)
length of barrel: 18.11 in (46 cm)
feed system: 35 or 50-round double-column magazines
weight (without magazine): 8.60 lb (3.90 kg)

CETME Model L Assault Rifle

country: Spain
action: delayed blowback
caliber: 5.56 × 45 mm (.223)
total length: 36.42 in (92.5 cm)
length of barrel: 15.75 in (40 cm)
feed system: 12 or 30-round double-column magazines
weight (without magazine): 7.50 lb (3.4 kg)

CETME Model LC Assault Rifle

country: Spain
action: delayed blowback
caliber: 5.56 × 45 mm (.223)
total length (with butt extended): 33.86 in (86 cm)
length of barrel: 12.60 in (32 cm)
feed system: 12 or 30-round double-column magazines
weight (without magazine): 7.50 lb (3.4 kg)

Heckler & Koch G11 Automatic Rifle

A highly progressive design. Apart from its very
compact appearance, the most interesting feature
of this weapon is the ammunition, based on
square-section cartridges with no case and consisting of a block of propellant (a suitably treated
high explosive) into which the bullet and primer
are inserted. This special type of ammunition
enables the weapon to be fed by 50-round magazines, ensuring a considerable volume of fire.

country: Federal Republic of Germany
caliber: 4.7 × 21 mm
total length: 29.52 in (75 cm)
length of barrel: 21.26 in (54 cm)
weight (empty): 1.42 lb (3.6 kg)

SUB-MACHINE GUNS

Ingram Model 10 and 11 Sub-machine Gun

This weapon has no silencer.

country: U.S.A.
action: blowback
caliber: .45 and .38
total length: 10.51 in (26.7 cm)
length of barrel: 5.74 in (14.6 cm)
feed system: 30-round double-column magazine
weight (without magazine): 6.26 lb (2.84 kg)

Viking Sub-machine Gun

country: U.S.A.
action: blowback
caliber: 9 × 19 mm Parabellum
total length (with butt extended): 23.62 in (60 cm)
length of barrel: 8.66 in (22 cm)
feed system: 20 or 36-round double-column magazines
weight (without magazine): 7.76 lb (3.52 kg)

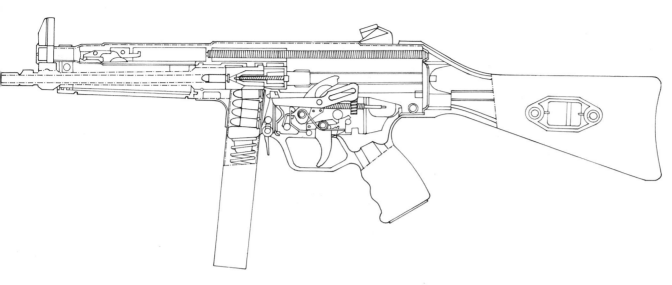

Heckler & Koch MP 5 Sub-machine Gun

country: Federal Republic of Germany
action: delayed blowback
caliber: 9 mm Parabellum
length of barrel: 8.86 lb (22.5 cm)
feed system: 15 or 30-round double-column magazines
weight (without magazine): 5.40 lb (2.45 kg)

The photo shows the MP 5K, short version.

Walther MP-K Sub-machine Gun

country: Federal Republic of Germany
action: blowback
caliber: 9 × 19 mm
total length (with butt extended): 25.70 in (65.3 cm)
length of barrel: 6.73 in (17.1 cm)
feed system: 32-round double-column magazine
weight (without magazine): 6.17 lb (2.8 kg)

255

Steyr MPi81 Sub-machine Gun

country: Austria
action: blowback
caliber: 9 mm Parabellum
length of barrel: 10.24 in (26 cm)
feed system: 25 or 32-round double-column magazines
weight (without magazine): 6.46 lb (2.93 kg)

UZI Sub-machine Gun of the Israeli Army
(first version)

country: Israel
action: blowback
caliber: 9 mm Parabellum
total length: 25 in (63.5 cm)
length of barrel: 10.24 in (26 cm)
feed system: 25, 32 or 40-round double-column magazines
weight (without magazine): 7.63 lb (3.46 kg)

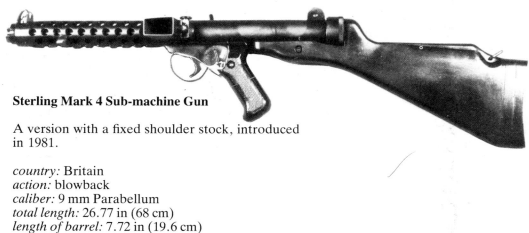

Sterling Mark 4 Sub-machine Gun

A version with a fixed shoulder stock, introduced in 1981.

country: Britain
action: blowback
caliber: 9 mm Parabellum
total length: 26.77 in (68 cm)
length of barrel: 7.72 in (19.6 cm)
feed system: 34-round double-column magazine

Beretta PM 12S Sub-machine Gun

country: Italy
action: blowback with a choice of burst or single-shot fire
caliber: 9 mm Parabellum
length with butt folded: 16.46 in (41.8 cm)
length with butt extended: 25.98 in (66 cm)
feed system: 32-round magazine
weight (without magazine): approx 6.60 lb (3 kg)

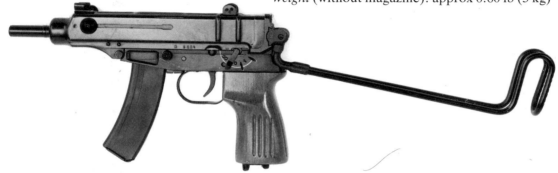

M 61 Skorpion Sub-machine Gun

The butt-extension fixed to the weapon can be folded over to allow the gun to be fired like a normal pistol.

The sub-machine gun can be fitted with a silencer and a luminescent sighting device for use at night.

country: Czechoslovakia
action: blowback, selective fire
caliber: 7.65 mm Browning
total length: 10.67 in (27.1 cm) with butt folded; 20.59 in (52.3 cm) with butt extended
length of barrel: 4.53 in (11.5 cm)
feed system: 10 or 20-round double-column removable magazines
weight: 3.41 lb (1.548 kg)

257

Carl-Gustaf Sub-machine Gun

country: Sweden
action: blowback
caliber: 9 mm Parabellum
total length (with butt extended): 31.93 in (81.1 cm)
length of barrel: 8.38 in (21.3 cm)
feed system: 36-round double-column magazine
weight (without magazine): 9.26 lb (4.2 kg)

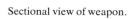

Sectional view of weapon.

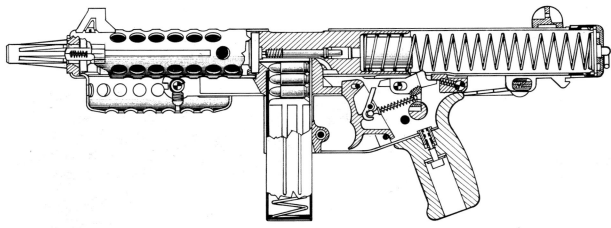

Star Model Z-62 Sub-machine Gun

country: Spain
action: blowback
caliber: 9 mm Parabellum; 9 mm Bergmann
total length (with butt extended): 27.56 in (70 cm)
length of barrel: 7.87 in (20 cm)
feed system: 20 and 30-round double-column magazines
weight (without magazine): 6.61 lb (3 kg)

PISTOLS

Walther Model P 38 Automatic Pistol

This is the post-war version of the P38 regulation model of the Army of the Third Reich, from which it differs in minor details.

country: Federal Republic of Germany
action: short recoil, double-action
caliber: .22 L.R.; 7.65 mm Parabellum; 9 mm Parabellum
total length: 8.50 in (21.6 cm)
length of barrel: 5.08 in (12.9 cm) for the .22 caliber L.R.; 4.92 in (12.5 cm) for the other two calibers
feed system: 8-round magazine
weight (without magazine): approx 1.75 lb (800 g)

Walther Model P 5 Automatic Pistol

country: Federal Republic of Germany
action: short recoil, double-action
caliber: 9 × 19 mm (9 mm Parabellum)
total length: 7.08 in (18 cm)
length of barrel: 3.54 in (9 cm)
feed system: 8-round magazine
weight (without magazine): approx 1.75 lb (795 g)

Walther Model PP Automatic Pistol

This is the old Walther of Zella Mehlis built at Ulma in the post-war period.

country: Federal Republic of Germany
action: double-action
caliber: 5.6 mm (.22 L.R.); 7.65 mm (.32); 9 mm (.380)
total length: 6.69 in (17 cm)
length of barrel: 3.85 in (9.8 cm)
feed system: 8-round magazine (7-round in 9 caliber)
weight (minus magazine) with steel frame: 1.41 lb (640 g) for 5.6 caliber; 1.45 lb (660 g) for 7.65 caliber.; 1.46 lb (665 g) for 9 caliber

Walther Model PPK Automatic Pistol

This is also a further edition of the Zella Mehlis weapon.

country: Federal Republic of Germany
action: double-action
caliber: 5.6 mm (.22 L.R.); 7.65 mm (.32); 9 mm short (.380)
total length: 6.10 in (15.5 cm)
length of barrel: 3.27 in (8.3 cm)
feed system: 7-round magazine (6-round in 9 caliber)
weight (minus magazine) with steel frame: 1.23 lb (560 g) in 5.6 caliber; 1.30 lb (590 g) in 7.65 and 9 caliber
weight (minus magazine) with light metal frame: 0.97 lb (440 g) in 5.6 caliber; 1.04 lb (470 g) in 7.65 caliber

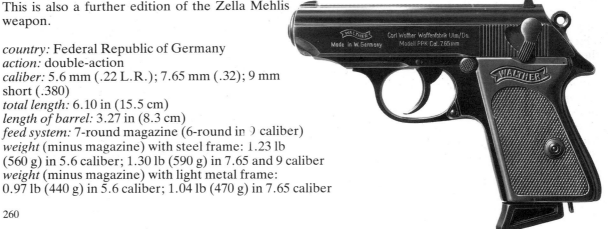

Heckler & Koch P 7 Automatic Pistol

country: Federal Republic of Germany
caliber: 9 mm Parabellum
total length: 6.53 in (16.6 cm)
length of barrel: 4.13 in (10.5 cm)
feed system: 8-round magazine
weight: 2.16 lb (980 g)

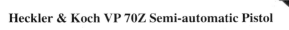

Heckler & Koch VP 70Z Semi-automatic Pistol

A civil version of the VP 70 automatic pistol; the Model VP 70M also offers automatic fire and can be converted to a pistol-carbine by fitting a holster-stock.

country: Federal Republic of Germany
action: semi-automatic double-action
caliber: 9 × 19 mm
total length: 8.03 in (20.4 cm)
length of barrel: 4.57 in (11.6 cm)
feed system: 18-round double-column magazine
weight: 1.81 lb (823 g)

Mauser Model HSc Automatic Pistol

This post-war version of the Mauser HSc, from which it differs in minor details, was distributed to the police of the Reich.

country: Federal Republic of Germany
action: blowback, double-action
caliber: 7.65 mm (.32)
total length: 5.98 in (15.2 cm)
length of barrel: 3.38 in (8.6 cm)
feed system: 8-round double-column removable magazine
weight (without magazine): 1.30 lb (590 g)

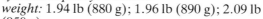

Manurhin MR 73 Revolver

country: France
action: double-action
caliber: .357 Magnum; 9 mm Parabellum (with special cylinder)
total length: 7.68 in (19.5 cm); 8.07 in (20.5 cm); 9.17 in (23.3 cm)
length of barrel: 2.50 in (6.35 cm); 3 in (7.62 cm); 3.98 in (10.1 cm)
cylinder capacity: 6 rounds
weight: 1.94 lb (880 g); 1.96 lb (890 g); 2.09 lb (950 g)

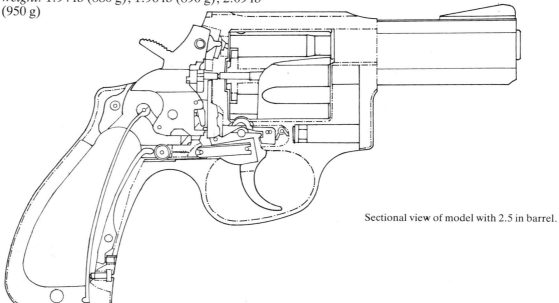

Sectional view of model with 2.5 in barrel.

PA 15 MAB Automatic Pistol

country: France
action: short recoil
caliber: 9 mm Parabellum
total length: 7.99 in (20.3 cm)
length of barrel: 4.49 in (11.4 cm)
feed system: 15-round double-column magazine
weight: 2.40 lb (1.09 kg)

Colt Detective Special Revolver

country: U.S.A.
action: double-action
caliber: .38 Special
total length: 6.85 in (17.4 cm)
length of barrel: 2 in (5.1 cm)
cylinder capacity: 6 rounds
weight (without ammunition): 1.33 lb (602 g)

Colt Python Revolver

country: U.S.A.
action: double-action
caliber: .357 Magnum; .38 Special
total length: 11.22 in (28.5 cm) with 5.98 in (15.2 cm) barrel
length of barrel: 2.48 in (6.3 cm); 3.98 in (10.1 cm); 5.98 in (15.2 cm)
cylinder capacity: 6 rounds
weight (without ammunition): 2.03 lb (924 g); 2.34 lb (1.06 kg); 2.68 lb (1.22 kg), depending on length of barrel

Colt Combat Lightweight Automatic Pistol

country: U.S.A.
action: short recoil
caliber: .445 ACP
total length: 8 in (20.3 cm)
length of barrel: 4.25 in (10.8 cm)
feed system: 7-round magazine
weight (without magazine): 1.63 lb (740 g)

Smith & Wesson Model 29 Revolver

country: U.S.A.
action: double-action
caliber: .44 Magnum; .44 Special; .44 Russian
total length: 11.85 in (30.1 cm) with 6.50 in (16.5 cm) barrel
length of barrel: 3.98 in (10.1 cm); 6.50 in (16.5 cm); 8.35 in (21.2 cm)
cylinder capacity: 6 rounds
weight (minus ammunition): 2.90 lb (1.32 kg) with 6.50 in (16.5 cm) barrel

Smith & Wesson Model 586 Distinguished Combat Magnum Revolver

country: U.S.A.
action: double-action
caliber: .357 Magnum; .38 Special
length of barrel: 4.33 in (11 cm); 5.87 in (14.9 cm)
cylinder capacity: 6 rounds
weight (minus ammunition): 2.62 lb (1.19 kg); 2.87 lb (1.30 kg)

Smith & Wesson Model 459 Automatic Pistol

country: U.S.A.
action: short recoil
caliber: 9 mm Parabellum
length of barrel: 4.01 in (10.2 cm)
feed system: 14-round double-column magazine
weight (without magazine): 1.90 lb (865 g)

Mod. no. S45N .44 caliber Magnum, in stainless steel

Mod. no. KBN-36 .357 caliber Magnum, in stainless steel

Ruger New Model Blackhawk Revolver

This was produced in twelve different versions.

country: U.S.A.
action: single-action
caliber: .30 Carbine; .38 Special; .357 Magnum; .41 Magnum; .44 Magnum; .45 Long Colt; 9 mm Parabellum
total length: from a minimum of approx 10¼ in (26 cm; Mod. no. BN-41 .41 caliber Magnum and Mod. no. BN-44 .45 caliber Long Colt) to a maximum of approx 13⅛ in (33 cm; Mod. no. BN-31 .30 caliber Carbine and Mod. no. BN-45 .45 caliber Long Colt)
length of barrel: from a minimum of 4⅝ in (11.7 cm; Mod. no. BN-34 .357 caliber Magnum; Mod. no. BN-41 .41 caliber Magnum; Mod. no. BN-44 .45 caliber Long Colt; Mod. no. KBN-34 stainless steel .357 caliber Magnum) to a maximum of 7½ in (19 cm; Mod. no. BN-31 .30 caliber Carbine; Mod. no. BN-45 .45 caliber Long Colt)
cylinder capacity: 6 rounds
weight: from a minimum of approx 1,080 g (38 ounces = 2.38 lb; Mod. no. BN-41) to a maximum of approx 1,250 g (44 ounces = 2.75 lb; Mod. no. BN-31)

Ruger "Old Army Cap and Ball" Revolver
(with front-loading cylinder)

A weapon produced in two versions: Model BP-7 (blued) and Model KBP-7 (in stainless steel).

country: U.S.A.
action: single-action, gunpowder
caliber: .44
total length: approx 13.75 in (35 cm)
length of barrel: approx 7.50 in (19 cm)
cylinder capacity: 6 rounds
weight: approx 2.86 lb (1.3 kg)

Ruger Redhawk Revolver

Produced in six versions, each sold in blued and stainless steel types.

country: U.S.A.
action: double-action
caliber: .357 Magnum; .38 Special; .41 Magnum; .44 Magnum; .44 Special
total length: approx 11 in (28 cm) or 13 in (33 cm), depending on the barrel
length of barrel: approx 5.5 in (14 cm) or 7.5 in (19 cm)
cylinder capacity: 6 rounds
weight: approx 52 ounces (1.47 kg)

KNR 5 version, with special cylinder for .22 WMR cartridge.

Ruger New Model Super Single-Six Six-Shot Revolver

A single-action revolver in the style of the famous Colt Peacemaker, but with adjustable sights and made out of modern materials. Available in six versions.

country: U.S.A.
caliber: the revolvers of this type are chambered for the .22 LR but also take the .22 short and .22 long, as well as the .22 Winchester Magnum Rimfire, by changing the cylinder.
total length: 9.76 in (24.8 cm); 10.70 in (27.2 cm); 11.69 in (29.7 cm); 14.72 in (37.4 cm), depending on length of barrel.
length of barrel: approx 4.57 in (11.6 cm) in NR-4 version; approx 6.42 in (13.8 cm) in NR-5 and KNR-5 versions; approx 6.42 in (16.3 cm) in NR-6 and KNR-6 versions; approx 9.40 in (23.9 cm) in NR-6 version.
weight: approx 6.42 lb (935 g) with 5.43 in (13.8 cm) barrel

Model KMK-6

Ruger Standard Model Mark II Automatic Pistol

Produced in blued types MK-4 and MK-6, and stainless steel types KMK-4 and KMK-6.
Trigger with surface for finger nearly ⅜ in (1 cm) wide.

country: U.S.A.
caliber: .22 Long Rifle
total length: 8.27 in (21 cm); approx 10 in (25.4 cm), depending on length of barrel
length of barrel: 4.72 in (12 cm); approx 6 in (15 cm)
feed system: 10-round magazine
weight: 2.25 lb (1,019 g) with 4.72 in (12 cm) barrel

Sterling .357 Magnum Revolver

country: Britain
action: double action
caliber: .357 Magnum; .38 Special
length of barrel: 2 in (5.1 cm) 4 in (10.2 cm)
cylinder capacity: 6 rounds

SIG – SAUER P 230

country: Switzerland
action: blowback, double-action
caliber: 9 mm Police and short; 7.65 mm
Browning
total length: 6.61 in (16.8 cm)
length of barrel: 3.62 in (9.2 cm)
feed system: 7-round magazine
weight (without magazine): 1.52 lb (690 g) for
9 mm Police; 1 lb (460 g) for 9 mm short; 1.02 lb
(465 g) for 7.65 mm

SIG – SAUER P 225 Automatic Pistol

country: Switzerland
action: short recoil, double-action
caliber: 9 mm Parabellum
total length: 7.09 in (18 cm)
length of barrel: 5.16 lb (13.1 cm)
feed system: 8-round magazine
weight (without magazine): 1.63 lb (740 g)

SIG – SAUER P 226 Automatic Pistol

country: Switzerland
action: short recoil, double-action
caliber: 9 mm Parabellum
total length: 7.72 in (19.6 cm)
length of barrel: 4.40 in (11.2 cm)
feed system: 15-round double-column magazine
weight (without magazine): 1.65 lb (750 g)

SIG – SAUER P 220 Model 75 Automatic Pistol

country: Switzerland
action: short recoil, double-action
caliber: 9 mm Parabellum; 7.65 mm Parabellum;
.45 ACP; .38 Auto Super; .22 Long Rifle
total length: 7.80 in (19.8 cm)
length of barrel: 4.40 in (11.2 cm)
feed system: 9-round magazine; 7-round (.45
ACP); 10-round (.22 Long Rifle)
weight (without magazine): 1.60 lb (750 g) for
9 mm Para; 1.68 lb (765 g) for 7.65 mm Para;
1.60 lb (730 g) for .45 ACP; 1.65 lb (750 g) for .38
Super Auto; 1.73 lb (785 g) for .22 Long Rifle

Beretta Model 93 R Automatic Pistol

country: Italy
action: semi-automatic or automatic with controlled burst of three shots; geometric, falling block closure
caliber: 9 mm Parabellum
total length: 9.45 in (24 cm)
length of barrel: 6.14 in (15.6 cm) with flash hider and muzzle brake
feed system: 20-round double-column magazine
weight (with magazine empty): 2.58 lb (1.17 kg)

special features: a folding metal crutch can be fitted to the grip for medium-range firing.

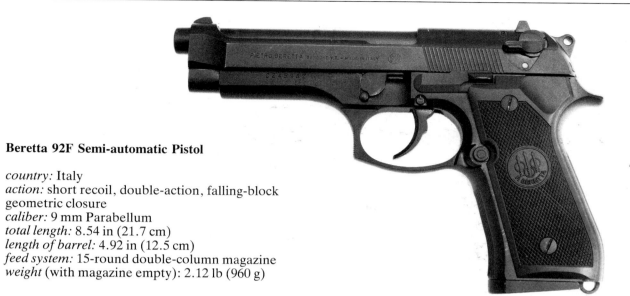

Beretta 92F Semi-automatic Pistol

country: Italy
action: short recoil, double-action, falling-block
geometric closure
caliber: 9 mm Parabellum
total length: 8.54 in (21.7 cm)
length of barrel: 4.92 in (12.5 cm)
feed system: 15-round double-column magazine
weight (with magazine empty): 2.12 lb (960 g)

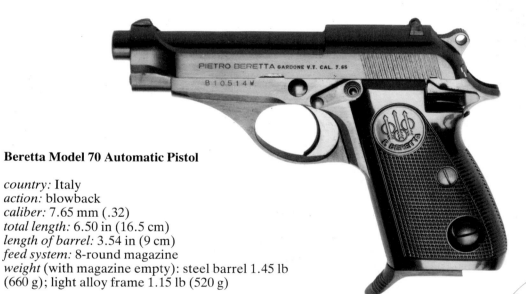

Beretta Model 70 Automatic Pistol

country: Italy
action: blowback
caliber: 7.65 mm (.32)
total length: 6.50 in (16.5 cm)
length of barrel: 3.54 in (9 cm)
feed system: 8-round magazine
weight (with magazine empty): steel barrel 1.45 lb
(660 g); light alloy frame 1.15 lb (520 g)

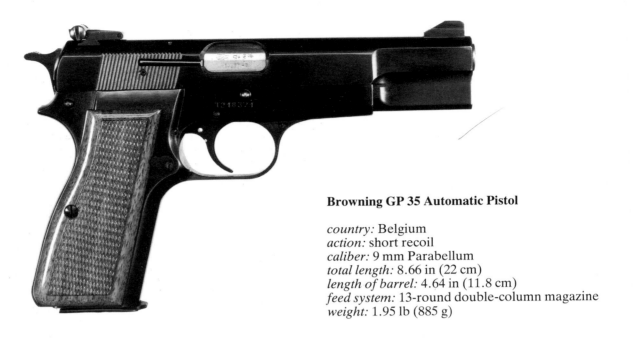

Browning GP 35 Automatic Pistol

country: Belgium
action: short recoil
caliber: 9 mm Parabellum
total length: 8.66 in (22 cm)
length of barrel: 4.64 in (11.8 cm)
feed system: 13-round double-column magazine
weight: 1.95 lb (885 g)

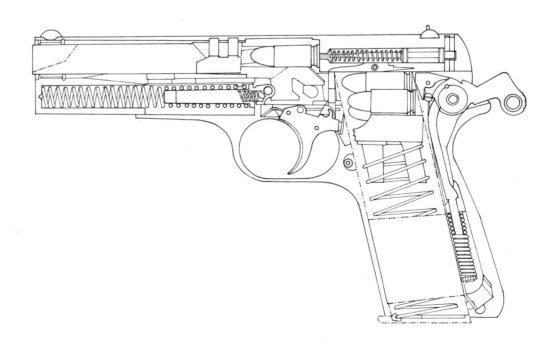

Cross-section of basic GP (*Grande Puissance*) model, the first version of which was produced in 1935.

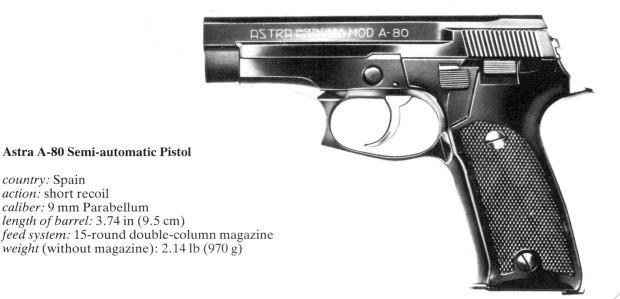

Astra A-80 Semi-automatic Pistol

country: Spain
action: short recoil
caliber: 9 mm Parabellum
length of barrel: 3.74 in (9.5 cm)
feed system: 15-round double-column magazine
weight (without magazine): 2.14 lb (970 g)

M 52 Automatic Pistol

This short recoil weapon uses the breech-block system of the German MG 42 machine gun.

It is chambered for the Czech version of the Soviet P Type (7.62 mm) cartridge, called Model 48 in Czechoslovakia and interchangeable with the 7.63 mm Mauser.

The German cartridge has a slightly smaller charge than the other two.

country: Czechoslovakia
caliber: 7.62 mm
total length: 8.27 in (21 cm)
length of barrel: 4.72 in (12 cm)
feed system: 8-round double-column removable magazine
weight: 2.20 lb (1 kg)

GLOSSARY
INDEX BY COUNTRY
ANALYTICAL INDEX
BIBLIOGRAPHY

GLOSSARY

arquebus: the generic name for all portable firearms at least 3.28 ft (1 m) long, used until the eighteenth century.

assault rifle: a translation of the German word *Sturmgewehr* adopted in the Second World War to indicate a new range of individual weapons which combined the characteristics of the repeating rifle (stability and accuracy) with those of the sub-machine gun (light weight and a considerable volume of fire). The assault rifles used by the armed forces of numerous countries were derived from the German models, for instance the Soviet AK 47, Belgian FAL and West German G3 (and subsequent models).

automatic musket: an Italian name for long automatic weapons which fire pistol cartridges (e.g., the MAB 38A). The distinction between automatic musket and *pistola mitragliatrice* (machine pistol) is not made in English-speaking countries and in Germany, where the terms sub-machine gun and *Machinenpistole* (MP) are used; it is, however, useful for distinguishing sub-machine guns of the Second World War which did not have a folding butt.

automatic weapon: a firearm in which continuous pressure on the trigger causes the uninterrupted fire of numerous projectiles (burst fire). This term is, however, also applied to semi-automatic weapons to distinguish them from ordinary repeating weapons (e.g., Beretta Model 1934 automatic pistol).

back sight: a device to control aiming of a weapon according to the distance.

back sight notch: a recess on the back sight or barrel. The firer looks through this notch when aiming. See *back sight, diopter, foresight* and *leaf.*

barrel: part of the weapon which serves to use the thrust of the gases of the propelling charge to send the projectile in the desired direction. Early barrels were forged of iron, various systems being used to ensure strength and durability. Modern barrels are made from cold-drawn and extruded steel.

barrel band: a metal band used to fix the barrel to the fore-end of the stock.

barrel closure: a system developed by J. Werndl and adopted by the Austrian Army from 1867. The breech-block (q.v.) consisted of a cylinder with an axis parallel to that of the barrel. To load the weapon, the cylinder was turned clockwise, uncovering the chamber, into which the cartridge was put. The shape of the breech-block was such that turning it anti-clockwise closed the breech tightly.

base: base of a modern cartridge. The primer (q.v.) is placed at the center of the base in center-fire cartridges and all around the edge in rim-fire cartridges.

blowback closure: this is a type of closure used in automatic weapons in which the breech-block, held by a spring (the return spring) inside the weapon, ensures closure until the projectile with most of the gases from the explosion have escaped. The recoil from firing and the thrust of the residual gases then drive back the breech-block, enabling the cartridge case to be expelled and a new cartridge to be chambered.

bolt: a type of breech-block (q.v.) consisting of a metal cylinder which is shifted by a handle to allow the cartridge to be fed into the chamber. It normally also contains the percussion mechanism.

bore: the interior of a gun barrel along which the projectile travels.

box lock: a type of lock fitted to short weapons from the mid eighteenth to the end of the nineteenth century, in which the cock and related mechanisms are housed in a "box" in a central position behind the barrel.

breech: rear end of the barrel where the charge is placed. The term is mainly applied to old weapons and artillery.

breech-block: part of a breech-loading firearm which closes the breech. See the various types of block and closure.

breech-loading: a system of loading from the breech (q.v.). Ever since the introduction of firearms, efforts have been made to develop breech-loading systems (see *chamber* and the sections on mechanisms in the historical and technical chapters), but significant breech-loading weapons have only been produced on an industrial scale since the nineteenth century, as a first step towards the development of modern weapons.

bullet puller: an instrument used in cleaning muzzle-loading weapons to remove bullets that got stuck in the barrel. It consisted of a steel screw tip fitted to a ramrod (q.v.), which was normally used for loading.

burst: a rapid sequence of shots from an automatic firearm.

butt: part of the stock of the gun, from the grip to the heel.

butt-plate: metal plate covering the heel.

caliber: diameter of the bore (q.v.) of the barrel, to which certain types of cartridge correspond. The caliber may be indicated in millimeters (e.g., 5.6 mm) or in thousandths of an inch (e.g., .220). In the case of weapons with rifled barrels, the caliber is measured between the lands (the parts of the bore not furrowed by rifling grooves). To distinguish between cartridges of the same caliber but with different characteristics, an "x" sign is used, followed by the length of the case. Further differences are expressed by letters or definitions (like R for rimmed). In shotguns, the caliber is expressed as the bore and corresponds to the number of balls of the correct caliber for the gun in question, which together would make up a pound of lead weight: e.g., "12 bore" means that 12 lead balls of that caliber weigh one pound.

carbine: a long weapon with a rifled barrel. It originated in the sixteenth century as a hunting weapon and was then used to arm elite mounted troops (who became known as carabineers). It was widely used as an infantry weapon too from the second half of the eighteenth century. When rifling became normal for all military firearms, some countries kept the word "carbine," e.g., Germany, where the abbreviation "*Kar*" stands for *Karabiner*, but is applied to weapons which other countries call rifles or muskets. In Austria, the long weapons of a few special units were called "carbines" regardless of whether they had long or short, smooth-bore or rifled barrels. In Italy, the term was used for a time to refer to the weapons of the Piedmontese *Bersaglieri*, while before Italy was unified a few or her states applied the name to some foreign imports, if they had been described as such by their country of origin. Nowadays, the word carbine is used (in Italy) for rifled hunting weapons, sporting guns and a few military weapons.

cartridge: nowadays, this comprises the primer, explosive charge and bullet, contained in a single case. The original cartridge was a strong paper container which was torn open at the moment of use. For further details, see text and entry under *primer*.

cartridge case: a paper, cardboard or metal tube containing the propelling charge and projectile. In breech-loading weapons, the case is the part of the cartridge containing the primer, charge and bullet. In modern weapons, the cartridge case is nearly always made of brass alloy. In shotguns, it is made of pressed cardboard or plastic, just the base being metal.

chamber: part of the breech where the charge (in old weapons) or the cartridge (in modern breech-loading weapons) is placed. In early breech-loading artillery pieces, it consisted of a hollow metal cylinder, or rather a type of pot with a handle, containing the charge and often the projectile as well, which was fitted into the breech of the weapon and secured by a wedge. The system was also used in the first breech-loading portable weapons, where the chamber consisted of a reusable cartridge case in the form of a metal tube containing the charge and projectile, which was also fitted into the breech by various systems of closure.

closing lugs: protrusions from the breech-block which, when the latter or part of it is turned, fit into corresponding slots in the breech, ensuring closure at the moment of firing.

cock: part of the mechanism of a firearm which, when actuated, fires the weapon. Restyled the *hammer*. Ignition is accomplished in wheel-lock weapons by friction against a piece of pyrites; in flintlock weapons by striking steel with a piece of flint; in percussion lock weapons by hitting a cap; and in modern weapons by striking the cartridge base with a firing pin. For further details, see sections on mechanisms. It was sometimes called a "dog" or "dog-head" in the early days, because of its shape with two jaws to hold the piece of pyrites or flint. On the continent, the name "dog" is used to this day, although with the introduction of the percussion system, its appearance changed considerably and it was renamed the hammer in English.

continuous action: revolvers (q.v.) are described as "continuous action" if pulling the trigger rotates the cylinder, cocks and activates the hammer; unlike "double action" revolvers (q.v.), this type cannot effect "single action" fire as an alternative.

cylinder: see **revolver**.

diopter: an aiming device normally fitted to the frame, with an adjustable aperture (see *leaf*) through which one collimates with the foresight (q.v.) to frame the target.

double action: apart from "single-action" firing (q.v.), a weapon with this type of mechanism can fire one round after another simply by pressing the trigger, without having to lift the hammer by hand. Firing under these conditions is obviously less accurate since the effort of pressing the trigger prevents one from taking careful aim, as is possible with single-action firing.

drilling: a triple-barrelled hunting gun, generally with two smooth-bore barrels at the top and a third, rifled barrel underneath.

dropping block: a vertically-sliding breech-block developed by the American Sharps. The trigger guard (q.v.) is moved forward, causing the breech-block to slide downwards along a special track; this opens the chamber, in which a fabric and paper cartridge is placed. When the trigger guard is returned to its original position, the breech-block rises back up and a blade attached to it cuts through the base of the cartridge, exposing the gunpowder inside it to the flash from the primer (q.v.). At a later date Sharps modified his patent to adapt it to metal cartridges with incorporated primers; further changes were introduced by the German Borchardt.

extractor: a device which takes hold of the base of the cartridge when the breech is opened, wholly or partially extracting the fired cartridge.

falling block: a type of breech-block (q.v.) which is mobile and hinged to the back of the breech of the weapon. Moving the trigger guard lowers the breech-block, enabling the cartridge to be introduced. Movement of the trigger guard also cocks the hammer and returns the breech-block to the original, closed position (but see notes on operation of Werder in the section on

mechanisms). Some authors apply the term "falling block" to all breech-blocks which are lowered to allow the cartridge to be inserted; others prefer to make a distinction between "falling block" and "tilting block" types, the latter name being reserved for breech-blocks which are hinged to the back of the barrel.

firing pin/striker: part, normally pointed, of the firing mechanism of breech-loading weapons. When the trigger is pulled, it strikes the base of the cartridge in the chamber, causing the primer to explode and thus igniting the propelling charge (which fires the shot).

flash hider: a truncated-conical tube fitted to the barrel of burst-fire weapons to hide the flash and make them harder to identify in combat.

flash shield: a shield to protect the firer from injury from a flare-up in the priming pan (q.v.).

fore-end: the part of the stock which supports the barrel.

foresight: a metal projection at the front of the barrel, used for aiming. The target should be at the end of the imaginary line connecting the foresight to the back sight notch (see *back sight*).

frame: metal container for repeater and trigger mechanisms (q.v.).

frizzen: the unit made up of the plate which is struck by the flint in a flintlock weapon and the pan cover (q.v.).

front-loading cylinder: in this method of loading, the propelling charge and projectile are inserted into each chamber (q.v.) of the revolving cylinder from the front. The chambers are closed at the back, apart from having a small hole communicating with the priming pan or nipple.

full cock: the position of the cock or hammer of a gun when it is ready for firing. See *cock* and *half cock*.

fulminate (powder or compound): a chemical compound which has the property of exploding with a powerful detonation when violently compressed between two hard surfaces. The properties of fulminates were exploited from the beginning of the nineteenth century in the production of percussion caps and primers (q.v.).

furniture: all the parts, usually of metal, which complete a weapon, such as the trigger guard (q.v.) and barrel bands (q.v.).

gas operation: a system employed in automatic weapons with high-power cartridges to use some of the gases from firing, which are generally channelled along a cylinder communicating with the barrel. These gases drive a piston which releases the breech-block, allowing it to move back, with the result that the cartridge case is expelled and a new cartridge is chambered.

grip: the part of the weapon held in the fist. In pistols it serves both to hold the weapon and to enable it to be used; in ordinary guns*, assault rifles and submachine guns, it serves to improve stability and accuracy of fire. (*In ordinary

long guns it is called the *hand*).

gunpowder: this is the name given to the chemical compound, the explosion of which fires the projectile. The first type was black powder, or a mixture of sulfur, charcoal and saltpeter. It remained in use until the end of the nineteenth century, when it was largely superseded by powders based on nitro-cellullose and described as "smokeless" because they did not generate the great clouds of smoke produced by black powder.

half cock: intermediate position of the cock, which serves to block it to enable the weapon to be loaded without any risk of accidentally firing the gun. See also *full cock*.

heel: the end of the butt, covered by the heel-plate.

holster: a leather holder for carrying pistols on foot or horseback and even guns (on horseback) in the old days. It is shaped to allow the weapon to be rapidly removed.

leaf: a metal strip, which is part of the rear sight (q.v.), with back sight notches (q.v.) which are fixed or adjustable according to the different distances of the targets.

lock: a mechanism for igniting the propelling charge of a firearm. See text for different types of lock; in this glossary, cf. *steel*, *pan cover*, *frizzen*, *nipple* and *wheel*.

lock plate: metal support which held the parts of the firing mechanism of an old firearm together. Nowadays it is only used for drop-barrel hunting weapons.

magazine: a metal container, usually in the form of a prismatic box, which holds the cartridges of repeating weapons. The magazine is fitted into a housing in the gun, from which it can be easily removed. Magazines are classified as single-column or double-column, depending on how the cartridges are arranged.

musket: this was originally a big match-lock arquebus for military use, common in the sixteenth and above all the seventeenth century, which needed a forked rest (see *musket rest*) or natural support for firing. Typically for a period in which artillery pieces were named after snakes or birds, the term musket is derived from the Italian *moschetto* or *muscetto*, meaning sparrow hawk. With the spread of flintlock weapons in the armies of the eighteenth century, many countries kept the name musket to refer to long, smooth-bore, individual infantry weapons. In Italy, for historical reasons, the term musket has been applied to cavalry carbines and weapons for special troops.

musket rest: a wooden shaft with a forked piece of iron or bronze at one end and iron tip at the other. It served as a rest for the arquebus and particularly the heavy musket in the sixteenth and seventeenth centuries.

muzzle: the technical term for the mouth of the barrel.

muzzle-loading: a system of loading through the mouth or muzzle of the gun (see *barrel*).

needle/pin: firearms with this system have a long point (the firing pin) which pierces through the paper cartridge until it strikes the primer (fulminate) inside it. See text for cartridges and needle guns; cf. entries under *fulminate* and *primer*.

nipple: a hollow support, screwed to the breech of a percussion lock weapon, on which the percussion cap was placed. When the hammer struck the cap, this caused a flare-up and the flash from this passed through the hole in the nipple, igniting the propelling charge inside the breech.

pan cover: a lid used in matchlock, wheel-lock and flintlock weapons, to stop the priming powder from falling out of the pan or being soaked by rain. It was shifted at the moment of firing. For further details see text.

patch puller: a tool whose purpose was somewhat similar to that of the bullet puller, and which served to remove the rags used to clean the weapon or wadding left in the barrel. It consisted of two spiral steel pincers, ready fitted or for fitting to a ramrod.

percussion cap: a squat cylinder of copper or brass, closed at one end, the inside of which was coated with a compound of fulminate (primer) and which was used in percussion lock weapons. It was placed over the nipple (q.v.) and as the hammer struck this, it crushed the cap, causing the primer to explode; the flash from this passed through the hole in the nipple, igniting the gunpowder charge.

pin: a small copper rod, the principal component of pin-fire cartridges, used from the mid nineteenth century, until gunpowder became obsolete. In pin-fire weapons, the hammer strikes this copper bar perpendicularly. One end of the bar projects from the breech while the other is inserted in the cartridge case in contact with a cap of primer at the base of the cartridge. The blow from the hammer pushes the bar against the cap, causing it and the propelling charge inside the cartridge to explode.

powder flask: a receptacle made of horn, wood, boiled leather or metal and used to hold gunpowder; it went out of use with the establishment of cartridges. Many powder flasks were beautifully decorated. Smaller versions were used to hold priming powder, which was finer than normal gunpowder.

primer: a substance or device which serves to ignite a propelling charge or explosive. Until the percussion method was employed, the primer consisted of gunpowder which was placed in a priming pan and ignited by various systems (slow match, wheel, flint; see text). After the introduction of fulminates

(q.v.), the primer was first contained in a cap or explosive tube and then, with the establishment of the modern cartridge, distributed around the base of the latter.

priming pan: a concave piece of metal, originally let into the barrel at the breech, then part of the lock mechanism; it held the priming powder in matchlock, wheel-lock and flintlock weapons.

propelling charge: the gunpowder charge placed behind the projectile. It is ignited by means of a primer (q.v.), causing the projectile to shoot out of the barrel (see *cartridge*).

ramrod: a wooden or steel rod used to push the projectile down the barrel of muzzle-loading weapons and to clean the barrel.

recoil: violent backward movement of a firearm, caused by the impact on the back of the chamber of the gases released by ignition of the propelling charge. The recoil can be partly attenuated by the shape of the weapon.

repeater system: a system of loading which allows several shots to be fired in sequence, without having to reload the weapon for each shot. For origins, see text. There are three types of repeating guns: manual or ordinary repeaters (where a lever has to be operated or the breech-block shifted manually after each round to expel the spent cartridge case and feed a new cartridge into the chamber); automatic repeaters (see *semi-automatic weapon*); and burst-fire repeaters (see *automatic weapon*).

revolver: a pistol with a cylinder subdivided into several chambers, each of which contains a cartridge. It is thus possible to fire several rounds in sequence before reloading the weapon. In some revolvers, the cylinder (q.v.) is front-loading; in others, it is breech-loading. Pin-fire (see *pin*), center-fire or rim-fire cartridges may be used. Single-action, continuous-action and double-action (q.v.) revolvers are found. In revolvers prior to the nineteenth century, the cylinder was normally rotated by hand.

rifling: roughly helical grooves cut into the inside of the barrel of a firearm to increase the accuracy of fire. For the origins of rifling, see text.

rolling block: a breech-loading system invented at the Remington factory in 1864. For operation, see text and section on mechanisms of repeating weapons.

safety catch: a device found on even the oldest weapons, to prevent accidental firing by blocking the cock or, in more recent times, the firing pin.

sear: the part of the mechanism in old weapons which released the cock or hammer from the stationary position, causing it to shoot down towards the pan or percussion cap.

semi-automatic weapon: a firearm in which pressure on the trigger causes the cartridge case to be expelled after firing

prior to insertion of a new cartridge in the barrel and cocking of the hammer or firing pin. Unlike automatic weapons, the trigger has to be pulled for every single shot.

short recoil: in most weapons with this type of mechanism, the barrel and breech-block recoil together for a few millimeters when the shot is fired, allowing the bullet to leave the barrel and the pressure of the gases to fall; then the barrel stops and the breech-block continues to recoil, compressing a spring known as the return spring; as this spring relaxes, it carries the breech-block forward, and as a result a new cartridge is fed into the chamber.

side-plate: a metal plate fitted to the stock (q.v.) opposite the lock plate (q.v.), to help support the latter.

sight: see *diopter*.

silencer: a tube which fits on to the end of the barrel, the interior of which is shaped so that the gases released by firing swirl around inside it, with the result that they decompress more gradually and the noise is reduced.

single action: revolvers are described as "single action" if the hammer has to be cocked by hand before firing (with the thumb or by passing the palm of the other hand over it). Cocking the hammer also causes the cylinder to rotate. Pulling the trigger causes the hammer to fall and fires the shot. The action must be repeated for every single shot.

sling swivel: ring to which the sling of a portable firearm larger than a pistol (rifle, assault rifle, sub-machine gun, etc.) is attached.

slow-match: a piece of cord treated in various ways beforehand (boiling in a saturated solution of saltpeter, or even just salt water) and used to ignite gunpowder in matchlock weapons, artillery and mines.

snuff-box closure: a system employed, among others, by J. Snider and used to convert muzzle-loading weapons to breech-loading. Snuffbox breech-loading systems are also found in weapons prior to the nineteenth century. The main part of the Snider system consisted of a cylindrical breech-block, hinged on the right-hand side of the weapon, behind the chamber. The breech-block was moved sideways with the thumb of the right hand; a metal cartridge was inserted in the chamber and the breech-block was then returned to the closed position.

Stecher: a German name for the set trigger, a double trigger device; the first trigger serves as a safety catch for the second during aiming; the second releases the hammer or firing pin on very slight pressure.

steel: a metal plate, often combined with the pan cover (q.v.) which, in flintlock weapons, is struck by the flint held between the jaws of the cock at the moment of firing. See also *frizzen*.

steel rod: a type of muzzle-loading system (see text).

stock: part of the firearm which holds the mechanisms and barrel together and enables the weapon to be handled and used. See *fore-end, grip* and *butt*.

stopping-power: the capacity of a projectile to neutralize the enemy by the force of its impact. The stopping-power is proportional to the weight and velocity of the projectile.

straight-pull bolt-action breech-block: a type of cylindrical breech-block, operated by a handle, which is slid forward for closure and blocked, in most cases because the front end (the head) can be turned sideways and has lugs which slot into special recesses in the breech (e.g., the Mannlicher Model 1895).

tilting block: see *falling block*.

touch-hole: a hole made in the side or back of the breech of old weapons, through which the flame from the primer (q.v.) could set light to the propelling charge.

trap-door: a type of breech-block used to convert muzzle-loading weapons to breech-loading. This type of breech-block is overturned along the axis of the barrel, to which it is hinged, to enable the cartridge to be introduced (for details, see section on mechanisms).

trigger guard: a strip, usually made of metal, to shield the trigger of a firearm from knocks. In various breech-loading (q.v.) and repeating (q.v.) mechanisms, the trigger guard is designed to be used during the loading process as well.

tumbler: an internal part of the firing mechanism, connected or fixed to the cock, which can assume various positions depending on the movement of other mechanical parts which act on the two or three notches with which it is provided. Depending on the position of the tumbler, the cock is prepared for firing (cocked), actuated or held in a safe position.

turn-bolt bolt-action breech-block: a type of cylindrical breech-block, operated by a handle, which is closed by sliding it forwards and blocked by turning it partly to the right, so that: (a) in the oldest weapons, the base of the handle slots into a recess in the breech (e.g., the Dreyse Model 1862); (b) lugs engage in special notches in the breech to hold or close it (e.g., the Mauser Model 1898).

turning block: a type of breech-block invented at the Remington factory in 1864. For operation, see section on mechanisms.

wheel: the principal component of a mechanism widely used between the sixteenth and eighteenth century, in which a knurled steel wheel struck sparks from a piece of pyrites to ignite the priming powder and, through this, the propelling charge. For further details, see section on mechanisms.

wheel spanner: an iron spanner, normally with a T-shaped head. At both ends of the head was a square hole which fitted on to the wheel-axle of wheel-lock weapons. The tool was used to wind up the wheel until it was blocked by a sear (q.v.).

Index by country

AUSTRIA

Carbine, cavalry, Mannlicher mod. 1890 190, *190*
Carbine, Hussars' mod. 1798 117, *117*
Carbine, Mannlicher mod. 1895 with experimental bayonet 191, *191*
Carbine, Werndl mod. 1867 164, *164*
Musket, light infantry mod. 1769 116, *116*
Musket, light infantry mod. 1796 116, *116*
Musket, light infantry mod. 1842 161, *161*
Musket, light infantry mod. 1854 162, *162*
Musket, light infantry Wänzel mod. 1867 165, *165*
Musket, Mannlicher mod. 1895 191, *191*
Musket with superimposed barrels mod. 1768 115, *115*
Pistol, automatic Mannlicher mod. 1905 193, *193*
Pistol, automatic Roth-Steyr mod. 1907 193, *193*
Pistol, automatic Steyr mod 1912 194, *194*
Pistol, cavalry mod. 1844 165, *165*
Pistol, cavalry mod. 1859 166, *166*
Revolver, Gasser mod. 1870 191, *191*
Revolver, Rast-Gasser mod. 1898 192, *192*
Rifle, automatic Steyr Aug A1 250, *250*
Rifle, compressed-air repeating mod. 1780 114, *114*
Rifle, infantry Lorenz mod. 1854 162, *162*
Rifle, infantry Wänzel mod. 1867 163, *163*
Rifle infantry and light infantry mod. 1873 165, *165*
Rifle, infantry and light infantry Werndl mod. 1867 164, *164*
Rifle, Lindner experimental 163, *163*
Rifle, Mannlicher mod. 1888 190, *190*
Rifle, Mannlicher mod. 1895 190, *190*
Rifle with chambered breech mod. 1842 161, *161*
Sub-machine gun, Steyr MPi81 256, *256*

BADEN

Carbine, cavalry, converted to percussion lock 132, *132*
Pistol, cavalry, converted to percussion lock 133, *133*

BAVARIA

Musket, Podewils mod. 1842/58 136, *136*
Rifle, infantry Werder mod. 1869 136, *136*

BELGIUM

Carbine, Mauser mod. 1889 213, *213*
Musket, Comblain mod. 1871 168, *168*
Pistol, automatic Bergmann-Bayard 214, *214*
Pistol, automatic Browning GP 35 272, *272*
Pistol, automatic Browning high-power (1935) 214, *214*
Rifle, light automatic FN FAL 247, *247*

BRITAIN

Carbine, Whitworth c. 1860 152, *152*
Musket, large lock mod. 1838 151, *151*
Musket, mod. 1839 151, *151*
Musket of the East India Company 121, *121*
Pistol, automatic Webley & Scott mod. 1904 209 *209*
Pistol automatic Webley MK I 209, *209*
Revolver, Adams Double-Action 206, *206*

Revolver, Colt 206, *206*
Revolver, Colt London Navy 1851 205, *205*
Revolver, Sterling .357 Magnum 268, *268*
Revolver, Webley no. 1 Mark VI 206, *206*
Rifle, Baker adopted in 1823 121, *121*
Rifle, Enfield mod. 1853 152, *152*
Rifle, Lee Enfield no. 1 Mark III 204, *204*
Rifle, Lee Enfield no. 4 Mark I 205, *205*
Rifle, Lee Enfield no. 5 205, *205*
Rifle, Lee Enfield XL70E3 automatic 247, *247*
Rifle, Lee Metford Mark II* 204, *204*
Rifle, semi-automatic L1A1 247, *247*
Rifle, Snider mod. 1853/66 153, *153*
Royal Ordnance Enfield Individual Weapon 242
Sub-machine gun, Lanchester Mark 1 207, *207*
Sub-machine gun, Sten MK II 207, *207*
Sub-machine gun, Sten MK IV mod. A 208, *208*
Sub-machine gun, Sten MK IV mod. B 208, *208*
Sub-machine gun, Sten MK VI(S) 208, *208*
Sub-machine gun, Sterling L2A3 242
Sub-machine gun, Sterling MK 4 256, *256*

CANADA

Ross Mark III Rifle 203, *203*

CZECHOSLOVAKIA

Pistol, automatic C2 mod. 1924 233, *233*
Pistol, automatic C2 M 38 233, *233*
Pistol, automatic M 52 273, *273*
Rifle, Mauser mod. 1924 233, *233*
Sub-machine gun, M 61 Skorpion 257, *257*

DENMARK

Carbine mod. 1829 122, *122*
Pistol, cavalry, first half of the nineteenth century 123, *123*

FRANCE

Carbine, light infantry mod. 1867 *à tabatière* 158, *158*
Carbine, mod. Anno XII (1803–04) Versailles Infantry 119, *119*
Carbine, mod. 1837 Tirailleur 154, *154*
Carbine, mod. 1846 154, *154*
Double-barrelled gun mod. 1850 159, *159*
Infantry weapon mod. 1822 119, *119*
Infantry weapon mod. 1853 155, *155*
Musket, artillery mod. 1829 119, *119*
Musket, artillery mod. 1829T 159, *159*
Musket, Chassepot mod. 1866 157, *157*
Musket, Mannlicher-Berther mod. 1892 211, *211*
Musket, Mannlicher-Berthier mod. 1892 M 1916 211, *211*
Musket mod. 1777, restyled Model Anno IX (1800–01) 118, *118*
Pistol, automatic PA 15 MAB 262, *262*
Pistol, cavalry mod. 1777 120, *120*
Pistol, cavalry mod. 1822 T 159, *159*
Pistol, cavalry mod. Anno XIII (1804–05) 120, *120*
Pisto, cavalry and Dragoon mod. 1763–66 120, *120*
Pistol, naval mod. 1849 160, *160*
Pistol, officer's mod. 1822 T 160, *160*
Pistol, staff officer's mod. 1855 160, *160*
Revolver, Lebel mod. 1892 212, *212*

Revolver, Lefaucheux Commercial mod. 212, *212*
Revolver, Manurhim MR73 262, *262*
Revolver mod. 1873 212, *212*
Rifle, automatic MAS 242, 248, *248*
Rifle, Chassepot mod. 1866 156, *156*
Rifle, Grenadier mod. 1822 119, *119*
Rifle, infantry Gras mod. 1874 158, *158*
Rifle, infantry mod. 1840 155, *155*
Rifle, infantry mod. 1867 *à tabatière* 157, *157*
Rifle, Lebel mod. 1866 M 93 210, *210*
Rifle, Mannlicher-Berthier mod. 1907/15 211, *211*
Rifle, M.A.S. mod. 1936 211, *211*
Rifle, naval Kropatschek mod. 1878 210, *210*
Rifle, semi-automatic RSC mod. 1918 213, *213*
Rifle, Voltigeur mod. 1853 156, *156*

GERMANY

Carbine, Mauser mod. 1871 138, *138*
Carbine, mod. 1888 181, *181*
Carbine, mod. 1898 182, *182*
Carbine, mod. 1898 A 182, *182*
Carbine, mod. 1898 K 182, *182*
Pistol, automatic Bergmann no. 3 187, *187*
Pistol, automatic Heckler & Koch P7 261, *261*
Pistol, automtic Mauser 1896/12 187, *187*
Pistol, automatic Mauser mod. HSc 261, *261*
Pistol, automatic mod. 1908 (P 08) 188, *188*
Pistol, automatic Saver M 38 189, *189*
Pistol, automatic Walther mod. 1938 (P 38) 188, *188*
Pistol, automatic Walther mod. P 5 260, *260*
Pistol, automatic Walther mod. P 38 259, *259*
Pistol, automatic Walther mod. PP 260, *260*
Pistol, automatic Walther mod. PPK 260, *260*
Pistol, automatic Walther PPK 189, *189*
Pistol, semi-automatic Heckler & Koch VP 70Z 261, *261*
Revolver, Mauser mod. 1878 183, *183*
Rifle, Mauser mod. 1871 137, *137*
Rifle, Mauser mod. 1871/84 180, *180*
Rifle, Mauser mod. 1898 181, *181*
Rifle, Mod. 1888 180, *180*
Rifle, assault mod. 1944 *Sturmgewehr* 44 185, *185*
Rifle, automatic Heckler & Koch G3A3 250, *250*
Rifle, automatic Heckler & Koch G11 253, *253*
Rifle, paratroop mod. 1842 184, *184*
Rifle, semi-automatic mod. 41 183, *183*
Rifle, semi-automatic mod. 43 186, *186*
Sub-machine gun, Heckler & Koch MP 5 255, *255*
Sub-machine gun, mod. 1940 186, *186*
Sub-machine gun, mod. 1941 (MP 41) 186, *186*
Sub-machine gun, Walther MP-K 255, *255*

GREECE

Musket, Mannlicher Schoenauer mod. 1903/14 227, *227*
Rifle, Mannlicher Schoenauer mod. 1903/14 226, *226*

HANOVER

Pistol with shoulder stock 108, *108*

HOLLAND

Mannlicher Model 1895 Musket 234, *234*

ISRAEL

Galil Assault Rifle 252, *252*
UZ1 sub-machine gun *243*, 256, *256*

ITALY

Carbine, Albini mod. 1868 for the Italian Royal Navy 145, *145*
Carbine, automatic Beretta mod. SC 70 249, *249*
Carbine, light infantry (Bersaglieri) mod. 1856 144, *144*
Musket, Mannlicher-Carcano mod. 91/385 TS 219, *219*
Musket, Mannlicher-Carcano mod. 1891 TS* 219, *219*
Musket, mod. 1891 for the Royal Carabineers of the King's Guard 218, *218*
Musket mounted R RCC (Royal Carabineer) converted to breech-loading using the Carcano system 146, *146*
Musket TS mod. 1870/87/16 217, *217*
Musket, Vetterli mod. 1870 Royal Carabineer 146, *146*
Musket, automatic Beretta mod. 38 A 221, *221*
Musket, cavalry Mannlicher-Carcano mod. 1891 218, *218*
Pistol, automatic Beretta mod. 70 271, *271*
Pistol, automatic Beretta mod. 93 R 270, *270*
Pistol, automatic Beretta mod. 1934 222, *222*
Pistol, automatic mod. 1910 222, *222*
Pistol, revolving Chamelot-Delvigne mod. 1874 220, *220*
Pistol, semi-automatic Beretta 92 F 271, *271*
Rifle, Carcano adopted in 1867 144, *144*
Rifle, Doersch-Baumgarten 143, *143*
Rifle, Mannlicher-Carcano mod. 1891 217, *217*
Rifle, Mannlicher-Carcano mod. 1891/41 219, *219*
Rifle, Terssen 143, *143*
Rifle, Vetterli-Vitali mod. 1870/87 217, *217*
Rifle, automatic Beretta mod. AR 70 249, *249*
Rifle, infantry French-style of 1812 109, *109*
Rifle, infantry Vetterli mod. 1870 (first type) 145, *145*
Rifle, infantry Vetterli mod. 1870 146, *146*
Rifle, semi-automatic Armaguerra mod. 39 221, *221*
sub-machine gun, Beretta mod. 38/44 221, *221*
Sub-machine gun, Beretta PM 125 257, *257*
Sub-machine gun, F.N.A.-B. mod. 43 222, *222*
Sub-machine gun, Villar Perosa mod. 1915 220, *220*

JAPAN

Pistol, automatic Nambu Type Taisho 14 (1925) 235, *235*
Pistol, automatic Type 94 235, *235*
Rifle, Arisaka Type 38, Meiji Era (1905) 235, *235*
Rifle, Murata Type 13, Meiji Era (1880) 235, *235*

PAPAL STATES

Carbine, Gendarmerie, Remington mod. 1868 141, *141*
Musket, Artillery, Remington mod. 1868 141, *141*
Rifle, infantry, Remington mod. 1868 141, *141*

POLAND

Pistol, automatic, Radom mod. 1935 232, *232*
Rifle, Mauser mod. 1929 232, *232*

PORTUGAL

Rifle, Mauser-Vergueiro mod. 1904 226, *226*

PRUSSIA

Carbine, cavalry Dreyse mod. 1857 135, *135*
Carbine, cavalry mod. 1811 107, *107*
Dreyse gun for "Fusilier-Regimenter" mod. 1860 133, *133*
Musket, light infantry mod. 1810 107, *107*
Pistol, cavalry mod. 1823 107, *107*
Pistol, internal-percussion, muzzle-loading needle, Dreyse system 135, *135*
Rifle, infantry mod. 1809 106, *106*
Rifle, infantry mod. 1809 converted to percussion lock 133, *133*
Rifle, infantry Dreyse mod. 1862 134, *134*
Rifle, light infantry Dreyse mod. 1865 135, *135*

ROMANIA

Musket, Mannlicher mod. 1893 234, *234*

RUSSIA/SOVIET UNION

Carbine, Cossack 169, *169*
Musket, cavalry of 1851 169, *169*
Musket, Cossack, of 1851 123, *123*
Musket, Mosin Nagant 1938 229, *229*
Musket, Winchester Military mod. 1895 228, *228*

Pistol, automatic TT mod. 1933 231, *231*
Pistol, cavalry of 1854 170, *170*
Pistol, Cossack Officer's of 1850 170, *170*
Revolver, Nagant mod. 1895 229, *229*
Rifle AK 47 *241*
Rifle AK 74S *241*
Rifle AKMS *241*
Rifle, Berdan II mod. 1871 169, *169*
Rifle, Berdan II mod. 1871 Cossack 170, *170*
Rifle, Cossack, of 1852, 169, *169*
Rifle, Mosin Nagant Dragoon mod. 1891 227, *227*
Rifle, Mosin Nagant mod. 1891/30 228, *228*
Rifle, semi-automatic Tokarev mod. 1938 230, *230*
Rifle, semi-automatic Tokarev mod. 1940 230, *230*
Snayperskaya Vintovka Dragunova (SVD) 249, *249*
Sub-machine gun PPSh M.1941 231, *231*

SARDINIA, Kingdom of

Blunderbuss with iron barrel 111, *111*
Carbine, infantry mod. 1860 140, *140*
Carbine, light infantry (Bersaglieri), mod. 1848 139, *139*
Carbine, light infantry (Bersaglieri) mod. 1856 139, *139*
Carbine, light infantry (Bersaglieri), La Marmora system 138, *138*
Carbine, light infantry (Bersaglieri) Thouvenin-rod 139, *139*
Musket, cavalry, mod. 1833 111, *111*
Musket of His Majesty's Guards mod. 1814 110, *110*
Musket of Royal Carabineers, mod. 1814 109, *109*
Pistol, cavalry, mod. 1814 112, *112*
Pistol, cavalry officer's adopted in 1848 140, *140*
Pistol of the Regia Marinaria, mod. 1814 111, *111*
Pistol of the Sardinian Royal Navy 140, *140*
Pistol-carbine 112, *112*
Rifle, infantry mod. 1814 109, *109*

SCHAUMBURG-LIPPE

Carbine, cavalry D & B mod. 1861 137, *137*

SPAIN

Carbine, light infantry mod. 1857/59 168, *168*
Pistol, automatic Astra mod. 400–1921, 224, *224*
Pistol, automatic Astra mod. 600 225, *225*
Pistol, automatic Astra mod. 902 225, *225*
Pistol, automatic Astra mod. 1921 224, *224*
Pistol, automatic Campogiro mod. 1913 223, *223*

Pistol, semi-automatic Astra A-80 273, *273*
Rifle, assault, CETME mod. L 252, *252*
Rifle, assault, CETME mod. LC 252, *252*
Rifle, short, Mauser mod. 1893 223, *223*
Sub-machine gun, Star mod. 2-62 258, *258*

SWEDEN

Sub-machine gun Carl-Gustaf 258, *258*

SWITZERLAND

Carbine, Federal mod. 1851 167, *167*
Carbine, Vetterli mod. 1872 216, *216*
Musket, Vetterli mod. 1871 215, *215*
Pistol, automatic SIG-SAUER P220 mod. 75 269, *269*
Pistol, automatic SIG-SAUER P225 268, *268*
Pistol, automatic SIG-SAUER P226 269, *269*
Pistol, automatic SIG-SAUER P230 268, *268*
Revolver, standard mod. 1882 (Schmidt system) 216, *216*
Rifle, assault, SG550 251, *251*
Rifle, assault, SG551 251, *251*
Rifle, infantry, Millbank-Amsler mod. 1859/67 167, *167*
Rifle, infantry mod. 1842 166, *166*
Rifle, Vetterli mod. 1869 215, *215*

TURKEY

Carbine, Mauser mod. 1871/84 232, *232*
Rifle, Mauser mod. 1871/84 231, *231*
Rifle, Peabody and Martini 171, *171*
TWO SICILIES, Kingdom of the Carbine for light infantry battalions with 32 in barrel (of 1849) 142, *142*
Musket, cavalry, French model 113, *113*
Musket for light infantry battalions with 28 in barrel (of 1860) 142, *142*
Rifle, French model 112, *112*
Rifle, mounted light infantry with 38 in barrel 142, *142*
Rifle, semi-breech-loading of 1831 113, *113*

UNITED STATES OF AMERICA

Carbine, M1 201, *201*
Carbine, M1 A1 202, *202*
Carbine, Sharps New mod. 1863 148, *148*
Carbine, Winchester mod. 1866 196, *196*
Carbine, Winchester mod. 1873 197, *197*
Carbine, cavalry Peabody 147, *147*
Carbine, cavalry Spencer mod. 1860 195, *195*
Pistol, M 1911 203, *203*
Pistol, automatic Colt Combat Lightweight 263, *263*

Pistol, Automatic Ruger Standard mod. Mark II 267, *267*
Pistol, automatic Smith & Wesson mod. 459 264, *264*
Revolver, Colt Army mod. 1860 199, *199*
Revolver, Colt Detective Special 263, *263*
Revolver, Colt Python 263, *263*
Revolver, Remington New mod. 1858 198, *198*
Revolver, Ruger New mod. Blackhawk 265, *265*
Revolver, Ruger New mod. Super Single-Six Six-shot 267, *267*
Revolver, Ruger "Old Army Cap and Ball" 266, *266*
Revolver, Ruger Redhawk 266, *266*
Revolver, Smith & Wesson mod. 29 264, *264*
Revolver, Smith & Wesson mod. 586 Distinguished Combat Magnum 264, *264*
Revolver, Smith & Wesson mod. 1869 200, *200*
Rifle, Enfield mod. 1917 198, *198*
Rifle, Garand M1 201, *201*
Rifle, Hall 147, *147*
Rifle, Springfield M 1903 197, *197*
Rifle, Springfield mod. 1903 197, *197*
Rifle, Springfield mod. 1903 A3 198, *198*
Rifle, automatic Armalite AR-15 (M16) *244*, 245, *245*
Rifle, automatic Ruger K AC-556F Selective Fire 246, *246*
Rifle, infantry Allin mod. 1866 149, *149*
Rifle, infantry mod. 1863 148, *148*
Rifle, naval Remington adopted in 1867, 150, *150*
Rifle, semi-automatic M21 245, *245*
Rifle, semi-automatic Mini-14/5R 246, *246*
Rifle, semi-automatic Ruger Mini-Thirty 246, *246*
Sub-machine gun, Ingram mod. 10 and 11 254, *254*
Sub-machine gun, M3 Grease Gun 202, *202*
Sub-machine gun, Thompson mod. 1928 A1 202, *202*
Sub-machine gun, Viking 254, *254*

VENICE, Republic of

Rifle of the Militia of the Venetian Republic 108, *108*

WÜRTTEMBERG

Carbine, cavalry 1829 105, *105*
Pistol, cavalry 1827 106, *106*
Rifle, infantry 105, *105*
Rifle, infantry converted to percussion lock 132, *132*

WÜRZBURG, Principality of

Carbine, Jäger-type 104, *104*

General index

A

Adams, John 206
Adams, Robert 70, 206
Adams, double action revolver 70, 206, *206*
AK (Avtomat Kalashnikova; Kalashnikov)
— 47, *241*, 248, *248*
— 74, *241*, 248, *248*
— 74S, *241*
AKMS *241*
Albini, carbine for the Italian Royal Family mod. 1868 145, *145*
Allin, E.S. 129, 149
—infantry rifle mod. 1866 149, *149*
Altenstetter, David 46
AR-15 (Armalite) *244*, 245, *245*
Argent, Monsieur d' 55
Ariosto, Ludovico 16
Arisaka, rifle type 38 (1905) 235, *235*
Armaguerra, semi-automtic rifle mod. 39 221, *221*
Armalite, automatic rifle AR-15 (M-16) *244*, 245, *245*
Armistead, Brigadier General 76
arquebus
— with Baltic lock *40*
— with Farnese wheel-lock *29*
— flintlock *40*, 42
— with internal wheel *32*
— Japanese matchlock *49*
— matchlock *15*, *16*, *25*, 44, 48–9, 50
— rifled wheel-lock *23*
— scavezzo *51*, *53*
— wheel-lock *18*, 24, *25*, *28*, 35, 38, 44, 51, 56
— wheel-lock, double-firing *33*
— wheel-lock with two cocks *30*
Astra
— automatic pistol mod. 400 224, *224*, 225
— automatic pistol mod. 600 225, *225*
— automatic pistol mod. 900 225
— automatic pistol mod. 902 225, *225*
— automatic pistol mod. 903 225
— automatic pistol mod. 1921 224, *224*
— automatic pistol Model F 225
— pistola 600/43 225
— semi-automatic pistol A-80 273, *273*
Astra-Unceta y Compania, S.A. 225
AUG A1 (Steyr) 250, *250*
Augustin, Vinzenz von 161
— percussion lock 126, *126*, 161, 162, 165
Auteroches, Comte d' 54
Avtomat Kalashnikova (AK)
— AK47 *241*, 248, *248*
— 74 *241*, 248, *248*
— 74S *241*

B

Bacon, Roger 9
Baker, rifle (1873) 62, 121, *121*
Barne, Harman 48
Baumgarten, Cramer von 137
Bayerisch Blitz (Bavarian Lightning) 128, *128*, 136, *136*
Beaumont, system *82*
Becker, Elias 46
Berdan, Hiram 169
— cartridge, rifle of 1866 *82*
— rifle *82*
— system *82*, 84
— II, rifle mod. 1871 169, *169*
— II, Cossack rifle mod. 1871 170, *170*
Beretta 47
— automatic carbine for special troops mod. SC 70 249, *249*
— automatic musket mod. 38 A (MAB 38 A) *90*, 221, *221*
— automatic pistol Model 70 271, *271*
— automatic pistol mod. 93 R 270, *270*
— automatic pistol mod. 1934 179, *179*, 222, *222*
— automatic rifle mod. AR 70 249, *249*
— PM 12S sub-machine gun 257, *257*
— semi-automatic pistol 92F 271, *271*
— sub-machine gun mod. 38/44 221, *221*
Bergier, Pierre 44
Bergmann, Theodor 84, 187
— automatic pistol no. 3 187, *187*
Bergmann-Bayard automatic pistol 214, *214*
Bernadelli 79
Berthier 211
Bisley (Colt) *70*
Black Berthold 9
Blackmore 42
blunderbuss *51*, 57
— with iron barrel (Kingdom of Sardinia) 111, *111*
Boccaccio 38–9
Bogardus, Adam 92
Bonomino, Domenico *51*
Borchardt 84
Borstorfer, Hieronymus 46
Boxer, E.M. *82*, 169
— cartridge *82*
Brown Bess 55, 61, 121, *121*
Browning, John Moses 84, 203, 214, 228
— 'Baby Browning' pistol 237, *237*
— GP 35 automatic pistol 272, *272*
— high-power automatic pistol, or Pistole 640 (b) 214, *214*
Buffalo Bill 92
Burton, James Henry 72, 73

C

Campogiro, Count of (Venancio Lopez de Caballos y Aguirre) 223
Campogiro
— automatic pistol mod. 1913 223, *223*, 224
— pistol mod. 1913/16 223
cannon, breech-loading *10*
Carbine, Bersaglieri
— La Marmora system (Kingdom of Sardinia) 138, *138*
— mod. 1848 (Kingdom of Sardinia) 139, *139*
— mod. 1856 (Kingdom of Sardinia) 139, *139*
— mod. 1856 converted to breech-loading using the Carcano system 144, *144*
— Thouvenin-rod light infantry (Kingdom of Sardinia) 139, *139*
Carbine, Cavalry
— 1811 (Prussia) 107, *107*
— 1829 (Württemberg) 105, *105*
— converted to percussion lock (Baden) 132, *132*
carbine, Cossack, (Russia) 169, *169*
carbine, Crespi system 147
carbine, Federal mod. 1851 (Switzerland) 167, *167*
carbine, hussars' mod. 1798 (Austria) 117, *117*
carbine, *Jager*-type (Würzburg) 104, *104*
carbine, Light Infantry
— mod. 1857/59 (Spain) 168, *168*
— mod. 1867 *à tabatière* (France) 158, *158*
carbine, light infantry battalions with 32 in barrel (Kingdom of the Two Sicilies) 142, *142*
carbine M1 (United States) 201, *201*
carbine M1 A1 (United States) 202, *202*
carbine mod.
— 1793 119
— 1829 (Denmark) 122, *122*
— 1846 (France) 154, *154*
— 1846 T (France) 154
— 1853 T (France) 154
— 1888 (Germany) 181, *181*
— 1898 (Germany) 182, *182*
— 1898 A (Germany) 182, *182*
— 1898 K (Germany) 182, *182*
carbine, percussion-lock hunting (Würzburg) 62
carbine, Taifun model free (USSR) 92
Carbine, Tirailleur mod. 1837 154, *154*
carbine, "Versailles" infantry mod. Anno XII (France) 119, *119*
carbine, wheel-lock *23*, 45
Carcano, Salvatore 144, 217
— rifle adopted in 1867 144, *144*
— system 144
Caron 69
Carver, Doc 92
Catlin, George 78
Česká Zbrojovka (C2)
— automatic pistol M38 233, *233*
— automatic pistol mod. 1924 233, *233*
CETME Model L Assault Rifle, 252, *252*
CETME Model LC Assault Rifle 252, *252*
Chaineux, J. 237
Chamelot Delvigne
— revolving pistol mod. 1874 220, *220*
— system 212
Charles I, King of England 48
Charles II, King of England 48
Charles V, Emperor *14*, 18, 26
Chassepot, Antoine-Alphonse 156
— cartridge *82*
— musket mod. 1866 157, *157*
— rifle 73, 84, 144
— rifle mod. 1866 156, *156*
Cicero, 38
Colonna, Prospero 49
Colt
— automatic pistol Combat Lightweight 263, *263*
— M 1911 84, 86, 203, *203*
— M 1911 A1 *85*, 86
— revolver 69, 73, 198, 206, *206*
— revolver Bisley *70*
— revolver Detective Special 263, *263*
— revolver double action 69
— revolver English Dragoon Pistol *70*
— revolver London Navy 1851 205, *205*
— revolver model 1860 Army *70*, 199, *199*
— revolver Peacemaker 267
— revolver Python 263, *263*
— "Single Action Army" *70*
— sporting gun *70*
Colt, Samuel 70, 199
Colt-Browning, system 231, 232
Combat Lightweight (Colt) 263, *263*
Comblain musket mod. 1871 168, *168*
Cominazzi family 46, 47
Cominazzo, Lazarino 45, 46
Console, Giuseppe 126
— system 126
Cookson 48, 174
— system 174
Cornaro, Giovanni Antonio 42
Corset *39*
Cromwell, Oliver 48
Cutlass/Revolver 237, *237*
CZ (Česká Zbrojovka)
— automatic pistol M 38 233, *233*
— automatic pistol mod. 1924 233, *233*

D

D & B (Doersch & Baumgarten)
— cavalry carbine mod. 1861 137, *137*, 144
— rifle 143, *143*
Danner, Wolf 34
Dante 38
D'Avalos, Ferrante (Marquis of Pescara) *12*, *14*, 17
Daw, system *82*
De Gheyn, Jacob 36
De Jonge *40*
de Milemete, Walter 8
Deane
— revolver Adams double action 70, 206, *206*
— revolver Adams mod. 1851 72
Delvigne, Gustave 72
— bullet 72
— rifle 72
— system 138, 140, 154, 161
Derringer, pistol 79, 236, *236*
Doersch & Baumgarten (D & B)
— cavalry carbine mod. 1861 137, *137*, 144
— rifle 143, *143*
Doersch, Joseph Carl 137
double-barrelled Italian 'hammerless' 79
double-barrelled percussion-lock hunting weapon 56
Dreyse
— cartridge *82*
— Cavalry carbine mod. 1857 135, *135*
— Infantry rifle mod. 1862 64, 134, *134*
— internal-percussion, muzzle-loading needle pistol 135, *135*
— Light Infantry mod. 1865 135, *135*
— rifle 64, 68, 70
— rifle mod. 1860 for "Fusilier-Regimenter" 133, *133*
— system 127, *127*
Dreyse, Johann Nikolaus von 64, 68, 80, 134
Dreyse, Rudolf von 68
D.W.M. (Deutsche Waffen-Munitions-Fabriken) 84
— automatic pistol mod. 1908 188, *188*
— Luger mod. 1917 84
— Luger Parabellum M 1900 84, 86

E

Egg, Joseph 64
Einhorn, cartridge *82*
Emanuele Filiberto, Duke of Savoy 42
Enfield
— rifle Mark 1 *86*
— rifle mod. 1853 73, 152, *152*
— rifle mod. 1917 198, *198*
— rifle no. 4 Mark 1 *89*
— rifle no. 1 Mark III *89*
English Dragon Pistol (Colt) *70*
ERMA, sub-machine pistol MP 38 186
Esperanza y Unceta 223
Este, family of *25*

F

Fabbrica Nazionale d'Armi di Brescia (F.N.A.-B.) 222
— sub-machine gun mod. 43, 222, *222*
Fallschirmjager Gewehr 42, 89
Famars 79
FAMAS (Fusil Automatique MAS) 242, 248, *248*
Farington, cartridge for rifle system *82*
Farnese, arquebus *28*, *29*
Fass 90 (SIG) 251
Ferdinand II, Grand Duke of Tuscany *23*
Ferdinand III of Hapsburg-Lorraine, Grand Duke of Tuscany 62
Ferguson 60–61
— rifle 60–61
— system 60

FG42 (rifle mod. 1942) 86, *89*
Fiat mod. 15 220, *220*
Flobert 150
F.N.A.-B. (Fabbrica Nazionale d'Armi di Brescia) 222
— sub-machine gun mod. 43 222, *222*
FN FAL Light Automatic Rifle 247, *247*
Foix, Gaston de 18
Forsyth, John 62–3
— percussion lock *126*
fowler *43*, 44
Francini family 46
Francino, Giovanni Battista 46
François I. King of France 12, *14*, 16, 18
Franz Ferdinand, Archduke *25*
Fraser, Simon 61
Frundsberg, Georg von *14*

G

G3A3 (Heckler & Koch) 250, *250*
G11 (Heckler & Koch) 253, *253*
Gal, Uziel 243
Galil assault rifle 243, *243*, 252, *252*
Gambara, Count Niccolò *16*
Garand, rifle M1 89, 197, 201, *201*
Gasser, revolver mod. 1870 191, *191*
Geiger, Leonard 150
Gheetels, J. *12*
Giovio, Paolo 17
Girardoni, Bartolomeo *52*, 114
— system *52*
Glisenti pistol 222, *222*
Graecus, Marcus 9
Gras 158
— infantry rifle mod. 1874 158, *158*
— system 84
Greener, W.W. 62, 79
Grimmelhausen, H.J.C. 31
Gustavus I, Vasa 41
Gustavus Adolphus of Sweden *40*, 41

H

Hall, John 147
— rifle 113, 147, *147*
Hammerli, pistol mod. 150 *92*
Hanger, George 62
Harttel, Johannes *23*
Hay, Lord Charles 54
Hayward 42, 46
Hebler, system *82*
Heckler & Koch
— automatic pistol P7 261, *261*
— automatic rifle G3A3 250, *250*
— G11 automatic rifle 253, *253*
— MP 5 sub-machine gun 255, *255*
— semi-automatic pistol VP 70Z 261, *261*
Henri IV, King of France *43*, 44
Henry VIII, King of England 46
Henry, A. 127
— lever-action rifle 196
— repeating rifle 175, *175*
— rifle 73, 195
Henry-Winchester 79
— system 215
Herman, J.J. *53*
Holland & Holland 79
Houiller 212
Hughes, B.P. 61
Huss, Jan 11

I

Ieyasu, Tokugawa 49
India Pattern 60, *61*, 121, *121*
Ingram
— sub-machine gun mod. 10, 254, *254*
— sub-machine gun mod. 11, 254
Isidoro of Seville 38

J

Jaquinet, C. 44
Johann Georg I, Elector of Saxony 35
Johann Georg II 35

K

KAC-556 F (Ruger) 246, *246*
Kalashnikov
— 47 241, 248, *248*
— 74 241, 248, *248*
— 74S *241*
— AKMS *241*
Kalthoff 48
— arquebus 196
— repeating rifle 48
— system 48
Kalthoff, Caspar 48
Kalthoff, Peter 48
Kentucky (Pennsylvania) rifle 61, *61*, *74*
Kerr, percussion revolver 72
Klett family 46
Knoop, Jan 48
Kollner, Gaspard 34
Kotter, August 34
Krag 79
Krag-Jorgensen, rifle mod. 1889 176, *176*
Krnka, Sylvester *82*
— rifle 84
Kropatschek, naval rifle mod. 1878 210, *210*
Kropatschek-Chatellerault, repeating rifle 74/82 *82*

L

L1A1 *242*, 247, *247*
L2A3 (Sterling) *242*
La Chaumette-Ferguson system *127*
La Chaumette, Isaac de 60
La Marmora, system 138
La Noue, François de 26, 30
Lanchester, George 207
— sub-machine gun Mark 1 207, *207*
Land Pattern 121
Le Bourgeois, Jean 44
Le Bourgeois, Marin *43*, 44
Le Hollandois 44
Lebel
— rifle mod. 1886 M 93 210, *210*, 211
— revolver mod. 1892 212, *212*
Lee, James Paris 84
Lee, Robert E 76
Lee Enfield
— automatic rifle XL70E3 247, *247*
— Jungle Carbine 205, *205*
— rifle no. 1 Mark III 204, *204*
— rifle no. 4 Mark I 205, *205*
— rifle no. 5 205, *205*
Lee-Metford
— rifle Mark II 204
— rifle Mark II* 204, *204*
Lefaucheux, Casimir 64
— cartridge with needle 64
Lefaucheux, Eugène 212
— commercial model revolver 212, *212*
Lefaucheux cartridge 64, *82*
Leonardo da Vinci 18
Lindner
— experimental rifle 163, *163*
— system *82*
Long Land Service 61
Lopez de Caballos y Aguirre, Count of Campogiro, Venancio 223
Lorenz 162
— bullet 166
— infantry rifle mod. 1854 162, *162*
Lorenzoni-Cookson repeater system 174, *174*
Lorenzoni system 48
Louis XIII, King of France 43
Loys, M.N. *38*

Luger 187
— automatic pistol mod. 1908 188, *188*
— pistol mod. 1917 *84*
— pistol Parabellum M 1900 84

M

M 3 Grease Gun 202, *202*
M 16 (Armalite Ar-15) 244, 245, *245*
M 38 (C2) 233, *233*
M 52 automatic pistol 273, *273*
M 93 (Lebel) 210, *210*, 211
M 1911 (Colt) 84, 86, 203, *203*
M 1911 A1 (Colt) 85, 86
MAB (Moschetto automatic Beretta) 86
MAB (Manufacture d'Armes Automatiques) 262
MAB (Moschetto automatico Beretta) 86
— 38 A *90*, 221, *221*
MacDowell, General *75*
Magnus, Albertus 9
Mannlicher, Ferdinand Ritter von 84
— automatic pistol mod. 1905 193, *193*
— carbine mod. 1895 191, *191*
— cartridge mod. 77, *82*
— cartridge mod. 1888, *82*
— cavalry carbine mod. 1890 190, *190*
— musket mod. 1893 234, *234*
— musket mod. 1895 191, *191*, 234, *234*
— repeating rifle of 1880 175, *175*
— repeating rifle of 1882 175, *175*
— rifle mod. 1888 190, *190*
— rifle mod. 1895 190, *190*
— rifle with turning-head, bolt-type breech-block 176, *176*
Mannlicher-Berthier
— musket mod. 1892 211, *211*
— musket mod. 1892 M 1916 211, *211*
— rifle mod. 1907/15 211, *211*
Mannlicher-Carcano
— cavalry musket 91/38 *89*
— cavalry musket mod. 1891 218, *218*
— musket 91/24 *89*
— musket TS mod. 91/38 "S" 219, *219*
— musket TS mod. 1891 219, *219*
— rifle model '91 *86*
— rifle model 91/38 *89*
— rifle mod. 1891 217, *217*
— rifle mod. 1891/41 219, *219*
Mannlicher Schoenauer
— musket mod. 1903/14 227, *227*
— rifle mod. 1903/14 226, *226*
Manton, Joseph 64
Manufacture d'Armes Automatiques (MAB) 262
— automatic pistol PA 15 262, *262*
Manufrance, Falcor Model with superimposed barrels 91
Manurhin revolver MR 73 262, *262*
Mariette 69
Marlin, Model 336C (repeating carbine) *91*
Marston, system *82*
Martini, Friedrich von 127, 128, 171
Martini-Henry breech loader 78, 79, *82*, 127, *127*
M.A.S.
— Modèle 38, 178, *178*
— rifle mod. 1936 211, *211*
— sub-machine gun mod. 1938 213, *213*
matchlock *11*, 12–18, *15*, *16*, *25*, 26, 35, 38
Mauser
— automatic pistol 1896/12 187, *187*
— automatic pistol mod. 712 187
— automatic pistol mod. 1899 177, *177*
— automatic pistol mod. 1912 *85*
— automatic pistol mod. 1932 187
— automatic pistol mod. HSc 261, *261*
— carbine 1871/84 232, *232*
— carbine mod. 1871 138, *138*
— carbine mod. 1889 213, *213*
— carbine mod. 1898 (KAR 98 K) 86
— revolver mod. 1878 183, *183*
— rifle mod. 1871 137, *137*
— rifle mod. 1871/84 180, *180*, 231, *231*

— rifle mod. '88 175, *175*
— rifle mod. 1898 181, *181*, 219
— rifle mod. 1924 233, *233*
— rifle mod. 1929 232, *232*
— short rifle mod. 1893 223, *223*
Mauser, Peter-Paul 79, 84
Mauser-Paravicino, rifle mod. 1891 217, *217*
Mauser-Vergueiro rifle mod. 1904 226, *226*
Maximilian I, Emperor 19
Meister der Tierkopfranken 24, 46
Merkel 79
Meunier family 48
Milbank-Amsler
— infantry rifle mod. 1859/67 167, *167*
— system 167
Milemete, Walter de 8
Mini-14/5R (Ruger) 246, *246*
Minié, Claude-Etienne 72
— bullet 72, *80*, 154
MKb 42 185
Monluc, Blaise de 16
Mont Storm, system *82*
Montigny, breech-loader 82
Montmorency, Duke of 17
Morgan, Daniel 61
Mosin, I.S. 176, 227
Mosin-Nagant
— Dragoon rifle mod. 1891 227, *227*
— musket mod. 1938 229, *229*
— rifle mod. 1891 176, *176*, 227, *227*
— rifle mod. 1891/30 228, *228*
MP 5 (Heckler & Koch) 255, *255*
MP 38 (ERMA) 186
MP 40 (ERMA) 186, *186*
MP 41 (ERMA) 186, *186*
MP 81 (Steyr) 256, *256*
MP K (Walther) 255, *255*
Murata, rifle type 13 171, *171*
musket, artillery
— mod. 1829 (France) 119, *119*
— mod. 1829 T (France) 159, *159*
musket cavalry
— "big" model 1814 (Kingdom of Sardinia) 110
— French model (Kingdom of the Two Sicilies) 113, *113*
— mod. 1833 (Kingdom of Sardinia) 111, *111*
— of 1851 (Russia) 169, *169*
musket, Cossack 1851 (Russia) 123, *123*
musket, East India Company (Great Britain) 61, *61*, 121, *121*
musket for the Royal Carabineers of the King's Guard mod. 1891 (Italy) 218, *218*
Musket, light infantry
— mod. 1769 (Austria) 116, *116*
— mod. 1796 (Austria) 116, *116*
— mod. 1810 (Prussia) 107, *107*
— mod. 1842 (Austria) 161, *161*
— mod. 1854 (Austria) 162, *162*
musket, light infantry battalions, with 28 in barrel (Kingdom of the Two Sicilies) 142, *142*
musket, mod. 1777 re-styled Anno IX (France) 61, *61*
musket mod. 1838 large locks (Britain) 151, *151*
musket mod. 1839 (Britain) 151, *151*
musket of His Majesty's Guards mod. 1814 (Kingdom of Sardinia) 110, *110*
musket of Royal Carabineers mod. 1814 (Kingdom of Sardinia) 109, *109*
musket of the Mounted RRCC converted to breech-loading (Italy) 146, *146*
musket TS mod. 1870/87/16 217, *217*
musket with superimposed barrels mod. 1768 (Austria) 115, *115*

N

Nagant 176, 227
— revolver mod. 1895 229, *229*
Nagant, Emile & Leon 141

Nambu
— automatic pistol type Taisho 14, 235, *235*
— Kiska model 235
New Model Blackhawk (Ruger) 265, *265*
Nobel, Alfred 84
Nobunaga, Oda 49
Nock, Henry 57

O

Old Army Cap and Ball (Ruger) 266, *266*
Olympia (Walther) *92*
Orley, Bernaert van *12*

P

pepperbox pin-fire revolver 236, *236*
pistol, American mod. 1911 A1 179, *179*
pistol, breech-loading *67*
pistol, "diapason" *36*
pistol, double-barrelled *24*
pistol, duelling 57, 60
pistol, flintlock *43, 45, 48*
pistol, pepper-box 69, 70
pistol, matchlock 20–21
pistol, percussion-lock duelling *67*
pistol, short-barrelled *24*
pistol, wheel-lock *18, 21, 22, 26, 32, 38*
pistol, with Catalan-style lock *38*
pistol, with turn-off barrel 47
pistol, automatic
— mod. 1910 (Italy) 222, *222*
— type 94 (Japan) 235, *235*
pistol-carbine (Kingdom of Sardinia) 112, *112*
pistol, cavalry
— converted to percussion lock (Baden) 133, *133*
— first half of XIX century (Denmark) 123, *123*
— mod. 1777 (France) 120, *120*
— mod. 1814 (Kingdom of Sardinia) 112, *112*
— mod. 1822 T (France) 159, *159*
— mod. 1823 (Prussia) 107, *107*
— mod. 1844 (Austria) 165, *165*
— mod. 1859 (Austria) 166, *166*
— mod. Anno XIII (France) 120, *120*
— of 1827 (Würtemberg) 106, *106*
— of 1854 (Russia) 170, *170*
pistol, cavalry and dragoon mod. 1763–66 (France) 120, *120*
pistol, internal-percussion, muzzle-loading needle 135, *135*
Pistol Model 39(t) 233, *233*
pistol, naval mod. 1849 (France) 160, *160*
pistol, officer's
— Cavalry (Kingdom of Sardinia) 140, *140*
— Cavalry (Russia) 170, *170*
— Cossack (Russia) 170, *170*
— mod. 1822 T (France) 160, *160*
— staff officer's mod. 1855 (France) 160, *160*
pistol of the Royal Navy
— mod. 1844 (Kingdom of Sardinia) 140, *140*
— mod. 1814 (Kingdom of Sardinia) 111, *111*
pistol with shoulder stock 108, *108*
Podewils, Philipp von 136
— musket mod. 1842/58 136, *136*
— rifle *82*
Pontacharra carbine 154, *154*
Poser, Paul *55*
Pottet, Clément 64
P 5 (Walther) 260, *260*
P 7 (Heckler & Koch) 261, *261*
P 38 (Walther) 86, 188, *188*, 259, *259*
PA 15 MAB 262, *262*
Pattern P-14 *89*, 198
Pauly, Johannes Samuel 64, 80
— cartridge 64, *82*

Peabody, Henry O., 79, 128, 147
— cavalry carbine 147, *147*
— falling-block breech-loader *78*, 127, *127*
— system *82*
Peabody & Martini 84
— American-built rifle 171, *171*
Peacemaker (Colt) 267
Pedro Unceta y Juan Esperanza 223
Peeters expanding bullet 130, *130*, 139
Perazzi 79
petrary, chambered *11*
Petrini, Antonio 43–4
Philip IV, King of Spain *34*
Philipp, needle gun *82*
Pickett, General 76, 77
Pieper, 214
PP (Walther) 260, *260*
PPK (Walther) 189, *189*, 260, *260*
PPSh M. 1941 sub-machine gun, 231, *231*
Purdey, James 64, 79
— Luxury model with over-and-under barrels *91*

R

Radom, automatic pistol mod. 1935 232, *232*
Rast-Gasser, revolver mod. 1898 192, *192*
Redhawk (Ruger) 266, *266*
Remington 73, 128, *128*
— artillery musket mod. 1868 141, *141*
— breech-loader *78, 79*
— gendarmerie carbine mod. 1868 141, *141*
— infantry rifle mod. 1868 141, *141*
— naval rifle of 1867 150, *150*
— revolver New Model 1858 198, *198*
Repetierwindbüchse 52, 114, *114*
Revelli, Bethel Abiel 220
— rifle 221
revolver 36, 65
— Belgian 20-shot 237, *237*
— cutlass/revolver 237, *237*
— mod. 1873 (France) 212, *212*
— mod. 1874 of the Italian Royal Army 178, *178*
— Montenegro 236, *236*
— pepper-box pin-fire 236, *236*
— standard mod. 1882 (Schmidt system) 216, *216*
Rheinmetall-Borsing 184
— FG 42, 86, *89*, 184, *184*
Richards, Westley 128
Rider, Joseph 150
rifle, breech-loading
— falling-block *78, 79*, 127, *127*
rifle, compressed-air repeating mod. 1780 (Austria) 114, *114*
rifle, Cossack, of 1852 (Russia) 169, *169*
rifle, double-barrelled percussion-lock 56
rifle, double-barrelled Wender system *52*
rifle, Girardoni system *52*
Rifle, Grenadier, mod. 1822 (France) 119, *119*
rifle, hunting 50
— with Florentine-style lock *34*
— with Roman-style lock *39*
rifle, infantry
— French model (Kingdom of the Two Sicilies) 112, *112*
— French style of 1812 (Kingdom of Italy) 109, *109*
— mod. 1809 (Prussia) 106, *106*
— mod. 1814 (Kingdom of Sardinia) 109, *109*
— mod. 1822 (France) 119, *119*
— mod. 1840 (France) 155, *155*
— mod. 1842 (Switzerland) 166, *166*
— mod. 1853 (France) 155, *155*
— mod. 1853 T (France) 155
— mod. 1857 (France) 155
— mod. 1863 (United States) 148, *148*
— mod. 1867 *à tabatière* (France) 157, *157*
— of 1809 converted to percussion lock (Prussia) 133

— of 1819 converted to percussion lock (Württemberg) 132, *132*
— of 1825 (Württemberg) 105, *105*
rifle, Jäger *55*, 56, 57, 61, 62
rifle, light infantry, with 38 in barrel (Kingdom of the Two Sicilies) 142, *142*
Rifle, Militia, Republic of Venice 108, *108*
rifle mod.
— 1777, restyled Anno IX (France) 61, *61*, 109, 112, 118, *118*, 119
— 1888 (Germany) 180, *180*
rifle, paratroop and light infantry mod. 1942 (Germany) 86, *89*, 184, *184*
rifle, Pennsylvania 61, *61*
rifle, self-defence 50
rifle, semi-automatic
— M 21 (USA) 245, *245*
— mod. 41 (Germany) 183, *183*
— mod. 43 (Germany) 186, *186*
— R.S.C. mod. 1918 (France) 213, *213*
rifle, semi-breech-loading (Kingdom of the Two Sicilies) 113, *113*
rifle, Voltigeur mod. 1853 (France) 156, *156*
rifle, with Catalan-style lock *34*
rifle with chambered breech mod. 1842 (Austria) 161, *161*
Rigby 69
Roberts
— breech-loader 1831 *82*
— rifle 1867 82
Ross, rifle Mark III mod. 1910 203, *203*
Roth-Steyr, automatic pistol mod. 1907, 193, *193*
Roux, Claude *52*
Royal Ordnance Enfield Individual Weapon *242*
Ruger
— automatic pistol mod. Mark I Target *92*
— automatic pistol Standard Model Mark II 267, *267*
— revolver New Model Blackhawk 265, *265*
— revolver New Model Super Single-Six Six-Shot 267, *267*
— revolver "Old Army Cap and Bell" 266, *266*
— revolver Redhawk 266, *266*
— selective fire automatic rifle K AC-556F 246, *246*
— semi-automatic rifle Mini-14/5R 246, *246*
— semi-automatic rifle Mini-Thirty 246, *246*
Rupert, Prince 48

S

Sauer 79
— automatic pistol M 38 189, *189*
Schmeisser, Hugo 185
Schneider 157
Schoenauer 226
Schwarz, Berthold 9, *9*
Schwarzlose 84
Schweizerische Industrie-Gesellschaft (SIG)
— 90 PE 251
— assault rifle SG 550 251, *251*
— assault rifle SG 551 251, *251*
— Fass 90 251
— Stgw 90 251
— Stgw 90 PE 251
Scott 79
SG 550 (SIG) 251, *251*
SG 551 (SIG) 251, *251*
Sharps, Christian 148
— breech-loading rifle 73
— carbine Model 1863 *73, 77*
— New Model 1863 carbine 148, *148*
Shaw, Joshua 64
SIG (Schweizerische Industrie-Gesellschaft)
— 90 PE 251
— assault rifle SG 550 251, *251*

— assault rifle SG 551 251, *251*
— Fass 90 251
— Stgw 90 251
— Stgw 90 PE 251
SIG-SAUER
— automatic pistol P 220 Model 75 269, *269*
— automatic pistol P 225 268, *268*
— automatic pistol P 226 269, *269*
— automatic pistol P 230 268, *268*
Sirani 39
Skorpion M 61 257, *257*
Smith & Wesson 70–71
— automatic pistol mod. 459, 264, *264*
— revolver mod. 29 264, *264*
— revolver mod. 586 Distinguished Combat & Magnum 264, *264*
— revolver mod. 1869 200, *200*
Snayperskaya Vintovka Dragunova (SVD) 249, *249*
Snider, Jacob 153
— rifle mod. 1853 153, *153*
— system 79
Spät, Caspar 45
Spät, Sadeler 45
Spencer, Christopher 195
— breech-loader of 1860 *73*
— cavalry carbine mod. 1860 195, *195*
— repeating rifle 73, 77
Springfield
— musket-rifle 72, 73, 77
— rifle mod. 1903 176, 197, *197*
— rifle M 1903 197, *197*
— rifle mod. 1903 A3 198, *198*
— rifle mod. 1855 138, *138*
Star, sub-machine gun mod. Z-62 258, *258*
Sten 86
— Mk II submachine gun *89*, 207, *207*, 208
— Mk IV Model A sub-machine gun 208, *208*
— Mk IV Model B sub-machine gun 208, *208*
— Mk V sub-machine gun 208
— Mk VI (S) sub-machine gun 208, *208*
Sterling
— revolver .357 Magnum 268, *268*
— sub-machine gun 22A3 242, *242*
— sub-machine gun Mark 4 256, *256*
Steyr
— automatic pistol mod. 1912 194, *194*
— automatic rifle AUG A1 250, *250*
— MPi81 sub-machine gun 256, *256*
StG 44 86, 185, *185*
Stgw 90 (SIG) 251
Stgw 90 PE (SIG) 251
Stockel, Johan F. 24
sub-machine gun
— Carl-Gustav (Sweden) 258, *258*
— M3 "Grease Gun" (United States) 202, *202*
— MP 38 186
— M 61 "Skorpion" (Czechoslovakia) 257, *257*
— mod. 1940 (Germany) 186, *186*
— mod. 1941 (Germany) 186, *186*
— PPSh M. 1941 (USSR) 231, *231*
SVD (Snayperskaya Vintovka Dragunova) 249, *249*

T

Taifun, Model free carbine 92
Takeda clan 49
Taylor, General 70
Terssen 143
— rifle 143, *143*
Thompson, Model 1928 A1 sub-machine gun *89*, 202, *202*
Thouvenin 72, 154
— system 139
Thuraine 44
Tokarev
— automatic pistol mod. 1933 (TT33) 86, 231, *231*

— semi-automatic rifle mod. 1938 230, *230*
— semi-automatic rifle mod. 1940 230, *230*
— TT1930 *86*
Tokugawa 48, 49
— arquebus *49*
Toschi family *47*
Tournier, J.C. 44
Trumbull, John 74
Tschinke 32, *23*, 24, 45
Twigg *51*

U

Unceta y Compania 225
UZ1 sub-machine gun *243*, 256, *256*

V

van Orley, Bernaert *12*
Vasto, Marquis of 17
Velasquez *34*
Vetterli, Friedrich 79, 215
— carbine mod. 1872 216, *216*
— infantry rifle mod. 1870 145, *145*, 146, *146*

— musket mod. 1871 215, *215*
— rifle mod. 1869 215, *215*
— Royal Carabineer Musket mod. 1870 146, *146*
Vetterli-Vitali, rifle mod. 1870/87 217, *217*
Vieille, Paul 84, 210
Viking, sub-machine gun 254, *254*
Villar-Perosa, sub-machine gun mod. 1915 220, *220*
Vis mod. 35 232, *232*
Vischer, Adam 46
Vitali 217
Volcanic repeating rifle 175, *175*
Voltaire 55
VP 702 (Heckler & Koch) 261, *261*

W

Walker, Sam 70
Wallhausen, J.J. *27*
Walther
— automatic pistol mod. 1938 (p 38) 86, 188, *188*, 259, *259*
— automatic pistol mod. P 5 260, *260*
— automatic pistol mod. PP 260, *260*

— automatic pistol mod. PPK 189, *189*, 260, *260*
— automatic pistol Model Olympia *92*
— semi-automatic rifle Mod. 41 183, *183*
— sub-machine gun MP-K 255, *255*
Wänzel
— infantry rifle mod. 1867 163, *163*
— light infantry musket mod. 1867 165, *165*
Webley
— automatic pistol Mark 1 209, *209*
— revolver no. 1 Mark VI 206, *206*
Webley & Scott, automatic pistol mod. 1904 209, *209*
Webley-Fosbery automatic revolver 179, *179*, 183
Weimar, Duke of 50
Wender, Felix 48
Wender system *52*
Werder, J.L. 128
— infantry rifle mod. 1869 (Bayerisch Blitz) 128, *128*, 136, *136*
— rifle mod. 1868 *82*
— system 128
Werndl, Josef 164
— carbine mod. 1867 164, *164*

— Infantry and Light Infantry rifle mod. 1867 164, *164*
— system *82*
Westley-Richards 79
— system *82*
Whitneyville-Walker 44 caliber 70
Whitworth, carbine of 1860 152, *152*
Wilkinson 162
Winchester, Oliver 195
Winchester
— carbine M1 201, *201*, 241
— carbine M1 A1 202, *202*
— carbine mod. 1866 73, 196, *196*, 197
— carbine mod. 1873 73, 197, *197*
— military musket mod. 1895 228, *228*
— repeating rifle mod. 1866 72, 195
— repeating rifle mod. 1895 177, *177*
— rifle 84, *91*
— rifle mod. 1894 73

Z

Z-62 (Star) 258, *258*
Zanotti family *47*
Zizka, Jan 11

Bibliography

GENERAL WORKS

AKEHURST, R., *The World of Guns*, Hamlyn, London 1972

ANGELUCCI, A., *Catalogo dell' Armeria Reale di Turin*, Candeletti, Turin 1890

BLACKMORE, H.L., *Guns and Rifles of the World*, Batsford, London 1965

BLAIR, C.A., *European and American Arms c.1100–1850*, Crown. London 1962

BLAIRE, C.A. et al., *Arms and Weapons*, London 1982

DEMMIN, A., *Guides des Amateurs d'Armes*, Renouard, Paris 1879

DIAGRAM GROUP, *Weapons*, Diagram Visual Information Ltd., London 1980

Enciclopedia Militare, Istituto Editoriale Scientifico (published by «Il Popolo d'Italia»), Milan 1933.

GELLI, J., *Guida del raccoglitore e dell'Amatore di Armi antiche*, Hoepli, Milan 1900, reprinted Milan 1968

GREENER, W.W., *The Gun and its Development*, London 1881, ninth ed. 1910, reprinted by Arms and Armour Press, London 1986

HAYWARD, J.F., *The Art of the Gunmaker*, Barrie & Rockliff, London 1962/1963

HELD, R./JENKINS, N., *The Age of Firearms – A pictorial History*, Harper & Bros., New York 1957

LUGS, J., *Handfeuerwaffen – Systematischer Überblick über Handfeuerwaffen und ihre Geschichte*, Militärverlag der DDR, Berlin 1986 (orig. ed. Prague 1956, first German edition Berlin 1968)

MANN, J., *European Arms and Armour*, Hertford House, London 1962

MILLER, M., *The Collector's Illustrated Guide to Firearms*, Barrie & Jenkins, London 1978

MORIN, M., *Armi antiche*, Mondadori, Milan 1982

MUSCIARELLI, L., *Dizionario delle Armi*, Mondadori, Milan 1971

NATIONAL RIFLE ASSOCIATION, *Gun Collector's Handbook*, Washington, D.C., 1959

PETERSON H.L., *The Treasury of the Gun*, Golden Press, New York 1962

PETERSON H.L., Editor, *Encyclopedia of Firearms*, Dutton, London & New York 1964

PETERSON, H.L./ELMAN, R., *The Great Guns*, Hamlyn, London 1971

REID, W., *Weapons Through the Ages*, formerly *The Lore of Arms*, Peerage Books, London 1984

ROSA, J.G./MAY, R., *An illustrated History of Guns and Small Arms*, Peerage Books, London 1984

SCHMIDT, R., *Die Handfeuerwaffen*, 1875–78, reprinted Akademische Druck- und Verlaganstalt, Graz 1968

SMITH, W.H.B./SMITH, J.E., *Small Arms of the World*, Stackpole, Harrisburg, 1962

THIERBACH, M., *Die geschichtliche Entwicklung der Handfeuerwaffen*, C. Hockner, Dresden 1886–87, reprinted Akademische Druck- und Verlaganstalt, Graz 1965

THOMAS, B./GAMBER, O./SCHEDELMANN, H., *Die schönsten Waffen und Rüstungen aus europäischen und amerikanischen Sammlungen*, Keysersche Verlagsbuchhandlung GmbH, Heidelberg-München 1963

ZUNIN, A., *Armi antiche e moderne*, Vallardi, Milan 1929

DOCUMENTS AND MONOGRAPHS

Abridgements of the Patent Specifications Relating to Firearms and Other Weapons, Ammunitions & Accoutrements, 1588–1858, reprinted Saifer, London 1960

ALBAUGH, W.A., III/SIMMONS, E.N., *Confederate Arms*, Stackpole, Harrisburg 1957

ALBAUGH, W.A., III/BENT, H./SIMMONS, N.E., *Confederate handguns*, Riling, Philadelphia 1963

APPIANO, E.L., *Fucili da caccia moderni, e loro munizioni*. F.lli Melita, CO.LI.PA., Rubano (PD), n.d.

APPIANO, E.L., *Revolver e Pistole Automatiche – notizie tecniche e storiche*, Fr.lli Melita, CO.LI.PA., Rubano (PD), n.d.

Armes à feu réglementaires françaises, 1717–1919. Series of pamphlets published under the direction of BOUDRIOT, J., Petitot, Paris 1960–1975

Armi e cultura nel Bresciano, 1420–1870. Reports delivered at the conference held in Brescia in 1980. Supplement to: *Commentari dell'Ateneo di Brescia*, Brescia 1981

ARNALDI, M., *Equipaggiamento, munizionamento ed armamento della fanteria*, Illustrazione Militare Italiana, Milan 1887

ASKINS, C., *The Shotgunner's Book*, Stackpole, Harrisburg 1958

BAILEY, D.W., *British Military Longarms 1715–1865*, Arms and Armour Press, London 1986

BARNES, F.C., *Cartridges of the World*, Follett Pub. Co., Chicago 1969

BARTOCCI, A./SALVATICI, L., *Armamento individuale dell'esercito piemontese e italiano 1814–1914*, Edibase, Florence 1978 (vol. I) – 1978 (vol. II)

BLACKMORE, H.L., *British Military Firearms 1650–1850*, Arco, London and New York 1961

BLAIR, C.-BOCCIA, L.G., *Armi e armature*, Fabbri, Milan 1981

BOCCIA, L.G./ROSSI, F./MORIN, M., *Armi e armature lombarde*, Electa, Milan 1979

BRUNELLI, V., *W come Winchester*, Editoriale Olimpia, Florence 1980

CAITI, P., *Fucili d'assalto*, Delta, Parma 1976

CALAMANDREI, C., *L'acciarino nei tempi*, Editoriale Olimpia, Florence 1976

CALAMANDREI, C., *Armi bianche militari italiane 1814–1950*, Editoriale Olimpia, Florence 1987

CAREY, M., *English, Irish and Scottish Firearms Makers*, Thomas & Cromwell, New York 1954

CARMICHAEL, J., *The Modern Rifle*, Winchester Press, New York 1975

CHIADARENO, G., *Guida ufficiale dell'Armeria di Torino*, compilata per cura della Direzione, Typography from the newspaper *Il Commercio*, Turin 1923

CIMARELLI, A.G., *Quattro secoli di armi da fuoco*, De Agostini, Novara 1972

CIMARELLI, A.G., *Storia delle Armi delle due guerre mondiali*, De Agostini, Novara

CLERGEAU, J.-R., *Restauration des Armes à Feu*, Office du Livre, Fribourg 1981

CORVETTO, G., *Il nuovo fucile rigato*, Cassone, Turin 1864

COTTY, H., *Mémoire sur la fabrication des armes portatives*, Magimel, Paris 1806

DARLING, A.D., *Red Coat and Brown Bess*, Museum Restoration Service, Ottawa, Ontario 1970

DE FLORENTIIS, G., *Tecnologia delle armi da fuoco portatili*, Hoepli, Milan 1963

DE LAMA, P., *Le fucine di Gardone nel 1794*, Bondavelli, Reggio Emilia 1883

DI CARPEGNA, N., *Firearms in the princes Odescalchi collection in Rome*, Marte, Rome 1975

285

DIETER, H., *Die Selbstlade – und automatischen Handfeuerwaffen*, Verlag E.S. Mittler & Sohn, Herford, Bonn 1986

DOLLECZEC. A., *Monographie der k. u. k. österr. -ung. Blank- und Handfeuerwaffen*, Vienna 1896, reprinted Akademische Druck- und Verlaganstalt, Graz 1970

DUCHARTE, P.-L., *Histoire des Armes de Chasse et de leurs Emplois*, Crépin Leblond, Paris 1955

DURDIK, J./MUDRA M./SADA M., *Firearms – a collector's guide: 1326–1900*, Hamlyn, London 1985

ECKARDT, W./MORAWIETZ, O., *Die Handwaffen des Brandeburgisch – Preussischdeutschen Heeres. 1640–1945*, H.G. Schulz, Hamburg 1957

EDWARDS, W.B., *Civil War Guns*, Stackpole, Harrisburg, Pa. 1962

EDWARDS, W.B., *Story of Colt's Revolver*, Stackpole, Harrisburg, Pa. 1954

EZELL, E.C., *Small Arms of the World*, revised and expanded edition of the work of the same title by SMITH, W.H.B./ SMITH, J.E., Stackpole, Harrisburg 1983

EZELL, E.C., *Handguns of the World, Military revolvers and selfloaders from 1870 to 1945*, Stackpole, Harrisburg 1981

FULLER, C.E., *The Rifled Musket*, Stackpole, Harrisburg 1958

GAIBI, A., *Arms da fuoco italiane*, Bramante, Busto Arsizio 1978

GARD, W., *The Great Buffalo Hunt*, University of Nebraska Press, Lincoln 1959

GATTIA, A., *Fucili e pistole*, Rizzoli, Milan 1969

GELLI, J., *Gli archibugiari milanesi. Industria, commercio, uso delle armi da fuoco in Lombardia*, Hoepli, Milan 1905

GEORGE, J.N., *English Guns and Rifles*, Stackpole, Harrisburg 1947

GEORGE, J.N., *English Pistols and Revolvers*, Samworth, Harrisburg, Pa. 1947, reprinted Holland Press, London 1961

GLUCKMAN, A., *United States Martial Pistols and Revolvers*, Stackpole, Harrisburg 1939

GLUCKMAN, A., *United States Muskets, Rifles and Carbines*, Stackpole, Harrisburg 1959

GRAELLES I PUIG, *Armes de foc de Ripoll*, Maideu, Ripoll 1975

GRANT, J.J., *Single Shot Rifles*, Morrow, New York 1947

GRANT, J.J., *More Single Shot Rifles*, Morrow, New York 1959

GRENNELL, A.D., *Pistol & Revolver Digest*, 3rd Edition, DBI Books, Northfield 1982

GUCCI, L., *Armi portatili*, Casanova, Turin 1915

HARDY, E., *Le Musée de l'Armée. Section des armes et armures*, Berger-Levrault, Paris 1911

HATCH, A., *Remington Arms in American History*, Holt, Rinehart & Winston, New York e Toronto 1956

HAYTHORNTHWAITE, P., *Weapons & Equipment of the Napoleonic Wars*, Blandford Press, Poole 1979

HELD, R./JENKINS, N., *The Age of Firearms*, Cassel, London 1955

HELD, R., *Oplologia italiana*, Editoriale Olimpia, Florence 1983

HELD, R., *Una rassegna di 162 armi antiche*, Acquafresca, Chiasso 1976

HICKS, J.E., *French Military Weapons*, Flayderman, New Milford, Conn. 1964

HINMAN, B., *The Golden Age of Shotgunning*, Winchester Press, New York 1971

HOGG, I.V./WEEKS, J., *Military small arms of the twentieth century*, Lionel Leventhal, London 1973

HOGG, I.V./WEEKS, J., *Pistols of the World*, Lionel Leventhal, London 1978

HOGG, I.V., *Le armi leggere da guerra*, volume from *Grande Enciclopedia delle Armi moderne*, Peruzzo, Milan 1985–1986

HOGG, I.V., *Encyclopedia of modern small arms*, Hamlyn, London 1983

HOGG, I.V., *German pistols and revolvers 1871/1945*, Arms and Armour Press, London 1971

HUNTINGTON, R.T., *Hall's Breechloaders*, G. Shuemwag 1972

JACKSON, H.J. et al., *European Hand Firearms of the Sixteenth, Seventeenth and Eighteenth Centuries*, Quadrangle, London 1933

JARLIER, P., *Répertoire d'arquebusiers et de fourbisseurs français*, F.P. Lobiès, Saint-Julien-du-Sault, 1976–1981

KARR, Jr., C.L./KARR, C.R., *Remington Handguns,* Stackpole, Harrisburg 1960 (fourth edition)

KAUFFMAN, H.J., *The Pennsylvania-Kentucky Rifle*, Stackpole, Harrisburg 1960

KENYON, C. Jr., *Lugers at random*, Handgun Press, Chicago 1969

KIESLING, P., *Bayonets of the World*, Military Collectors Service, F. van Gelder, Kedikem n.d.

KINDIG, Jr., J., *Thoughts on the Kentucky Rifle in its Golden Age*, Hyatt, Wilmington 1960

KIST, J.B. et al., *Dutch Muskets and Pistols*, Den Haag 1974

LAMARMORA, A., *Alcune norme sul fucile di fanteria*, Cassone, Turin 1848

LAVIN, J.D., *A History of Spanish Firearms*, H. Jenkins, London 1965

LENK, T., *Flintlaset: dess uppkomst och utveckling*, Stockholm 1939. Trans. of G.A. Urquhart, *The Flintlock, Its Origin and Development*, ed. by Hayward, J.F., Holland Press, London 1964

LIND, E., *The Complete Book of Trick and Fancy Shooting*, Winchester Press, New York 1972

LINDSAY, M., *Histoire des Armes à feu du XV au XX siècle*, Office du Livre, Fribourg 1972

LINDSAY, M., *One Hundred Great Guns*, Walker & Co., New York 1967

LOGAN, H.C., *Underhammer Guns*, Stackpole, Harrisburg 1960

LUPI, G., *Il fucile a cani esterni – Origine ed evoluzione*, Editoriale Olimpia, Florence 1975

LUPI, G., *I primi fucili a ripetizione*, Editoriale Olimpia, Florence 1976

LUPI, G., *La doppietta italiana – L'ingegno dei nostri armaioli dell'ultimo secolo*, Editoriale Olimpia, Florence 1978

LUPI, G., *Toschi e Zanotti, antichi artisti armaioli*, Editoriale Olimpia, Florence 1979

MANGEOT, H., *Traité du Fusil de Chasse et des Armes de Précision*, Tanera, Paris 1858

MARCIANÒ, E./MORIN, M., *Dal Carcano al FAL*, Editorial Olimpia, Florence 1974

MAROLLES, M. de, *La Chasse au fusil*, T. Barrois, Paris 1788, reprinted 1836

MARZOLI, L., *L'industria delle armi nel territorio bresciano e particolarmente nella Valle Trompia*, Apollonio, Brescia 1931

MASINI, S./ROTASSO, G., *L'arte della fortificazione in Italia e la realtà della cinta ferrarese*, in *Le mura di Ferrara – immagini e storia* (in the thirtieth edition of *Italia Nostra*, 1955–1985), Panini, Modena 1985

MASINI, S./ROTASSO, G., *Le armi nella storia*, in *Le armi degli Estensi – La collezione di Konopistê* (catalogue from the exhibition mounted by the Province of Ferrara in the Castello Estense, 1986–1987), Cappelli, Bologna 1986

MEZZANO, G.M./PARODI, A., *Le pistole d'ordinanza piemontesi (Regno di Sardegna 1720–1861)*. Alessandria 1983

MORIN, M., *Le armi portatili dell'Impero austroungarico*, Editoriale Olimpia, Florence 1981

MORIN, M./HELD, R., *Beretta, la dinastia industriale più antica al mondo*, Acquafresca, Chiasso 1980

Mostra delle armi da fuoco anghiaresi e dell'Appennino toscoemiliano, catalogue edited by M. Terenzi, Anghiari 1968

MYATT, F., *Modern Small Arms*, Salamander Books, London 1978

NEAL, W.K., *Spanish Guns and Pistols*, G. Bell & Sons, London 1955

NEGRI, F., *Il fucile da caccia. Armi, munizioni, tiro*, Editoriale Olimpia, Florence 1961

NUTTER, W.E., *Manhattan Firearms*, Stackpole, Harrisburg 1958

OAKESHOTT, R.E., *The Archaeology of Weapons*, Lutterworth Press, London 1960

O'CONNOR, J., *The Big Game Rifle*, A.A. Knopf, New York 1952

PARSONS, J.E., *The First Winchester*, Morrow, New York 1955

PARSONS, J.E., *Henry Deringer's Pocket Pistol*, Morrow, New York 1952

PARSONS, J.E., *The Peacemaker and its Rivals*, Morrow, New York 1950

PARSONS, J.E., *Smith & Wesson Revolvers*, Morrow, New York 1957

PARTINGTON, J.R., *A History of Greek Fire and Gunpowder*, W. Heffer, Cambridge 1960

PAULIN-DESORMEAUX, M.A.O., *Nouveau manuel complet de l'armurier, du fourbisseur et de l'arquebusier*, first edition. Paris 1825, Manuels Roret, reprinted. L.V.D.V. Inter livres, Paris 1984

PETERSON, H.L., *Arms and Armor in Colonial America, 1526–1783*, Stackpole, Harrisburg 1956

PETERSON, H.L., *Pageant of the Gun*, Doubleday, New York 1967

PINTI, P., *Antiche armi da fuoco*, Tolentino 1985

POPE, D., *Guns – From the invention of gunpowder to the 20th century*, Weidenfeld & Nicolson, London 1965

REYNOLDS, E.G.B., *The Lee-Enfield Rifle*, Arco, London 1960

ROBERTS, N.H., *The Muzzle-Loading Cap Lock Rifle*, Stackpole, Harrisburg 1958 (third edition)

ROOSEVELT, T., *African Game Trails*, Syndicate Publishing, New York, London 1909

ROSSI, F./di CARPEGNA, N., *Armi antiche del Museo Civico L. Marzoli*, Milan 1969

ROTASSO, G., *La baionetta nella storia delle guerre*, in *Studi storico-militari-1984*, S.M.E.-Ufficio Storico, Rome 1985

ROTASSO, G., *L'armamento dell'uomo d'arme dal XV al XVI secolo*, in *Studi storico-militari-1985*, S.M.E.-Ufficio Storico, Rome 1986

ROTASSO, G., *L'armamento portatile dell'esercito piemontese negli anni della Restaurazione*, in *Studi storico-militari-1986*, S.M.E.-Ufficio Storico, Rome 1987

RUSTICUCCI, L., *I fucili da guerra di tutti gli eserciti del mondo*, Colitti, Campobasso 1917

RUSSELL, C.P., *Guns on the Early Frontiers*, Bonanza Books, New York 1957

SAINT-RÉMY, P.S. de, *Mémoire d'Artillerie*, Rollin Fils, Paris 1746

SALVATICI, L., *Pistole Militari Italiane – Regno di Sardegna e Regno d'Italia – 1814–1940* Editoriale Olimpia, Florence, n.d.

SCHEDELMANN, H., *Die grossen Buchsenmachern-Leben, Werke, marken vom 15.bis 19. Jahrhundert*, Klinkhardt & Biermann, Braunschweig 1972

SELL, D.E., *Collector's Guide to American Cartridge Handguns*, Stackpole, Harrisburg 1957

SERVEN, J.E., *Colt Firearms from 1836*, Serven, Santa Ana 1954

SERVEN, J.E., *The Collecting of Guns*, Stackpole, Harrisburg 1964

SIMONE, G./BELOGI, R./GRIMALDI, A., *Il '91*, Ravizza, Milan 1970

SMITH, W.H.B., *Gas, Air and Spring Guns of the World*, Stackpole, Harrisburg 1957

SMITH, W.H.B., *The Book of Pistols and Revolvers*, Stackpole, Harrisburg 1962 (fifth edition)

SMITH, W.H.B./SMITH, J.E., *The Book of Rifles*, Stackpole, Harrisburg 1963 (third edition)

SMITH, W.H.B., *Mannlicher Rifles and Pistols*, Stackpole, Harrisburg 1947

SMITH, W.H.B., *Walther Pistols and Rifles*, Stackpole, Harrisburg 1962

STEPHENS, F.J., *Bayonets – an illustrated History and Reference Guide*, Lionel Leventhal, London 1968

STOCKEL, J.F., *Haandskydevaabens Bedommelse*, Udgivet A.F. – Tojhusmuseet, Copenhagen 1938, Revised and expanded edition in German, of HEER, E., entitled *Der neue Stockel*, Schweizerisches Waffeninstitut, Grandson

1978; distributed by Journal Verlag, Schwäbisch Hall

SUTHERLAND, R.Q./WILSON, R.L., *The Book of Colt Firearms*, Kansas City 1971

TAYLERSON, A.W.F., *The Revolver, 1865–1888*, Jenkins, London 1966

TAYLERSON, A.W.F., *Revolving Arms*, Jenkins, London 1967

TAYLERSON, A.W.F., *The Revolver, 1889–1914*, Barrie & Jenkins, London 1970

UGOLINI, L., *Il libro del cacciatore*, Vallecchi, Florence 1935

WALTER, J.- *The German Bayonet*, Arms and Armour Press, London n.d.

WALTER, J.- *Luger: an illustrated history of the handguns of Hugo Borchardt and Georg Luger, 1875 to the present day*, Arms and Armour Press, London 1977

WATERMAN, C.F., *Hunting in America*, Ridge Press/Holt, Rinehart and Winston, New York 1973

WATERMAN, C.F., *The Treasury of Sporting Guns*, Ridge Press, New York 1979

WATROUS, G.R./RICKHOFF, J.C./HALL, T.H., *The History of Winchester Firearms*, Winchester Press, New York 1966

WEBSTER, Jr., D.B., *Suicide Specials*, Stackpole, Harrisburg 1958

WILKINSON, F., *The World's Great Guns*, Hamlyn, London 1977

WILLIAMSON H.F., *Winchester, The Gun That Won the West*, Barnes, Washington, D.C. 1952

WILSON, J.L./du MONT, J.S., *Samuel Cold Presents*, Hartford 1961

WILSON, R.L., *Colt – An American Legend*, Abbeville Press

WINANT, L., *Early Percussion Firearms*, Morrow, New York 1959

WINANT, L., *Firearms Curiosa*, St. Martin's Press, New York 1955

WINANT, L., *Pepperbox Firearms*, Greenberg, New York 1952

HISTORY OF ARMIES

Various authors *Histoire Universelle des Armées*, Laffont, Paris 1964

—*Il Gioco della Guerra – eserciti, soldati e società nell'Europa pre-industriale* (Catalogue of the exhibition at Prato in 1984 under the patronage of the Assessorato alla Cultura), Conti, Calenzano 1984

CARDINI, F., *Quell'antica festa crudele*, Sansoni, Florence 1982

FALLS, C. et al., *Great Military Battles*, Weidenfeld and Nicolson, London 1964

FUNCKEN, L. et F., *Le costume, l'Armure et les Armes au temps de la Chevalerie*, Casterman, Tournai 1977

FUNCKEN, L. et F., *L'Uniforme et les Armes des soldats de la guerre en dentelle*, Casterman, Tournai 1975

FUNCKEN, L. et F., *L'Uniforme et les Armes des soldats des États-Unis*, Casterman, Tournai 1979

HALE, J.R., *War and Society in Renaissance Europe (1450–1620)*, Fontana, London 1985

HOWARD, M., *War in European History*, Oxford University Press, London – New York 1976

MACDONALD, J., *Great Battlefields of the World*, Michael Joseph, London 1984

PIERI, P., *Il Rinascimento e la crisi militare italiana*, Einaudi, Turin 1952

PIERI, P., *Guerra e politica negli scrittori italiani del Rinascimento*, Mondadori, Milan 1975

PRESTON, R.A./WISE, S., *Men in Arms*, Praeger, Toronto 1970

PUDDU, R., *Eserciti e monarchie nazionali nei secoli VX–XVI*, La Nuova Italia, Florence 1975

RIVISTA MILITARE, *Il soldato italiano dell'Ottocento nell'opera di Quinto Cenni*, text by MASINI, S./ALES, S., – Rome 1986

TURNBULL, *The Book of the Samurai*, Bison Books, London 1984

Picture sources

Arnoldo Mondadori Editore, archives: 8, 9, 34
Astra-Unceta y CIA, S.A.: 223, 224, 225, 273
Benvenuti: 240, 241, 242, 243
Beretta: 221, 222, 249, 257, 270, 271
Carl Walther GmbH: 255, 259, 260
Colt Collection of Firearms, Connecticut State Library,
    Museum of Connecticut History; 69, 71
Edibase-Enrico Bartocci Editore: 129, 130, 131
Empresa Nacional Santa Barbara de Industrias Militares S.A.: 248, 252
FN-Fabrique Nationale Herstal: 214, 247, 248, 272
Gettysburg National Military Park: 76
Greg Martin Collection: 71
Heckler & Koch GmbH: 250, 253, 255, 261
Hogg, I.V.: 202, 203, 204, 205, 206, 207, 208, 209, 211, 213, 254
Jane's Infantry Weapons: 248, 249, 256, 257
Library of Congress: 75
Matra Manurhin Defense: 262
Oesterreichische Nationalbibliothek: 11
SIG Swiss Industrial Company: 251, 268, 269
Steyr: 256
Springfield Armory Inc.: 201, 245
Sturm, Ruger & Company Inc.: 246, 265, 266, 267
Webley and Scott Ltd.: 209
Yale University Art Gallery: 74